D1458180

Practical Counselling Skills

A psychological skills approach for the helping professions and for voluntary counsellors

Richard Nelson-Jones BA, MA, PhD, FBPsS, NAPS

1983

HOLT, RINEHART AND WINSTON

London · New York · Sydney · Toronto

Holt, Rinehart and Winston Ltd: 1 St Anne's Road,
Eastbourne, East Sussex BN21 3UN

British Library Cataloguing in Publication Data

Nelson-Jones, Richard
    Practical counselling skills.
    1.   Counselling—Handbooks, manuals, etc.
    I. Title
    361.3'23   BF637.C6

ISBN 0-03-910478-8

Photoset in 10/12 point Linotron Times by Alan Sutton Publishing Ltd, Gloucester.
Printed and bound in Great Britain by Biddles Ltd, Guildford and King's Lynn

Last digit is print number: 9 8 7 6 5 4 3 2

Preface

The aim of this book is to provide a down-to-earth introduction to practical counselling skills for the helping professions and for voluntary counsellors. An important assumption throughout is that practical counselling skills are not just used by professional counsellors and psychologists. Instead, they are also used by voluntary counsellors and by many other people who use these skills as part of different roles: for example, doctors, managers, nurses, social workers, teachers and the clergy. Consequently I hope this book is helpful to trainees, trainers and to those who use counselling skills in a wide range of settings.

There is no getting away from the fact that practical counselling skills are at the heart of counsellor training. Though people can learn by reading, writing and talking about counselling, if they are to become competent counsellors, sooner or later they have to learn by *doing* it. Furthermore, since there is a very strong case for not using clients as guinea pigs for inexperienced counsellors, trainees need to develop their skills in practical training groups prior to being allowed responsibility for their own clients. This book is not only written to support such counsellor training groups, but also to help those who do not have the time or resources for, or ready access to, formal training. Additionally, I hope this book is used in conjunction with placement supervision, when the time comes for trainees to counsel their own clients.

My experience was that, in the early to mid-1960's, when I was a counsellor trainee at Stanford University in California I felt that their programme would have been much stronger if it had approached skills training in a more thorough and systematic way. The programme was unbalanced by too academic an emphasis. Indeed I learned more about practical counselling skills by enrolling as a client in both individual and group counselling in the University's counselling and medical centres, respectively, than I learned from the counsellor training programme itself. When, therefore, from 1970 to 1982, the poacher turned game-keeper and I was a counsellor trainer at the University of Aston in Birmingham, I tried to rectify the deficiencies I had perceived in my own training by always striving for a sizeable practical component. This was partly achieved by laboratory skills training conducted in small groups of approximately six trainees and partly by then providing trainees with the opportunity to counsel real clients under supervision.

I have written this book using what might be termed a micro-counselling approach. By this I mean that I have attempted to identify some central practical counselling skills and, if necessary, have broken them down into their component parts. Some of these skills are better thought of as appropriate to specific clients in specific situations, though as such they may constitute important elements within the counsellor's reper-toire of skills. The approach to each skill or component part of a skill is to start by describing it and then to provide an exercise involving using it. You will find that there are nearly sixty exercises in this book. I have included the exercises for two main reasons. First, as an adjunct to the text in the hope that the exercises might further clarify the concepts which have just been described. Second, as a way of building your practical counselling skills by getting you involved in learning by doing. In most cases I have been able to design the exercises in such a way that they may be done in a number of ways: on your own, in pairs or in a training group. A further skill that I have tried to deal with in the text rather than in any specific exercise is that of appropriate judgement or appreciating just what is appropriate when. This is a skill that also needs both experience and good supervision for its development.

As on a packet of cigarettes, I present this book with a 'health warning'. I warn you against being too slavish in your approach to the exercises. Listen to your own reactions and, if in a training group, work in consultation with your trainer. Undoubtedly you will find that some of the exercises are more important than others, some are better designed than others, and some also get you to diminishing returns sooner than others. Let me make an analogy with playing the piano. Though it is very important to learn technique, it is also vital not to let technique smother your ability to make emotional contact with others. I hope that working with the exercises does not result in your becoming wooden, but rather helps you to possess disciplined yet expressive counselling skills. There is a danger in a mechanistic focus on skills or techniques at the expense of a person-to-person relationship with your clients.

In writing this book I have become very aware of how psychologists like myself often use language in ways that are distancing. Stimulated by comments from those who read the first draft of the book, I rewrote many parts of it trying to use more simple and clear sentences and terminology. I hope that, to a large extent, I have succeeded in communicating in a direct way.

I thank the following people who have, in various ways, contributed to the writing of this book. My editor, Helen Mackay, who had faith in the book and conscientiously and tactfully worked to improve its quality. It is a salutary experience for psychologists to work with editors who have degrees in English! The reviewers of the first draft of the book whose comments contributed to its being substantially rewritten and expanded. They were Karen and Paul Lyons, Steve Murgatroyd, Joan Sullivan and Brian Thorne. The reviewers of the second draft, Paul Brown, Peter Daws, Audrey Newsome, Rita Mintz and Rob Ward. The two typists of drafts of the manuscript, Wendy Bayliss and Ann Aland. Also, my mother who provided 'office space' in her flat for me to write part of the book when I was in the process of moving back to London.

I hope that you find the book useful. Please feel free to make suggestions to me about how it, or individual exercises in it, might be improved.

Wimbledon
London

Richard Nelson-Jones
April 1983

Contents

PREFACE   **iii**

LIST OF EXERCISES   **viii**

1 **Counselling and Helping Relationships**   **1**
   What is counselling? 1;   *Kinds of counselling and*
   helping relationships 3;   *A model for counselling*
   and helping relationships 11;   *The counselling skills*
   debate 15;   *References* 16

2 **Observing and Listening**   **17**
   Understanding the client's world 18;   *Understanding*
   yourself as a listener 27;   *Helping the client to talk*
   34;   *References* 39;   *Responses for exercises* 39

3 **Empathic Responding**   **40**
   Defining empathic responding 40;   *Discriminating*
   empathic responding 41;   *Communicating empathic*
   responses 48;   *References* 62;   *Responses for*
   exercises 62

4 The Initial Session and Beginning Skills **65**
The initial session 65; *Beginning skills* 73

5 Focusing on Thinking **91**
When to focus on thinking 92; *Counsellor interventions for thinking difficulties* 94 *References* 115

6 Facilitating Changes in Behaviour **116**
Setting goals 116; *Managing anxiety* 120; *Developing specific behaviours* 126; *Decision-making, problem-solving and planning* 138; *Postscript* 142; *References* 142

7 Further Considerations and Skills **143**
Routine interview considerations and skills 143; *Handling crises* 155; *Counsellor self-disclosure* 163; *Medical considerations* 169; *References* 175

8 Group Counselling and Life Skills Training **177**
Group counselling 177; *Life skills training* 196; *Role decisions* 203; *References* 205

9 Developing Your Counselling and Helping Potential **206**
Practical, personal and academic dimensions 206; *Concluding comment* 216; *References* 216

APPENDIX — THEORIES UNDERLYING PRACTICAL
COUNSELLING SKILLS **218**

A GLOSSARY OF COUNSELLING TERMS **229**

NAME INDEX **241**

SUBJECT INDEX **242**

List of Exercises

Chapter 2   Observing and Listening
2.1 *Identifying the counsellor's frame of reference* 20;
2.2 *Vocal communication* 23;   2.3 *Bodily communication* 24;   2.4 *Exploring your counselling attitude* 28;
2.5 *Listening to your reactions* 31;   2.6 *Identifying your secrets* 32;   2.7 *Sharing your secrets* 33;   2.8 *Seating and body position* 35;   2.9 *Developing your disciplined listening skills* 38

Chapter 3   Empathic Responding
3.1 *Assessing empathic responding* 46;   3.2 *Reflection of content* 49;   3.3 *Exploring your 'feelings talk' vocabulary* 51;   3.4 *Reflection of feeling* 53;   3.5 *Reflection of content and feeling* 54;   3.6 *Making a succession of empathic responses* 57;   3.7 *Empathic responding with role-played clients* 58;   3.8 *Evaluating your empathic responding skills* 61

Chapter 4   The Initial Session and Beginning Skills
4.1 *Identifying and experiencing questioning errors* 75;
4.2 *Developing your questioning skills* 79;   4.3 *Making transition statements* 81;   4.4 *Developing your summarizing skills* 83;   4.5 *Developing your structuring skills* 87;   4.6 *Conducting an initial session* 90

Chapter 5 Focusing on Thinking
5.1 *Exploring unrealistic standards* 95; 5.2 *Formulating realistic standards* 99; 5.3 *Exploring the attribution of responsibility* 102; 5.4 *Exploring anticipating risk and gain* 104; 5.5 *Exploring self-protective thinking* 107; 5.6 *Exploring alternative frames of reference* 108; 5.7 *Encouraging specificity* 110; 5.8 *Developing your challenging skills* 113; 5.9 *Providing information* 115

Chapter 6 Facilitating Changes in Behaviour
6.1 *Setting goals* 119; 6.2 *Instructing oneself with coping statements* 124; 6.3 *Assertive training* 129; 6.4 *Using modelling* 131; 6.5 *Identifying rewards* 134; 6.6 *Using rewards with clients* 136; 6.7 *Using self-reward* 137; 6.8 *Developing problem-solving skills* 141

Chapter 7 Further Considerations and Skills
7.1 *Making referrals* 145; 7.2 *Keeping records* 151; 7.3 *Using written, audio and visual aids* 155; 7.4 *Crisis counselling* 163; 7.5 *Counsellor self-disclosure: sharing experiences* 167; 7.6 *Counsellor self-disclosure: sharing feelings* 169

Chapter 8 Group Counselling and Life Skills Training
8.1 *Deciding on whether or not to recommend group counselling* 181; 8.2 *Planning a counselling group* 186; 8.3 *Intake interviewing for a counselling group* 187; 8.4 *Structuring at the start of a counselling group* 189; 8.5 *Empathic responding to members' communication in group counselling* 191; 8.6 *Focusing on members' manner of relating in group counselling* 193; 8.7 *Handling aggression in a counselling group* 195; 8.8 *Designing a life skills training programme* 202; 8.9 *Making role decisions* 204

Chapter 9 Developing your Counselling and Helping Potential
9.1 *Developing your practical counselling skills* 215

Appendix Counselling Theory
A.1 *Exploring your theoretical preferences* 219

Für meinen liebsten Adoptivsohn Karli

1 Counselling and Helping Relationships

WHAT IS COUNSELLING?

Since definitions of counselling abound, I start by drawing together some of the terms and then present a definition for this book. Very often counselling is defined as a *relationship* by means of which counsellors help their clients to live more effectively and to cope better with their problems of living. In particular the 'person-centred' or 'client-centred' approach to counselling takes this viewpoint.[1] It sees an effective counselling relationship as one in which the counsellor exhibits a high degree of non-possessive warmth, genuineness and a sensitive understanding of the client's thoughts and feelings. The central quality of this counselling relationship tends to be known by terms such as 'empathic understanding', 'empathic responding' and, more colloquially, 'active listening'. I focus on its component parts in Chapters 2 and 3.

Another way of viewing counselling is as a *repertoire of skills*, including those of a fundamental counselling relationship. Counsellors' ideas of which skills they wish to offer differ according to their theoretical orientation. Counselling theories are really intellectual models designed to explain and predict human behaviour. The fact that counsellors operate from different theoretical assumptions means that counselling can be defined by innumerable different skills. For instance, a psychoanalytic counsellor might emphasize the interpretation of a client's dreams[2] and a behavioural counsellor might systematically use rewards as a means of helping a client to acquire or strengthen a specific behaviour,[3] whereas for some, but by no means all, humanistic counsellors a fundamental counselling relationship is both necessary and sufficient in itself for changes in clients to occur. Counsellor skills may also differ according to various areas of counselling. For example, a careers counsellor may need to be skilled in the use of occupational interest measures and knowledgeable about sources of occupational information; a disablement counsellor may need to understand the special problems and emotional difficulties of disabled people; and a marital counsellor's skills include those of helping clients who have sexual dysfunctions.

In this book, rather than presenting the skills of any single counselling approach or school, I have selected what I consider to be some of the most useful skills of a number of different approaches. Indeed some of the skills are so central that they are part of most counselling approaches. Furthermore, these skills are relevant to many different groups of clients, though additional skills may be required which are specific to the special group with whom you are working as a counsellor. Though a good relationship is fundamental, counselling may be quicker and more effective if, depending on the needs of individual clients, the counsellor is also prepared to offer the following skills: assessing clients (Chapter 4), helping them to understand and alter their self-defeating patterns of thinking (Chapter 5), and facilitating their attempts to take action and to change their behaviour (Chapter 6). Furthermore, counsellors are likely to be more effective if they possess the additional skills required for handling crises (Chapter 7) and for counselling groups of clients and training them in life skills (Chapter 8).

With the increasing recognition that psychological problems and difficulties in living are widespread and not confined solely to a seriously disturbed minority, there has been a growing demand for counselling services. Traditionally the helping professions, like psychiatry, clinical psychology and social work, have focused on the most vulnerable sectors of the population. However, these professions have neither the inclination nor the resources to provide sufficient services for less vulnerable sectors. Consequently, though counselling skills may be used with vulnerable groups like psychiatric patients, counsellors work mainly with less seriously disturbed people in non-psychiatric settings: education, marriage guidance councils, industry, churches, etc. Furthermore, people frequently seek counselling when making major decisions, for example choice of career, or at transition points in their lives, for example after a bereavement. In short, a further way of viewing counselling is in terms of *the provision of services to less seriously disturbed people* in predominantly non-psychiatric settings.

Perhaps a fourth approach to defining counselling is that it is a helping process with the *overriding goal of helping clients to help themselves*. Another way of stating this is that all clients, to a greater or lesser degree, have problems in taking effective responsibility for their own lives. The notion of personal responsibility is at the heart of the process of effective self-help. Such responsibility involves *self-awareness* or responsiveness to experience. It also involves the capacity for flexibility and *freedom of choice* in how to feel, think and act, a dimension sometimes presented as response-ability. Additionally, personal responsibility involves the *ability to act effectively* or to manipulate and deal with oneself and the environment in such a way that goals may be achieved and needs met.

A further characteristic of counselling is that it is a *predominantly psychological process*. The word 'process' in this context denotes movement, flow and the interaction of at least two people in a relationship in which each is continuously being affected in some way by the behaviour of the other. Though for the sake of simplicity I use the term 'counselling' in this book, the process to which I am referring might be better termed 'psychological counselling'. Reasons for this include the fact that these processes are based on psychological theories; for example, Rogers' person-centred approach is a prime example of the practical application of a psychological theory. Furthermore, psychological research may go some way towards assessing the value of different counselling skills, and in some counselling settings psychologically based tests and measures are often used, for example the use of measures of occupational interest by careers counsellors. Though psychology is the fundamental discipline underlying counselling, it is by no means the only relevant discipline. Biology, medicine, sociology and anthropology are other disciplines that contribute to a deeper understanding of the counselling process.

Below I draw together the five characteristics mentioned above into a composite definition of counselling which underlies the remainder of the book.

> Counselling aims to help clients, who are mainly seen outside medical settings, to help themselves. The counsellor's repertoire of psychological skills includes both those of forming an understanding relationship with clients and also skills focused on helping them to change specific aspects of their feeling, thinking and behaviour.

KINDS OF COUNSELLING AND HELPING RELATIONSHIPS

The people who use practical counselling skills encompass: professional counsellors, for example school and student counsellors; people who use counselling skills as part of their professional roles, for example nurses, doctors, social workers and the clergy; voluntary counsellors, for example marital counsellors and youth counsellors; and people in everyday relations, for example marital partners and parents relating to their children. Another way of looking at the use of counselling skills is that they may be used both in *counselling relationships*, based on an interview format in which counselling is the primary activity, and in a host of *helping relationships*, which may or may not take place in interview settings and where the use of counselling skills is likely to be only part of the helper's relationship with the client. In other words, *counselling relationships* involve the use of practical counselling skills in formal *counselling interviews*, whereas *helping relationships* may use many of the same practical counselling skills in more informal *helping contacts*. Some of the different kinds of counselling interviews and helping contacts are reviewed below.

Kinds of Counselling Interviews

Counselling interviews may be conducted by either professional or voluntary counsellors. There are many differing kinds of counselling interviews depending on such matters as the needs of the client, the theoretical orientation of the counsellor and time considerations, for example whether or not the client is leaving the district soon. Here I identify five main kinds of counselling interviews, though in practice they overlap.

The developmental interview

Although sometimes the term 'developmental counselling' is used in relation to helping people to confront and deal with specific developmental tasks in their life-cycle, a different meaning of the term is suggested here. In the developmental interview the major emphasis is on the development of the person rather than on any specific problem or decision. Rogers made a similar point in 1942 when he wrote of the newer psychotherapy that he was proposing: 'It aims directly towards the greater independence and integration of the individual rather than hoping that such results will accrue if the counsellor assists in solving the problem. The individual and not the problem is the focus. The aim is not to solve one particular problem, but to assist the individual to *grow*, so that he can cope with the present problem and later problems in a better integrated fashion.'⁴ Developmental interviewing often involves providing the client with a nurturing emotional relationship to remedy real or imagined deficiencies in previous relationships, especially those provided by parents. Rogers views all clients as having lost contact with their biological selves because they have internalized too many of the ideas and values of other people in order to avoid loss of love. The desirable counsellor-offered conditions of empathy, non-possessive warmth and genuineness are seen as those which will provide the acceptance and understanding which clients have lacked in the past, so that they can discover their true selves. Developmental relationships and interviews, however, are not restricted to Rogers' person-centred approach. The distinction between these and other kinds of interviews is that they are part of what is likely to be a long-term counselling relationship (possibly six months or more) with the aim of a fundamental alteration in clients' attitudes and approaches towards themselves and life. Below is a vignette of a typical client for whom developmental counselling might be appropriate.

> Joe grew up a solitary boy in a family where hard work, achievement and a puritan life-style were valued. Most people outside the family were considered deficient because they did not live up to his parents' high standards. When he came to college Joe found himself depressed, lonely, apathetic and getting increasingly behind in his work.

The problem-focused interview

This type of interview is one where the counselling relationship is based on helping clients to overcome or to learn to cope better with one or more specific problems in their lives. Sometimes this kind of counselling is called problem management or problem solving. Though the distinction is slightly artificial, developmental interviewing emphasizes changing the *person* whereas problem-focused interviewing deals solely with *problems*. The sorts of problems that might be presented to a counsellor are many and varied; examples are the communication problems of marital partners, the various learning difficulties of pupils and students, adjusting to a bereavement, the stress problems of an executive, and learning to come to terms with a physical disability. The behavioural approach to counselling is based on a problem-focused style of interviewing. Not surprisingly, problem-focused or problem-management interviewing often starts with asssessment in order to understand and define the problem areas and to set goals. Below is a vignette of a possible candidate for problem-focused counselling.

Jill is a middle-aged woman who finds that her job is getting too much for her and, on at least one occasion, she has had to leave work early because of this. Basically she enjoys her work, which is in the catering service of a large factory. However, she does find it difficult to talk to people on the phone and to direct the work of subordinates. She also worries a lot about not always being able to attain the high standards she would like at work. She indicates that she is not interested in long-term counselling, but just wants to focus on her problems at work.

The decision-making interview

The decision-making interview is one in which the focus is on helping clients to make one or more specific decisions. Much occupational counselling is concerned with clients' decisions in such areas as choosing: a career; the educational route to obtain qualifications; whether or not to accept redundancy or early retirement; whether or not to change jobs in mid-career; and what to do when retired. There are many other important decisions in people's lives that they may wish to think through with the help of a skilled and unbiased counsellor, for example getting married or getting divorced. Sometimes decision-making interviewing attains a broader focus than that of a specific decision by teaching clients how to make decisions wisely or by helping them to handle any anxiety which interferes with a rational approach to their decision-making. Below is a vignette of someone for whom decision-making interviewing would seem appropriate.

Roger, a married man with one child, has been a school-teacher for the last 20 years. It has recently been announced that his school is to be closed and that a voluntary redundancy scheme is available to him, with reasonable compensation payments for loss of employment based on length of service. Though the possibility of leaving school-teaching evokes some anxiety in him, even before the cuts he had reservations about his job and now wonders whether it is best to 'take the money and run'. He would like his decision to be as rational as possible and based on a systematic exploration of options.

The crisis interview

This type of interview is one in which the client feels that his or her coping resources are under great strain, if not overwhelmed. Such interviews are often characterized by heightened emotionality on the part of the client. These interviews tend to require the counsellor to make an immediate assessment of the situation, including degree of suicide risk, the client's coping resources, availability of support and whether medication is desirable. Furthermore, the counsellor is likely to work with the client on problem-solving, at least to the extent of getting him or her through the worst of the crisis.

A couple of days ago Barbara's boyfriend, with whom she had been living for the past eighteen months, left her. She thinks that there is another woman involved. Since then she has been increasingly anxious, agitated and depressed. She was brought to the counsellor by a friend to whom she had mentioned that she felt like killing herself. As soon as she came into the counselling room she started sobbing convulsively.

The supportive interview

The supportive interview is one where clients, while not going through a major crisis, nevertheless consider that some extra support may be necessary to help them through an awkward phase in their lives. This kind of counselling relationship is likely to be relatively brief and indeed may last for only one interview. Such interviewing can be very valuable to clients who may wish for the opportunity to express and then start sorting out their thoughts and feelings in a safe environment. Ideally, supportive interviews quickly put clients back in touch with their own resources so that they feel better able to cope with life without the counsellor.

Helen is a housewife with three children. Though she gets on well with her husband, recently he has not been at home much, since he has had an unusual number of sales trips abroad. Added to the pressures of looking after her children, she has been spending a lot of time helping her in-laws, both of whom are elderly and infirm. For the past couple of weeks she has been feeling that she has not been herself and decides that she would like to talk things over with a counsellor.

Kinds of Helping Contacts

In the above section on different kinds of counselling interviews, I assumed that they were labelled as such. However, counselling-type relationships and practical counselling skills may be useful in many situations which are not formal counselling interviews. Helping contacts may be made by people who use counselling skills as part of different or more complex roles. Furthermore, all close personal relationships could be regarded as having the potential for helping contacts, though obviously there will also be other forms of communication. Like counselling interviews, helping contacts may have either a developmental, problem-solving, decision-making, crisis or supportive focus at any given time.

Developmental helping contacts

Probably parenthood and education are the two main areas for developmental helping contacts. In fact, developmental interviews conducted by counsellors tend to be necessary in order to provide the nurture and emotional affirmation that should have been provided by good relationships with parents. For instance, in our previous example, had Joe been reared in an emotional climate where he felt understood and respected as a person, it is unlikely that he would have needed a series of counselling interviews. Perhaps the ability to listen to their children and to respond to them so that they feel that they are understood is the most important counselling skill that parents can possess. Similarly, teachers need to know how to offer a good human relationship to their pupils as well as how to impart knowledge. Counselling skills may be useful to teachers both for understanding and relating to individual pupils, and for communicating with classroom groups. Below is an example where a teacher might use counselling skills in a helping contact relevant to a pupil's emotional development.

> Iain is a teacher in a school where there is no counsellor. Ann is a ten-year-old girl whose parents are currently going through an acrimonious separation and divorce process. She has divided loyalties between her parents and is very distressed by their conflict. Recently Ann has not been looking happy in school and her work has been much poorer than usual. Iain tells Ann that he is concerned about her lack of progress and asks if there is any reason for it.

Problem-focused helping contacts

Problem-focused helping contacts occur within many different roles and in many different settings. For instance Jill, our earlier example of a woman who was finding her job too much for her, might have gone to discuss her problem with a supervisor or manager rather than with a counsellor. Supervisors and managers who have some counselling skills may be in a stronger position to identify and cope with the personal problems that employees bring to them than those who do not. Doctors are another example of people who are not primarily counsellors, but who use counselling skills as part of their professional roles, for example in helping their patients to understand and cope with problems in their health and in their personal lives. Similarly, nurses may engage in many helping contacts of a problem-focused nature since they are in the 'front line' in being available to patients. For example, a patient may wish to discuss the problems her family will face when they find out that she has been diagnosed as having terminal cancer. Much of the work of social workers involves helping contacts of a problem-focused nature.

> Isabel is a social worker in an area where there is high unemployment. Recently she has been asked to assist the Smith family, a couple with four school-aged children. Geoff Smith, the father, was laid off work a month ago and since then has started to drink heavily and have violent arguments with his wife. Jane Smith, the mother, is also unemployed. Both parents are concerned that their family life seems to be disintegrating both financially and emotionally.

Decision-making helping contacts

There are numerous opportunities for decision-making helping contacts. For instance, though relatively few young people will spend much time with a careers counsellor, most are likely to discuss their choice of job or career with their parents. Also, pupils and students may go to appropriate teachers and lecturers to discuss both educational and job decisions. Social workers may also engage in many decision-making counselling contacts with their clients. These may include decisions about whether or not a child or older person should be placed or place themselves in residential care and decisions about how a person on probation is going to lead his or her life.

> Paul is a probation officer who is trying to assist and befriend Tom, a fifteen-year-old who was found guilty of stealing a stereo radio cassette from a local store. As Paul gets to know Tom he finds that he has many decisions to make, including whether or not to go straight and how to make some money of his own.

Crisis helping contacts

People in virtually all walks of life may have the opportunity for helping contacts with people who are going through a crisis. Probably most people in a crisis are likely to turn to their friends and relatives, who may react in either helpful or harmful ways or, most probably, a mixture of the two. Doctors, nurses, social workers, lawyers and the clergy are all members of professional groups to whom people might turn in crises.

Policemen and policewomen are another group who deal with people in crises.

> Mary is an elderly spinster who had been living for the past thirty years with her widowed sister, Elizabeth. After a brief illness Elizabeth died. The next day Mary, in a very agitated and depressed state, came to see Mike, her parish priest. She said that the only thing that was keeping her going was her Christian faith.

Supportive helping contacts

Again, people in virtually all walks of life may have the opportunity for offering supportive helping contacts. Managers and supervisors in private industry and the public sector are likely to obtain greater productivity from their workers if they are perceived as supportive of them as people than if they are not so perceived. Similarly, in the educational, medical and social services there are many opportunities for supportive helping contacts from such people as school heads, matrons and senior social workers. Furthermore, employees and workers may have occasion to offer supportive helping contacts to their 'bosses' as well as to each other. Additionally, in any close personal relationship, for example in a marriage, there is much opportunity for the informal supporting of each partner by the other provided that each has the requisite skills for sending and receiving such communications.

> Sue is a 45-year-old woman who has decided that, now her children are grown up, she would like to have a career. On the surface she seems quite confident about her success, but the more she talks to Peter, her husband, the more she is able to confront her doubts and uncertainties about working outside the home. Peter sees his role as mainly listening, but now and then he shares his own opinions in an unthreatening way.

I have tried to indicate in the above section that the practical application of counselling skills is far wider than the formal counselling interview. In fact, like several other writers on counselling and psychotherapy, I consider that many of the skills of counselling are the skills of good human relating. As such, it is important that they do not become the preserve of a small group of full-time counsellors and psychologists but are far more widespread in our workplaces, communities and families. A further reason for the dissemination of counselling skills is that they are appropriate not only for helping others but also for self-help.

A MODEL FOR COUNSELLING AND HELPING RELATIONSHIPS

In the remainder of this book, for the sake of simplicity and to avoid repetition, I discuss counselling and helping relationships more in terms of the counselling interview than of other helping contacts in which counselling skills are used. Furthermore, I use the terms 'counsellor' and 'client', though I hope that this does not cause difficulty for readers who use counselling skills without labelling themselves counsellors and the people they are helping as clients.

Counselling Relationships as Processes

The counselling interview is an ever-changing relationship process between two *people* who influence each other. Fig. 1.1 indicates that both counsellor and client bring many characteristics *into* the interview as well as experiencing many thoughts and feelings *during* the interview. Indeed the counsellor–client relationship is likely to continue *after* the interview, even though the participants are not in physical contact. This

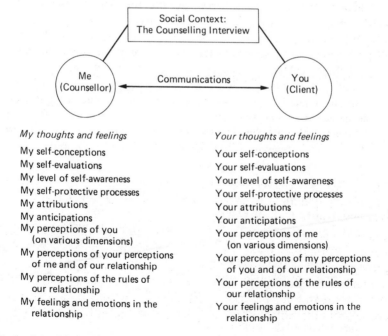

My thoughts and feelings	*Your thoughts and feelings*
My self-conceptions	Your self-conceptions
My self-evaluations	Your self-evaluations
My level of self-awareness	Your level of self-awareness
My self-protective processes	Your self-protective processes
My attributions	Your attributions
My anticipations	Your anticipations
My perceptions of you (on various dimensions)	Your perceptions of me (on various dimensions)
My perceptions of your perceptions of me and of our relationship	Your perceptions of my perceptions of you and of our relationship
My perceptions of the rules of our relationship	Your perceptions of the rules of our relationship
My feelings and emotions in the relationship	Your feelings and emotions in the relationship

Figure 1.1   Illustration of some relevant elements in the counselling interview.

is likely to be especially so for clients as they work through issues in their lives.

The following are brief descriptions of some elements of the counselling interview. They are not described separately for counsellor and client since they are elements of a person-to-person relationship with the emphasis on people rather than on roles.

1. *Self-conceptions.* Self-conceptions, sometimes called the self-concept, refer to the ways in which people see themselves and about which they use terms like 'I' or 'me'. Both counsellors' and clients' psychological selves may be viewed as groups of self-conceptions relating to such topics as their bodies, sexuality, personal relations, feelings and emotions, tastes and preferences, educational and occupational lives, and philosophy and values.

2. *Self-evaluations.* A person's self-evaluations represent the positive and negative values that they place on their personal characteristics. For instance, a client may feel 'I am a worthless person' or a counsellor may feel 'I am a competent counsellor'.

3. *Level of self-awareness.* People's levels of self-awareness refer to how conscious they are of their significant thoughts, feelings and actions. Many counsellors consider that their clients are preventing themselves from a full awareness of significant material in their lives.

4. *Self-protective processes.* The idea here is that people have a psychological self consisting of a group of self-conceptions that they wish to sustain. Self-protective processes are the means by which counsellor and/or client may 'operate' on incoming information which is inconsistent with their self-conceptions. Basically, self-protective processes consist of either denying or distorting the discrepant information. 'Defence mechanisms' is another term for these self-protective processes.

5. *Attributions.* Attributions here refer to the ways in which people are attributing or ascribing causes for their own thoughts, feelings and actions and for external events. For example, the client may feel 'I am a worthless person because my parents mistreated me' or the counsellor may feel 'I am a competent counsellor because I have worked very hard'.

6. *Anticipations.* Anticipations refer to the ways in which counsellor and client view the future. An example of a client anticipation is 'Whenever I meet people for the first time I get tense; therefore this will always happen'.

7. *Perceptions of the other.* Both counsellor and client perceive each

other and characteristics of each other. It is possible that, though some of these perceptions may be accurate, others may be inaccurate. For instance, especially at the beginning of counselling, the client's view of the counsellor may be distorted by seeing him or her in terms of a previous relationship, perhaps with a parent.

8. *Perceptions of the other's perceptions.* In counselling there tends to be an emphasis on personal disclosure on the part of the client who, consequently, is likely to be concerned with how the counsellor is perceiving these disclosures. Both counsellor and client are in a process of reacting to each other in terms of their perceptions of what the other person is thinking and feeling about what is happening in the counselling relationship.

9. *Perceptions of rules.* All relationships are heavily influenced by the social context in which they take place. Both counsellor and client perceive that there are certain rules, usually unstated, about what constitutes appropriate behaviour in the counselling interview. These rules may concern such matters as dress, amount of physical contact, extent of personal disclosure by each party and degree of confidentiality, to mention but a few. Since counselling interviews take place in many different social contexts, there are many variations in rules.

10. *Feelings and emotions.* People's emotions allow them to have shades of positive and negative feelings about what is going on in their lives. In the counselling relationship both counsellor and client will experience a range of feelings about themselves, about each other and about what is being discussed.

The above description of some elements of the counselling interview should be sufficient to indicate that the communications involved in it are more complex than they may seem on the surface. Table 1.1 is a diagrammatic representation of the counselling interview which further attempts to show that the processes of counselling relationships take place both *within* the counsellor and the client as well as *between* them. Only some of what is going on within either party is shared, and even this sharing may be unintentional, picked up by the other person through bodily and vocal cues rather than through the words themselves. To make matters even more complicated, both counsellor and client may be misperceiving themselves and each other. Furthermore, the client may be struggling to attain a greater degree of self-awareness and, even given this awareness, may still be debating whether to conceal or reveal information.

Table 1.1   *Diagrammatic representation of the counselling interview*

Counsellor: private	Counsellor and client: public	Client: private
Private thoughts and feelings Internal dialogue Level of self-awareness	Counsellor's intentional and unintentional verbal, vocal and bodily communications Client's intentional and unintentional verbal, vocal and bodily communications (Accuracy of client's perceptions of counsellor's verbal, vocal and bodily communications) (Accuracy of counsellor's perceptions of client's verbal, vocal and bodily communications)	Private thoughts and feelings Anticipation of advantages and disadvantages in self-disclosure Internal dialogue Level of self-awareness

The Counsellor as a Decision-maker

The counsellor may be viewed as a decision-maker engaged in making *role, treatment* and *responding* decisions. Role decisions relate to how counsellors distribute their time between various activities such as individual counselling, group counselling and running life-skills training programmes. Treatment decisions refer to *what* method or methods to adopt with *which* client or clients and *when*. The nature of the treatment decisions to be made varies according to the theoretical orientation of the counsellor and the concerns presented by the client. Treatment decisions, which can be made in collaboration with the client, imply some form of assessment on the part of the counsellor. All counsellors continually make responding decisions as a result of either individual or a series of client statements. Much of the counsellor's internal dialogue during the counselling interview is likely to consist of deciding how best to respond at the immediate moment to what the client is saying. The counselling skills covered in this book are primarily those concerned with responding decisions, although, especially in Chapters 4 and 8, I cover treatment decisions and role decisions.

Clients are also decision-makers both in collaboration with the counsellor and in their own right. For instance, in collaboration with the counsellor, the client may decide on the goals for counselling and on which treatment method or methods are acceptable. On a more negative note, the client may decide to collude with a counsellor in avoiding exploration of certain painful areas. In their own right, clients may decide what topics they wish to discuss, when and how. A final point is that not only is counselling a process in which counsellor decisions influence client behaviour, but it is very much a process in which client decisions influence counsellor behaviour. Some clients are capable of training their counsellors very well!

THE COUNSELLING SKILLS DEBATE

Counsellors tend to differ on how much they subscribe to the notion of counselling skills. In fig. 1.2, Position A and Position B represent two extremes in what might be regarded as a debate. In Position A it is the quality of the human relationship offered by the counsellor which is important. The emotional climate of safety and freedom created for the client is emphasized, and achieved only if the counsellor respects the client's need to live his or her own life. The counsellor needs to have a high level of self-acceptance in order to be able to accept the client as a unique and growing person. Sometimes the Greek word *agape*, meaning unselfish love, is used to describe the attitude of the ideal counsellor. Given the correct counsellor attitude and emotional climate in the interview, counsellor skills become secondary, since the client's own capacity for self-direction is released.

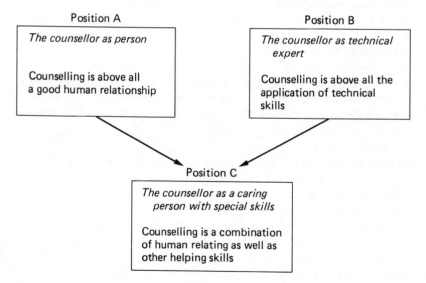

Figure 1.2 Three views of the counsellor and of counselling.

In Position B the counsellor–client relationship is that of teacher and learner. The counsellor possesses a range of specific skills or techniques and decides when and how best to employ them. Whereas Position A might be viewed as a *developmental* model, Position B is very much a *problem-focused* model in which the direction of the counselling interview is largely in the hands of the counsellor, who is the technical expert, with the relationship being considered as secondary to the application of technical skills. If anything, Position A focuses on understanding and facilitating clients' experiencing of their feelings, whereas Position B emphasizes teaching them to think and act more effectively.

In Position C a good human relationship is seen as consisting of a number of skills, for example the ability to understand the other person and to communicate to them that they are understood. These skills of good human relating involve both self-awareness and technique, with neither being sufficient on its own. Here self-awareness and a caring attitude to clients are sharpened by a more disciplined approach to treatment and responding decisions. The assumption is also that technical expertise is likely to be enhanced if used in the context of a good human relationship. The effective counsellor is able to work in each of the three areas of feelings, thinking and action, and also to make good decisions about where the emphasis should be placed at any given time. This book, with its three emphases of understanding feelings, focusing on thinking and facilitating action, represents Position C.

REFERENCES

1. Further information, including selected references, on the 'person-centred' or 'client-centred' approach to counselling is contained in Chapter 9.
2. Further information, including selected references, on the psychoanalytic approach to counselling is contained in Chapter 9.
3. Further information, including selected references, on the behavioural approach to counselling is contained in Chapter 9.
4. Rogers, C.R. (1942) *Counseling and Psychotherapy*. London: Constable.

2 Observing and Listening

The capacity to be a good and understanding listener is perhaps the most fundamental counselling skill of all. Good listening is more complicated than it seems on the surface, since it involves your own level of self-awareness as well as your awareness of the spoken and unspoken cues of the other person. Furthermore, you need to be able to respond to the speaker in such a way that he or she feels understood. Thus being a good listener entails both receiver and sender skills. You need to receive the other person's information accurately and then be able to send a message that you have received it accurately so that the other person feels that he or she is being understood. In counselling circles, these composite skills of being a good and understanding listener are termed accurate empathy, empathic understanding or, more collo-quially, active listening. Though the sender and receiver skills of accurate empathy are interrelated, in this chapter I focus more on receiver skills and the next chapter has more emphasis on sender skills.

You may already be wondering why accurate listening is so important when there are many opportunities for the client to be listened to outside counselling. Here, at risk of overstating the case, it is possible to make a distinction between a social and a counselling or therapeutic conversation. A *social* conversation is geared towards meeting the psychological needs of both participants. In fact, social conversations have been facetiously described as 'two people, each of whom is taking turns to exercise their ego'. Very often, for some of the reasons mentioned in this and the next chapter, the quality of listening in such a conversation is low. A *counselling* or *therapeutic* conversation, however, emphasizes meeting the psychological needs of clients rather than those of their counsellors. Many clients find it difficult to engage in social conversations outside counselling, especially if the conversations are of an intimate nature or otherwise involve subjects which are threatening to their self-image. However, given the safety and psychological space of a good counselling relationship, possibly for the first time in their lives these clients are given the opportunity to explore and listen to themselves and thereby to be affirmed as unique human beings.

Below are a couple of illustrations, one serious and the other humorous, which illustrate some of the after-effects when people feel that they have not been adequately listened to while growing up.

Julia, aged 26, has a number of problems concerning her relationships, particularly her marriage, which she feels is about to break up. Although she feels that some of her relationships have been fairly intense, she has never really been able to get close to anybody, particularly to anyone of the opposite sex. She describes herself as very inhibited, lacking confidence, unable to get on with people, full of indecision about herself and her future, and states: 'I'm unable to express myself physically or emotionally'. She describes her background as one in which her teacher father's rigid moral values were ruthlessly imposed on the family.

The second illustration comes from a cartoon of Jules Feiffer where a man is relating his life experiences of not being adequately heard. First he was an insecure, anxious and unhappy kid and his parents told him he would grow out of it. As an insecure young man, his friends told him he would grow out of it. As an insecure husband, his wife told him the same. He is now an insecure father, with his kids being anxious and unhappy, and he tells them that they will grow out of it and states 'Pass the word'.

UNDERSTANDING THE CLIENT'S WORLD

In Chapter 1 I stated that the counselling interview takes place between two people, each of whom has his or her own private thoughts and feelings, only some of which become public. Here I develop this notion of the psychological separation or differentness between counsellor and client and emphasize the importance of the counsellor's acknowledging the reality of the client's differentness and having the capacity to understand the client 'through his or her own eyes'.

At the heart of counselling is a basic distinction between 'me' and 'you' and, consequently, between 'my view of me' and 'your view of me' and between 'your view of you' and 'my view of you'. Now 'my view of me' and 'your view of you' are both inside or internal viewpoints, whilst 'your view of me' and 'my view of you' are both outside or external viewpoints. These two viewpoints, which acknowledge the counsellor's and client's psychological differentness, are often termed the *internal frame of reference* and the *external frame of reference*.

Internal and External Frames of Reference

The skill of really listening to and understanding another person is based on the internal rather than the external frame of reference. The *external* frame of reference involves looking at the client from outside. For instance, the following would be external frame of reference comments:

> 'She's a bright pupil.'
> 'All patients are a nuisance.'
> 'He has paranoid tendencies.'
> 'I like you.'
> 'Why don't you pull your socks up?'
> 'You seem all right to me.'

The *internal* frame of reference involves understanding clients on their own terms. This may involve careful listening and allowing the client the psychological space to tell his or her own story. The following are comments by a counsellor which attempt to reflect the client's internal frame of reference.

> 'You would really like to have more energy and not feel so low all the time.'
> 'You're really delighted to be off the dole at last.'
> 'You're wondering whether to go into mechanical or production engineering.'
> 'You feel this excruciating pain in your abdomen.'
> 'You are pretty scared at the thought of getting married.'

Whatever their other differences, all counselling approaches acknowledge the importance of understanding the client's internal frame of reference. Client-centred or person-centred counselling is the approach which most strongly emphasizes the importance of the client's or person's subjective perceptions and personal meanings. Sometimes this approach to clients and to people in general is known as the 'perceptual' viewpoint, in which behaviour is seen as the outcome of the subjective perceptions of each individual.

The first exercise in this book is on identifying the counsellor's frame of reference. As with a number of the other exercises, I have made suggestions about how Exercise 2.1 can be done individually, in pairs, or in a training group of, say, six to ten members plus a trainer. The answers to Exercise 2.1 are provided at the end of the chapter.

Exercise 2.1   Identifying the counsellor's frame of reference

This exercise may be done in a number of ways.

A   *On your own*
   This exercise consists of a number of client statements in various counselling settings. Three counsellor responses have been provided for each client statement. On a piece of paper write IN or EX for each of the counsellor responses according to whether you consider each response to be in the internal or external frame of reference.
B   *In pairs*
   There are a number of options. One possibility is to rate independently the three counsellor responses to the first client statement and then share and discuss your answers. Follow this by independently rating the responses to all the remaining client statements, then sharing and discussing your answers.
C   *In a training group*
   This is similar to B above, except that the group meets as a whole and the trainer leads or facilitates the sharing and discussion of answers by group members.

Example
Parishioner to clergyman
Client: There was a time when my faith was the most important thing in my life. Recently, however, I have been having doubts and now I don't know where I stand.
Counsellor:
(a)   You will find your way to God again.
(b)   Your faith used to be extremely important, but now you are having doubts and feel confused.
(c)   Your husband said that you had not been feeling yourself recently.
Suggested answers and comments:
(a)   External. This is what the clergyman is thinking.
(b)   Internal. This is what the parishioner is communicating.
(c)   External. This is what the clergyman is saying that the parishioner's husband is thinking.

Exercise
1.   Youth to youth counsellor
   Client: People round here just don't seem to understand that I am not lazy. I go for job interviews, but keep getting rejected. This is really getting me down. No wonder I get bitter.
   Counsellor:
   (a)   You feel really let down since, despite trying hard, you have not succeeded in getting a job and people still see you as lazy. It's not surprising you get bitter.

(b) The job market should get better as the next election gets nearer.
(c) Have you ever considered that the reason you have not yet got a job is that you don't possess the right skills?

2. Student to tutor
   Client: At last I've been able to start writing up my project. I know that it's cutting it fine, but it's good to be making real progress at last.
   Counsellor:
   (a) Well it's about time . . . don't let it happen again.
   (b) You're really pleased to be under way at last.
   (c) I doubt if you have sufficient time left really to do justice to the topic.

3. Patient to general practitioner
   Client: Ever since I've known I've got terminal cancer I've started worrying about death . . . both about whether it will be painful and about what will happen to my family when I die.
   Counsellor:
   (a) A lot of people feel the way you do, but it just has to be faced and I think I was right to tell you.
   (b) Keep your courage up.
   (c) You wonder how painful your illness will be and worry about how your family will get on without you.

4. Client to marital counsellor
   Client: It's hard to talk about, but we no longer seem to enjoy sex together. I don't know which one of us is to blame or whether it is both of us.
   Counsellor:
   (a) Now let's take a psychosexual history for each of you.
   (b) You are having problems in your sex life, which now you're finding it difficult to discuss, and you wonder who is to blame for the problems.
   (c) Well, how do you get on with each other apart from sex?

The above exercise has been designed for didactic purposes. I do not wish to imply that counsellors and others who use counselling skills need always stay in their clients' frame of reference, but emphasize that this is important much of the time. Also, it is always important to have the capacity for insight into when and why you became partially or wholly external.

Observing the Client

Listening to clients is not just a matter of receiving *what* they say, but also receiving *how* they say it. Sometimes how they communicate is much more revealing than what they actually say, which may be more concealing than revealing. The client's communications consist of both verbal messages and vocal and bodily 'framing' messages which may or may not match the verbal messages. Sometimes, also, bodily communication may be used to replace language and express emotions. Consequently, to understand the client's internal frame of reference, the counsellor must *observe* as well as *listen*.

Table 2.1 *Some dimensions of vocal or para-verbal communication*

Dimension	Illustrative characteristics
Volume	Loudness, quietness, audibility
Stress	Modulated, unmodulated
Pitch	High, low
Clarity	Good enunciation, mumbling, slurring
Pace	Fast, slow, ease of following
Speech disturbances	Stammering, repetition

Table 2.1 illustrates some dimensions of vocal or para-verbal communication. These dimensions provide a commentary on each utterance made by a speaker. Much of the emotional content of what is being said will be conveyed by vocal characteristics of the way it is being said. For example, a comment like 'You're a cheeky boy' can be either affectionate or disparaging depending on the way it it said.

Table 2.2 *Some dimensions of bodily communication*

Dimension	Illustrative characteristics
Proximity	Closeness, distance, ability to touch
Posture lean	Forwards, backwards
Posture orientation	Facing, turned away
Posture focus	Tense, relaxed, rigid, slouched
Clothes	Conforming, rebellious, attractive, dull, showing group identification
Physique	Thinness, fatness, muscularity
Hair	Length, styling
Grooming	Neat, unkempt, clean, dirty
Face	Expressive, blank
Gaze	Staring, avoidance of eye contact
Gesture	Amount, variety
Smell	Body odour present, deodorized, fragrant, pungent
Touch	Intimacy, aggression, part of a social ritual

Table 2.2 illustrates some dimensions of bodily communication. Both counsellors and clients continuously attribute thoughts and feelings to each other on the basis of vocal and bodily communications. Counsellors need to be careful not to misinterpret client's vocal and bodily communications. However, if counsellors are able to perceive such framing messages accurately they are in a much more powerful position to understand their clients. Indeed, sometimes counsellors respond only to bodily communication, for example the counsellor who acknowledges the pain and depression of a client by observing his or her slouched body posture and facial expression with ends of the mouth turned down. Facial cues are particularly important for distinguishing emotions. Feelings of dejection may also be conveyed by vocal characteristics, for example a flat voice tone and sighing. Sometimes it may be helpful for counsellors to check with clients what their vocal and bodily cues are really trying to communicate. Exercise 2.2 focuses on vocal communication, while Exercise 2.3 focuses on bodily communication.

Exercise 2.2   Vocal communication

The exercise can be performed in a number of different ways.

A   *On your own*
Write out an assessment of your vocal communication on each of the dimensions listed in Table 2.1.

B   *In pairs*
Speaking as close to your usual manner as possible, hold a conversation with your partner for 2 to 5 minutes. It may help to audio-record the conversation. At the end of this period, on each of the dimensions listed in Table 2.1, give feedback to your partner on his or her vocal communication and then allow your partner to give similar feedback to you. Both of you may wish to illustrate your feedback with examples from the recording.

C   *In a training group*
One option is to break the group down into pairs and perform the exercise as in B above, but come back together at the end for a plenary sharing and discussion session. Another option, especially if group members have had some prior contact, is to ask one member to assess his or her vocal communication on the Table 2.1 dimensions, then to get the other members to provide feedback on how they see that person's vocal communication. Each group member should have the opportunity to be the focus of attention.

Exercise 2.3 Bodily communication

This exercise can be performed in a number of different ways.

A *On your own*

Write out an assessment of your bodily communication on each of the dimensions listed in Table 2.2.

B *In pairs*

Seated, hold a conversation with your partner for 2 to 5 minutes. It may help to video-record the conversation. At the end of this period, on each of the dimensions listed in Table 2.2, give feedback to your partner on his or her bodily communication and then allow your partner to give similar feedback to you. Both of you may wish to illustrate your feedback with examples from the recording.

C *In a training group*

One option is to break the group down into pairs and perform the exercise as in B above, but come back at the end for a plenary sharing and discussion session. Another option, especially if group members have had some prior contact, is to ask one member to assess his or her bodily communication using Table 2.2 as a guide, and then to get the other members to provide feedback on how they see that person's bodily communication. Each group member should have the opportunity to be the focus of attention.

Open and Covert Communication

The notion of open and covert communication provides another way of looking at verbal, vocal and bodily communication. The Johari window, a modified version of which is shown in fig. 2.1,[1] helps to illustrate the issues of open and covert communication which are likely to occur in counselling and in other relationships. Area A may be viewed as the open area; area B, the blind; area C, the secret; and area D, the 'unconscious'. In general, the purpose of counselling is to increase area A, which entails greater self-awareness and more open and honest communication. For instance, a client like Julia, mentioned at the beginning of this chapter, is more likely before than after counselling to be giving out messages of which she is unaware (area B), to be secretive and inhibited about saying what she really thinks and feels (area C), and to be disguising and not acknowledging to herself many of her significant emotions (area D).

Communication is sometimes viewed as entailing an encoder, a

A	B
Known to others	Known to others
Known to ourselves	Not known to ourselves
C	D
Not known to others	Not known to others
Known to ourselves	Not known to ourselves

Figure 2.1   Modified version of the Johari window.

message and a decoder. Encoding involves saying what you mean indirectly by camouflaging the real message so that it has to be decoded through understanding the context in which it takes place and its accompanying vocal and bodily communication. With someone who is functioning well, there is relatively little encoding of messages. This relieves the necessity for much decoding and makes it easier to be accurately understood. Thus open messages are conducive to good listening. However, with a client at Julia's level of disturbance, much of the communication is likely to be covert or fairly heavily encoded. This makes it more difficult not only for the listener to understand the communication but also for the sender to undersand herself.

There are many reasons why clients and some counsellors engage in covert communication: an example would be the smile which hides embarrassment. This kind of communication is sometimes colloquially expressed as 'letting it come out sideways'. First, the person may be very uncertain of who they are or what they really think and feel. Second, as with Julia, it may not have been safe to communicate directly in the past and so she learned to 'manipulate' her environment less openly. Third, the client needs to learn to trust the counsellor and know that it is safe to communicate openly in the counselling interview. Fourth, the rules of many social situations are not conducive to open communication; for instance 'politeness' may be valued.

The concept of *genuineness* means that people, whether counsellor or client, are communicating openly. Verbal, vocal and bodily communications match each other and no real decoding is necessary to understand the message. There is an absence of facade and you feel that you are relating to people as they truly are rather than to their image of how they should be. Lack of genuineness, or incongruence, implies that people, either consciously or unconsciously, are 'presenting a self' and not really communicating openly. The skilled counsellor is able, with some success, to listen to and understand covert communications. This is a skill which is hard to present in a book such as this, since so many of the relevant cues are vocal and bodily rather than verbal.

Client Self-exploration

Empathic listening can be used either as a skill to help the counsellor assess a client or as part of a specific problem-management procedure. However, in developmental counselling especially, empathic listening is used to help clients to listen to themselves. This kind of listening requires letting clients have the acceptance and psychological space to do their own exploring. There is a beautiful saying of Lâo-Tsze which indicates the effects of such listening:

> It is as though he listened
> and such listening as his enfolds us in a silence
> in which at last we begin to hear
> what we are meant to be

Client self-exploration, helped or facilitated by the counsellor, involves examining self-referent thoughts, feelings and experiences. It is sometimes called inward searching or focusing. Self-exploration is not just an intellectual, thinking-through process, but one in which the counsellor attempts to help clients to acknowledge their own emotions and experiencing. The aim of such self-exploration is to cut through or dissolve false self-conceptions based on the internalization of other people's values. This helps clients to become in touch with and trust their own feelings.

Many counsellors view clients who come to counselling as being at varying degrees of distance from the core of their personality or true selves. Effective listening by the counsellor is likely to help clients to overcome their blocks to experiencing themselves as fully human. At first clients may be reluctant both to disclose personally relevant material and to explore certain emotionally tinged experiences, especially those that differ from their picture of themselves. Later they are likely to be more secure or centred in themselves and to have an inner point of reference for their thoughts and feelings. Empathic listening helps clients to listen to themselves, which in turn helps the counsellor to listen to them at a deeper level, which in turn further helps their self-exploration and experiencing of themselves. Here counselling may be seen as, on the one hand, an *interactional process between counsellors and clients* with the counsellors doing most of the listening. On the other hand, counselling may be viewed as an *internal* or *private process within clients*, both inside and outside the interview, in which there is an unfolding of their own significant thoughts, feelings and emotions as they become freer and less afraid to listen to themselves.

UNDERSTANDING YOURSELF AS A LISTENER

Most of us probably have the illusion that we are good listeners. However, really receiving another person's communications accurately is much more difficult than it seems. This is because not only is it a matter of technical skill but it goes to the root of our own level of self-acceptance and self-awareness.

Again I provide a couple of illustrations, one serious and one humorous, about issues that may interfere with a person's capacity to be a good listener.

> Graham is a counsellor in his mid-forties whose second marriage has just broken up. He is under a lot of strain at work and feels that he is neither adequately understood nor adequately appreciated by the educational institution that employs him. He sees himself as a sensitive and perceptive person who is something of an 'innocent in a cruel world'. He has always had a strong desire to help others and for a time was a priest. His own early life was difficult since his father died when he was four and he felt he never knew where he stood in relation to his mother's mood swings.

The above vignette illustrates, albeit in a rather simple way, that counsellors, like their clients, are human beings. As such, they bring into the counselling relationship their emotional histories and learned ways of dealing with the world. Incidentally, the early life histories of many famous counsellors, for example Rogers,[2] Ellis[3] and Perls,[4] indicate that they experienced a good deal of psychological pain. Furthermore, counsellors' capacity to listen is likely to be affected by their capacity to handle the current stresses of their everyday lives. It should be added that counsellors also bring many positive qualities to their work, such as warmth, caring and a genuine interest in other people.

The second example is a counselling joke. Two counsellors meet each other in the lift after a day of counselling: the first is very tired, while the second looks fit and spruce. First counsellor to second counsellor: 'I don't know how you manage to look so fresh after all that listening'. Second counsellor: 'Who listens?'

Laziness is far from the only reason why counsellors do not hear their clients. Some of the reasons concern clients' abilities to communicate openly, audibly and clearly. However, here I focus on the counsellor and suggest that blockages to counsellor listening can occur in three main interrelated areas: inadequate *skills*, the wrong *attitude*, and counsellor *anxiety*.

Listening and Skills

Since much of this and the subsequent chapter focuses on listening skills, perhaps the only point that needs to be made here is that it is very hard to listen when you are talking. In the training of counsellors, it is common for counsellor trainers to listen to audio-tapes of their trainee's work. However, one very experienced counsellor trainer used to quip that 'adhesive tape is much more important than audio-tape for beginning counsellors'. What he meant was that many inexperienced counsellors do not give their clients sufficient time and psychological space to generate material so that they can listen. Instead, they keep butting in and interrupting, which has the effect of upsetting the client's flow of talk.

Listening and Attitude

The emotional climate of the counselling interview is very important. An emotional climate conducive to client disclosure and counsellor listening is likely to be one in which the client feels safe and accepted in a non-judgemental environment. Sometimes in the counselling literature such an emotional climate is described as one in which the client experiences feeling prized, cared for and respected as a person in his or her own right. Exercise 2.4, the answers to which are at the end of the chapter, explores the dimension of counsellor attitude.

Exercise 2.4   Exploring your counselling attitude

This exercise can be done in a number of ways.

A   *On your own*
B and C   *In pairs or in a training group*
   One option is to complete the questionnaire independently and then together discuss the answers to each item in turn. Another option is to go through the questionnaire independently answering single items, each of which is discussed before moving on to answering and discussing the next item.

Exercise
After considering each statement, write down on a piece of paper whether or not you are in basic agreement (A), disagree (D), or cannot decide (?). Do not

use (?) unless absolutely necessary and do not spend too much time on any one item. Answer all items.

1. The counsellor should permit the client to solve his/her problem in his/her own way.
2. The counsellor should try to help the client see his/her problems in a logical way.
3. The successful counsellor is one who is able to suggest solutions to the client's problems in such a way that the client feels that they are his/her own.
4. In order for the client to benefit most from counselling he/she must be given unconditional acceptance by the counsellor.
5. The counsellor does not have the right socially or professionally to allow a client to choose an inadequate or antisocial solution to his/her problem.
6. The client should be allowed to indulge in self-pity.
7. The more information the counsellor has about the client prior to the counselling interview, the better he/she will be able to understand the client.
8. If counselling is to be successful, the counsellor must depend, for the most part, on the client's own potential for growth.
9. When the client makes conflicting statements, the counsellor should stay and get at the true facts in the situation.
10. When the client does not understand the meaning of a particular piece of behaviour the counsellor should explain it to him/her.
11. The counsellor should never take a client's statements at face value, since the client is not aware of the hidden import behind them.
12. The goal of counselling is to make people better adjusted to society.

The above items were taken from a Counsellor Attitude Scale based on the central idea of the person-centred school of counselling that clients have sufficient capacity to deal with all aspects of their lives which can potentially come into conscious awareness.[5] Essentially, 'correct' answers to the items are based on absence of counsellor direction (being client-centred) whereas 'incorrect' answers imply counsellor direction (being counsellor-centred). Some counsellors would regard the degree of non-interference contained in the scale as being more appropriate for developmental interviews with moderately disturbed clients rather than for more focused problem-management or decision-making interviews. The point nevertheless remains that counsellors who wish to control their clients' lives are likely to be blocked from really listening to them, since they do not respect their separate individuality. A rule of thumb in counselling is that counsellors' capacity to accept and respect their clients is closely related to their capacity to accept and respect themselves. I consider, however, that it is possible for counsellors to provide an emotional climate of acceptance and respect their clients and yet, on occasions, make focused interventions in regard to their thinking and actions. The purpose of such interventions is, however, to help clients to meet *their own* rather than their counsellors' goals.

Listening and Anxiety

Counsellor anxiety or feelings of threat to their psychological well-being can be present in counselling interviews for a number of reasons and, therefore, contribute to poor and sometimes downright bad listening. Sometimes, however, counsellor anxiety can be used constructively to identify something in themselves, their clients or the interview situation which needs attention. Here, however, the focus is on how it may create blockages to good listening.

Pressures to get on with clients and to achieve results are felt by many counsellors, especially those who are relatively inexperienced, since they are uncertain of their skills and do not have the evidence from many previous clients so that they can assess their own effectiveness. Anxiety, however, is likely to be present even in the counselling interviews of experienced counsellors, since everyone has areas of defence, self-protection and pain. Often it is a help with beginning counsellors to explore with them the limits of their responsibility in relation to their clients so that it relieves them of the pressure of feeling that they have to be responsible for their clients' as well as for their own behaviour.

Some specific *situations* which may generate anxiety include: the initial interview, where both parties are getting to know each other; handling silences in interviews; not knowing how to approach a problem area presented by a client; clients in crises; and being confronted with a client's dissatisfaction with counselling. Many counsellors find group counselling more anxiety-evoking than individual counselling, since there they have to be attentive to the communications and emotions of a number of people and, also, the situation is more unpredictable than when working with individual clients.

Different *characteristics* and *emotions* of clients may be anxiety-evoking for different counsellors. For example, counsellors may feel less comfortable with clients whose social characteristics, for example class and race, are very different from their own. Also, it may be threatening if the client is expressing strong anger against another person, even more threatening if the anger is directed at the counsellor, and more threatening still if the anger of the group is focused on the counsellor. The client's expressions of positive emotions towards the counsellor may also be threatening. These may range from declarations of love to those of liking, or just appreciation for doing a good job.

Some counsellors may find that discussion of certain *topic areas* is difficult or painful. If in the past a counsellor has had a similar experience to a client, this might heighten, impede or simultaneously heighten and impede his or her capacity to listen. Some counsellors find discussion of sexual matters difficult: for example, details of a client's heterosexual or homosexual activities. In such instances the counsellor may both fail to listen accurately and respond in such a way that these matters are not properly discussed.

Exercise 2.5   Listening to your reactions

The following exercise may be done in a number of ways.

A *On your own*
   After reading each of the following vignettes about a client, write down the sorts of feelings that the client might generate in you and identify those which might interfere with your effectiveness as a counsellor.

B *In pairs*
   Go through each vignette, first giving yourself time to listen to your own reactions then discussing your reactions together. Use your own experience to identify and explore your reactions to other situations, emotions, client characteristics and topic areas which might interfere with the quality of your listening.

C *In a training group*
   As for B above. The trainer can get group members to share any experiences they have had of their own anxieties getting in the way of their listening. Furthermore, trainers can highlight common anxieties which may affect listening in the situations for which they are training counsellors, for example death anxiety in bereavement counselling.

Exercise
1. Mick is a 55-year-old, working-class Irishman who dresses poorly, swears a lot and is extremely depressed. He looks unshaven and haggard and says that he never pays tax on his earnings.
2. Kate is a very prim and proper 30-year-old single woman with a strong upper-middle-class accent. She continuously refers to herself as 'one', controls her emotions, and says that she cannot stand uncertainty in her

life. Her political views are strongly right wing.

3. Khalid is a 23-year-old gay man who now leads and describes to you a promiscuous sex life based on finding partners in gay clubs and pubs. Three months ago he attempted suicide when the older man with whom he had been living for three years ended the relationship.

4. Sue is a 27-year-old married woman who, three years ago, discovered that she had multiple sclerosis. Recently her health has deteriorated rapidly and she is now having trouble both seeing and walking. She is also very anxious.

5. Rita is a 35-year-old married woman who is in conflict with her husband and family. She gets very angry indeed in the interview, keeps blaming everyone but herself and clearly sees you as a potential ally in her war against the rest of the family.

6. Dick is an 18-year-old unemployed man who has been on the dole for the last six months. He says that he spends much of the day in bed and that, while he would like a job, it is really the Government's fault that he hasn't got one.

Below are two further exercises focused on exploration of areas which might cause you difficulty in listening to your clients and seeing them clearly as separate people. Both Exercise 2.6, an individual exercise, and Exercise 2.7, a group exercise, are based on the notion that areas of ourselves about which we feel uncomfortable when talking to others are areas in others about which we may experience some anxiety when they discuss them with us.

Exercise 2.6   Identifying your secrets

This is an exercise, best done on your own, about how threatening you anticipate it would be for you to disclose and discuss your behaviour on a one-to-one basis with a specific acquaintance or friend of your choosing. Threat involves the degree to which you anticipate you might feel uncomfortable and/or be esteemed less as a result of your disclosures. Using the following rating scale, rate each area and, if any area is not true for you, rate it as though it were true for you.

Discussing in some detail with a specific friend or acquaintance of your own choosing your thoughts and feelings about yourself in ——— area would be:

5   Impossible, much too threatening
4   Very threatening
3   Moderately threatening
2   Slightly threatening
1   Not threatening at all

Areas	Rating for each area

Family relationships
Things that make you happy
Your body
Feelings about death

Social relationships
Use of leisure
Sexual feelings and behaviour
Feelings of depression

Political preferences
Intellectual capacity
Homosexual tendencies
Socioeconomic background

Your work
Things that make you angry
Fears and anxieties
Religious beliefs

Exercise 2.7 Sharing your secrets

This is a group exercise. The trainer gives each group member a standard piece of paper and a pencil and mentions that nobody is allowed to divulge that they have a specific secret. The trainer then asks the group members to print a one-sentence statement about themselves that they would ordinarily consider to be too threatening for the group to know. Each piece of paper is then folded twice, collected by the trainer, and shuffled. The 'secrets' are then distributed so that nobody has his or her own secret. If anyone has, the secrets should be reshuffled. The trainer uses the following procedure. First, he or she gets a member to read out someone else's secret; second, that member is asked to say how he or she would feel if the secret were true of him or her; and third, the remaining group members are asked to disclose how they would feel if the secret were true of them. The procedure is repeated for each secret. The trainer facilitates members' exploration of their reactions and ensures that no-one is ridiculed because of his or her secret.

By now this section should have established that empathic listening is not only a matter of technique, but also involves you as a whole person.

The existentialist counsellors use the term *presence* to describe the quality of a person who is accessible to another human being through his or her own capacity for self-awareness and awareness of the separate existence of the other.[6] Good listening requires just such presence or being present in the relationship. This is the opposite of the distance created by people who are so busy listening and responding to what is going on in themselves that they are unable to listen and respond to what is going on in others.

HELPING THE CLIENT TO TALK

Setting the Scene

Counselling interviews are best conducted in quiet, comfortable, well-decorated rooms which allow for absolute privacy and absence of interruption. The reception area is likely to be the client's first point of contact with most counselling agencies, and therefore the need for tactful and sympathetic receptionists is emphasized. Also, it gives a friendly impression if the counsellor goes out to bring the client from the reception area into his or her office rather than standing at the door. Often, however, counselling interviews are conducted in less than ideal circumstances through no fault of the counsellor, who is then faced with minimizing the impact of adverse working conditions. Furthermore, the counselling contacts of such people as nurses, pastoral care teachers and the clergy will often take place in very informal settings, for example in hospital wards, school classrooms and parishioners' homes.

There are a number of considerations regarding the seating arrangements for counselling. Some counsellors work sitting at a desk, while others prefer a more informal setting similar to a living-room in a private house, with chairs and a coffee table. Especially in encounter groups, some counsellors may settle for cushions and a carpeted floor.

Demonstrating your Attentiveness

Your bodily communication is an important indication of your interest in and attention to the client. Sometimes this is referred to in the counselling literature as attending behaviour. For example, details of your seating position can be important, since if the counsellor is too close the client may feel that his or her territorial space is being invaded by an overwhelming and possibly over-intimate counsellor: remember that at close distances touch is possible. If, however, counsellor and client are too far apart this may generate feelings of emotional distance. Though there is no absolutely right distance, if the counsellor's and the client's heads are about five feet apart, this should be comfortable for most people. Counsellor and client need to be seated at the same level, since if the client is lower than the counsellor this may indicate an inferior–superior emotional relationship as well. The angle of their chairs is also important. Clients can be very sensitive about too much eye contact, so rather than sitting squarely opposite the client it is better to sit at a slight angle. This will allow both client and counsellor to be flexible about eye contact.

Posture, trunk lean and eye contact all convey information about counsellor attentiveness and interest. Behavioural psychologists would view good counsellor body position as helping to reward or reinforce 'self-talk' on the part of the client, thus increasing the probability of the client being able to continue talking. A good starting position is an open posture with legs uncrossed, appearing moderately but not too relaxed, and with a slight forward trunk lean. Eye contact should be intermittent and not too obtrusive. As the counselling relationship progresses, clients get to know whether or not their counsellors are interested in them and then there should be less need for the counsellor to have to focus consciously on an attentive body position.

The purpose of Exercise 2.8 is to develop your awareness of non-verbal considerations in interviewing by getting you to experience good and bad bodily communication. Good attending behaviour is conducive to making the client feel that the counsellor is interested and wants to listen.

Exercise 2.8   Seating and body position

This exercise may be performed in pairs or in a training group.

A   *In pairs*
1.   *Seating position*
(a)   Distance. You sit in a chair and listen to your partner talking: (a) with your heads 18 inches apart; (b) with your heads 6 to 8 feet apart; then start moving in until your partner says it feels a comfortable distance for being counselled. You and your partner then reverse roles, followed by discussion.

    (b) Height. Your partner talks and you listen while you: (a) sit in a noticeably higher chair; (b) sit in a noticeably lower chair; and (c) sit in a chair which is the same height. You and your partner reverse roles, then discuss.

    (c) Angle. Your partner talks and you listen while: (a) sitting squarely opposite so that your right shoulder is directly across from your partner's left shoulder; (b) sitting at 90 degrees so that the front of your chair faces the right side of your partner's chair; and (c) you move your chair until your partner indicates that this is a comfortable angle for being counselled. You and your partner reverse roles, then discuss.

2. *Body position*

    (a) Posture. Both seated, your partner talks and you listen while you: (a) have your arms and legs tightly crossed; (b) sprawl loosely in your chair; and (c) try to adopt a relaxed and attentive body posture. You and your partner reverse roles, then discuss.

    (b) Trunk lean. Both seated, your partner talks and you listen while you: (a) lean right back; (b) lean far forward; and (c) lean slightly forward. You and your partner reverse roles, then discuss.

    (c) Eye contact. Both seated, your partner talks and you listen while you: (a) avoid your partner's gaze completely; (b) stare at your partner; and (c) maintain good eye contact, yet look away every now and then. You and your partner reverse roles, then discuss.

3. *Seating and body position*

    Your partner talks for a few minutes while you listen in a correct seating position, combining a relaxed posture, slight forward trunk lean and good eye contact. You and your partner reverse roles, then discuss.

B *In a training group*

    One option is to break the training group down into pairs, get the pairs to go through the exercise, then bring the whole group together for a plenary discussion session. Another option is for the trainer to get two group members at a time to demonstrate each part of the exercise in front of the rest of the group. With each option, the trainer can help group members to draw on their own experiences of good and bad bodily communication, both by others and by themselves, in interviews.

Making Opening Remarks and Continuation Responses

Good television interviewers or chat-show hosts are skilled in making remarks which open an interview or conversation. Furthermore, they are good at keeping the conversation going both by demonstrating attentiveness through their bodily communication and by making responses which encourage the speaker to continue. Perhaps you may wish to observe how they operate more closely, since some of the skills you need as a counsellor are similar to theirs.

Table 2.3   *Opening remarks and continuation responses*

Opening remarks	Continuation responses	

Hello, I'm ————. Would you care to:
  tell me why you've come to see me
  tell me what is concerning you
  tell me how you see your situation
  put me in the picture
	Um-hum
	Please continue
	I see
	Then
	Oh
	Indeed
	That's interesting
		And
		So
		Go on
		Really
		Ah
		Yes

You've been referred by ————.
  Now how do you see your situation?
  Where would you like to start today?		

Table 2.3 gives some examples of *opening remarks*, though this list is far from comprehensive and not necessarily appropriate to all counselling contexts. The message contained in all these statements is: 'I'm interested and prepared to listen, and would like you to share with me your view of yourself and your concerns'. These statements ask the client to let you as counsellor understand his or her frame of reference. The last of the openers, 'Where would you like to start today?' is more appropriate for later interviews, especially if conducted within a person-centred framework.

Continuation responses are designed to keep clients talking. The message they provide is: 'I am with you. Please go on'. I have listed verbal responses in Table 2.3, but stress that there are many non-verbal continuation responses, with perhaps the main one being the head nod. Counsellors need to be very sensitive to the power of continuation responses. On the one hand, they may greatly facilitate a client's exploration of his or her frame of reference, but on the other hand they may range from crude to subtle attempts to take clients out of their frame of reference so that they respond to the counsellor rather than to themselves. An obvious example is the counsellor who says 'Um-hmm' whenever the client says something that fits into his or her pet theoretical framework.

Good listening skills are not something which most beginning counsellors 'naturally' possess. They require a disciplined approach to the counselling interview and, for most people, much practice and experience. A good way to learn counselling skills is to practise with a partner, with one of you counselling the other for a period of time and then reversing roles. You may wish to do this for progressively longer periods until you are counselling each other for a whole interview, though as your sessions get longer you will probably need a break before reversing roles. This peer role-reversal approach is known as co-counselling, and our next exercise uses this format.

Exercise 2.9 is an integrative listening exercise combining bodily and vocal communication, listening to and understanding the client's internal frame of reference, and using opening remarks and continuation responses. You should consciously try to develop your skills in each of these areas, perhaps by using audio or video feedback.

Exercise 2.9   Developing your disciplined listening skills

This exercise may be done in pairs or in a training group.

A   *In pairs*
You act as counsellor to your partner for 2, 5 or 10 minutes, by using an opening remark, listening within his or her frame of reference, and using body language and continuation responses, but *not* using additional words. Your partner should talk about a current concern or role-play a client. At the end of this period, summarize for your partner what he or she was saying and ask your partner to comment on the accuracy of your feedback. You and your partner reverse roles, then discuss, possibly using audio or video feedback.

B   *In a training group*
First the trainer should act as counsellor and demonstrate or model the whole exercise with one of the group members. Then the group might be divided into twos or threes to do the exercise. If the group is divided into threes, one person should observe while the others act as counsellor and client, with all three discussing at the end, though members should rotate roles. The trainer should visit each group and ensure that there is a real focus on disciplined listening. After the pairs or subgrouping, there might be a plenary session of the whole training group in which members are encouraged to explore their listening abilities.

REFERENCES

1. Luft, J. and Ingham, H. (1955) *The Johari Window: A Graphic Model for Interpersonal Relations*. University of California at Los Angeles, Extension Office: Western Training Laboratory in Group Development. The word 'Johari' is derived from a combination of the Christian names of Joe Luft and Harry Ingham.
2. Rogers, C.R. (1980) *A Way of Being* pp. 5–26. Boston: Houghton Mifflin.
3. Gregg, G. (1973) A sketch of Albert Ellis. *Psychology Today*, **7**, (2), 61.
4. Perls, F.S. (1969) *In and Out of the Garbage Pail*. New York: Bantam Books.
5. Nelson-Jones, R. & Patterson, C.H. (1975) Measuring client-centred attitudes. *British Journal of Guidance and Counselling*, **3**, 228–236.
6. Further information, including selected references, on the existential approach to counselling is contained in Chapter 9.

RESPONSES FOR EXERCISES

Exercise 2.1
1. (a) internal; (b) external; (c) external
2. (a) external; (b) internal; (c) external
3. (a) external; (b) external; (c) internal
4. (a) external; (b) internal; (c) external

Exercise 2.4
1. A; 2. D; 3. D; 4. A; 5. D; 6. A; 7. D; 8. A; 9. D; 10. D; 11. D; 12. D. This scale is scored by summing correct answers and ignoring incorrect and (?) answers.

3 Empathic Responding

In Chapter 2 I focused more on the listening than on the responding dimensions of the composite skill of accurate empathy. In this chapter I focus more on how the counsellor actually responds to the clients' utterances to help them feel that they are understood.

DEFINING EMPATHIC RESPONDING

Empathic responding involves accurately understanding, from the internal frame of reference, what your client is telling you and then sensitively communicating back your understanding in a language attuned to your client's needs. More coloquially, empathic responding involves being a good listener and then responding with understanding. Though virtually all counsellors consider empathic responding necessary, the person-centred school of counselling particularly emphasizes it. In the person-centred approach, the three 'core' counsellor-offered conditions of accurate empathy, non-possessive warmth and genuineness are considered to be both *necessary* and *sufficient* for client changes to occur. In 1975 Rogers published an updating of his views on the process of being empathic. What he termed his current definition of empathy includes the following:

> . . . entering the private perceptual world of the other and becoming thoroughly at home in it.
> . . . being sensitive, moment to moment, to the changing felt meanings which flow in this other person . . .
> . . . sensing meanings of which he/she is scarcely aware, but not trying to uncover feelings of which the person is totally unaware since this would be too threatening . . .
> . . . communicating your sensings of his/her world as you look with fresh and unfrightened eyes at elements of which the individual is fearful . . .
> . . . frequently checking with him/her as to the accuracy of your sensings, and being guided by the responses you receive . . .

. . . pointing to the possible meanings in the flow of his/her experiencing you help the person to focus on this useful type of referent, to experience the meanings more fully, and to move forward in the experiencing.[1]

Below are two examples of clients for whom empathic responding might be appropriate, though in rather different ways. The first client may require long-term developmental counselling in which empathic responding will be used to help her to understand and experience herself more fully. This is because she appears to have grown up in an insufficiently nurturing environment where she was discouraged from being a person in her own right.

> Shirley, aged 22, comes for counselling having felt depressed for a long time. She has no self-confidence, considerable feelings of inferiority and great difficulty in coping. She is obsessed by minor details and cannot cope with major problems. Recently she has become extremely apathetic and she dreads her final examinations in six months' time. She studies in a very obsessional and time-consuming way and has great difficulty in concentrating. She says her parents, in particular her father, cannot understand her and her failure to achieve, and consider her behaviour childish. She has always been a poor mixer, rather solitary and introverted.

The second example comes from a medical setting where a male patient is speaking to a nurse. The nurse's response is an attempt to show respect for the patient as a *person* and to deal with rather than to deny his feelings.

> Patient: Will the doctor have the laboratory results soon? I still don't feel well and this is not like me.
> Nurse: You're keen to get to the bottom of what's causing your sickness. We expect your results tomorrow.

In the above example, not only has the patient's overt request for information been granted, but also some attempt has been made to respond to his covert request to have the personal meaning of obtaining his results understood as well.

On other occasions the counsellor may use empathic responding as one of the skills of clarifying a problem or a decision. Also, there are numerous opportunities for empathic responding to be used in everyday life, for instance by marital partners in informal situations of supporting each other or by parents who are helping their children to discuss what has happened in their day at school.

DISCRIMINATING EMPATHIC RESPONDING

A useful distinction is made in counsellor training between discriminating and communicating the various counsellor-offered conditions. Discrimination involves *assessing* how well other counsellors or you yourself are responding, while communication involves actually *responding*. Discriminations are sometimes made from audio-recordings of counselling interviews.

Some Common Mistakes

In our culture there are many common ways of responding which demonstrate lack of rather than presence of empathy. Most of these are similar to mistakes which both beginning and experienced counsellors should beware of. Sometimes they are obvious, but at other times they are much more subtly manipulative.

Directing and leading

Taking control of what the client can talk about:

> 'I would like you to talk about this today.'
> 'I do not think we should be spending so much time discussing your feelings about your parents.'
> 'I expect you to allow me to decide how we spend our time together.'

Judging and evaluating

Making evaluative statements, especially ones which imply that the client is not living up to your own standards:

> 'You are overpossessive.'
> 'I find your manner very defensive.'
> 'I can't accept that she really behaved that way to you.'

Moralizing, preaching and patronizing

Telling clients how they ought to be leading their lives:

> 'Sex is not everything in life.'
> 'Honesty is a virtue.'
> 'You should always respect your teachers.'

Labelling and diagnosing

Placing a diagnostic categorization on the client or on some of his or her behaviour:

'You have an inferiority complex.'
'You have paranoid tendencies.'
'You have an obsessive-compulsive neurosis.'

Reassuring, diverting and humouring

Trying to make clients feel better, yet not really acknowledging their true feelings:

'We all feel like that sometimes.'
'You can get by . . . I know you can.'
'You'll be all right.'

Not accepting the client's feelings

Telling the client that his or her positive and negative feelings should be different from what they are:

'You shouldn't boast.'
'Don't let yourself get so depressed.'
'I don't see why you are feeling so pleased with yourself.'

Advising and teaching

Not giving clients the space to arrive at their own solutions to their own concerns:

'Why don't you have a coffee with her and talk things over?'
'If he behaves like that to you, surely it's time you found another boyfriend.'
'I would be inclined to make a decision about where I wanted to live before I looked for a specific job.'

Interrogating

Using questions in such a way that the client feels as though he or she is 'in the dock' and is always responding to the counsellor's probing:

'I want a detailed account of the history of your problem.'
'Tell me who all your teachers are.'
'Now tell me about your sex life.'

Over-interpreting

Offering explanations of clients' behaviour which bear little relationship to what they might have thought of by themselves:

'Your reluctance to socialize may indicate some unresolved conflicts, possibly sexual.'
'Your indecision about getting a job is related to your fear of failure, which in turn is related to your fear of being in the public eye if you succeed and get promoted.'
'Your failure to do well at school is because you feel that your parents will not love you unless you succeed and this is making you much too nervous.'

Inappropriately self-disclosing

Talking about yourself either when clients do not want to listen or when listening to you stops them from really listening to themselves:

'My relationship with my mother had these features.'
'I think I'm pretty good at finding the solutions to other people's problems.'
'When I work I plan everything very carefully and start only when I know precisely where I'm going.'

Putting on a professional facade

Trying to make yourself seem an expert and thereby communicating in a defensive or otherwise inauthentic way:

'Your lack of progress is due to your resistances.'
'As your counsellor I'm telling you that you have severe problems.'
'You shouldn't direct your anger at a professional person like me.'

Encouraging dependence

Responding to your clients in ways focused on meeting your needs rather than facilitating their independence:

'Now the moment you get into any trouble come back and see me.'

'As far as I'm concerned you can always keep coming for counselling.'
'I like having you as a client and want you to keep coming.'

When reading the above section, you may have noted that all the counsellor statements were from the external rather than from the client's internal frame of reference. Almost all of them indicate that the counsellor has some difficulty accepting the client as a separate individual with his or her own life. Additionally, most of these statements show a lack of acceptance or are 'put-downs' of the client. Consequently the emotional climate of the counselling interview becomes less safe than ideal, with the amount and level of intimacy of the client's self-disclosures and self-exploration being diminished. Other results of this may be that the client edits and tends to disclose only material that wins counsellor approval or the client terminates counselling.

Assessing Empathic Responding

Good empathic responding indicates a basic acceptance of clients as people. It does not act as a 'stopper' on their flow of talk and their emotions, or make them feel inadequate, inferior, defensive or as though they are being talked down to. Good responses are made in easily comprehensible language and have a clarity and freshness of expression. They are accompanied by good vocal and bodily communication, something which the next exercise is unable to incorporate since it is in written form. Implicit in good empathic responding is the fact that the counsellor is *working in collaboration with* the client to understand his or her frame of reference and personal meanings. In such a collaborative companionship counsellors are always covertly or overtly checking the accuracy of their understandings. Furthermore, clients feel secure enough to mention if their counsellors are inaccurate and thus help them to stay accurate.

In assessing empathic responding it is sometimes helpful to think of a three-link chain: client statement–counsellor response–client statement. The adequacy of the counsellor's response can partly be ascertained not just be relating it to the original client statement but by imagining its impact on the next client statement. Good empathic responses provide the opportunity for the subsequent statement to be a continuation of the client's original train of thought and experiencing, while bad responses do not.

In the light of the above discussions on good empathic responding and on common mistakes which act as blockages, work through Exercise 3.1. Some answers are suggested at the end of the chapter.

Exercise 3.1   Assessing empathic responding

This exercise may be done in a number of ways.

A   *On your own*
Empathic responding involves accurately understanding, from the internal frame of reference, what your client is telling you and then sensitively communicating back your understanding in a language attuned to your client's needs. Take a piece of paper and rate the three counsellor responses to each of the client statements using the following scale:

5   Very good empathic response
4   Good empathic response
3   Moderate empathic response
2   Slight empathy in the response
1   No empathy at all

Write down the reason or reasons for each rating.
B   *In pairs*
With a partner, either rate individual responses or segments of the exercise and then discuss, or go through the whole exercise making independent ratings and then discuss.
C   *In a training group*
See B above, with the differences that the group meets as a whole and that the trainer both gives ratings and leads or facilitates the sharing and discussion of rating by group members.

Example
Pupil to careers officer
Client: You know I find it really hard to decide what I want to do. My father wants me to join him in the family electrician's business. My mother wants me to be a professional person. Frankly, I can't please both of them and neither of them may be right.
Counsellor:
(a)   Well, it's your life and your decision.
(b)   You're confused and finding it difficult to decide what's right for you. You are subject to family pressures but wonder whether they really provide the best solution.
(c)   Let's explore why you would like to please your parents. One of them is bound to be disappointed.
Suggested ratings and comments:
(a)   1; External frame of reference, advising, patronizing.
(b)   4; Communicates good understanding.
(c)   2; Slight chance of being in internal frame of reference, leading, interpreting.

Exercise

1. Youth to probation officer

   Client: I'm really fed up with getting into trouble with the law. Me and my mates used to think that nicking things from shops was a bit of a lark, but now I reckon its not worth the bother.

   Counsellor:

   (a) I am sure that this will please your parents. It's been a terrible worry for them.

   (b) You are right to be fed up and I'm glad that you have decided to go straight.

   (c) You now feel that getting into trouble with the law is more trouble than its worth . . . taking things from shops is not the same game it used to be.

2. Patient to doctor

   Client: I know I'm being stupid but I'm worried about my operation, both whether something will go wrong with it and whether I will be in pain afterwards.

   Counsellor:

   (a) It's common for people to worry, but worrying about it doesn't really help that much.

   (b) I am sure that you will be able to cope . . . I doubt if it will hurt that much.

   (c) You feel foolish about your concerns over your operation and would like reassurance that it will not give you too much pain.

3. Employee to industrial counsellor

   Client: I've always been an active person and I'm both excited and frightened that I will be retired at the end of next month. Part of me says that it's a great opportunity to do the things that I have always wanted to do, but every now and then I find myself getting very anxious and, on a few occasions, have even woken up at night thinking about it.

   Counsellor:

   (a) Your retirement presents exciting challenges, since you will then have the freedom to engage in some really rewarding activities, but you have an undercurrent of fear and anxiety.

   (b) You like being busy and now is your opportunity to be busy doing the things that you like. Why does this worry you?

   (c) Not being able to sleep at night and getting very anxious indicates that you need to plan for your retirement much more thoroughly so that you can make sure to spend your time in fulfilling endeavours.

4. Wife to husband

   Wife: It's depressing to see one's parents getting very old and unable to look after themselves properly. I don't know what to do about dad now that mum's got this spell in hospital coming up.

Husband:
(a) I'm sure that we will manage one way or the other.
(b) Yes, your dad never has learned to look after himself and this is even harder now he is old.
(c) You're sad seeing them so old and vulnerable and are wondering how best to handle mum's absence.

COMMUNICATING EMPATHIC RESPONSES

This section adds to the previous exercises by focusing on the use of words in responding. Along with the text there are seven exercises: reflection of content, exploring your 'feelings talk' vocabulary, reflection of feeling, reflection of content and feeling, making a succession of empathic responses, empathic responding to role-played clients, and evaluating your empathic responding.

Reflection of Content

'Mirroring' is another word for reflection. A distinction in counselling is often made between reflection of *content* and reflection of *feeling*. In reflection of content the counsellor mirrors only the verbal content of the client's communications by restating or paraphrasing them. Reflection of content is one way in which people can build up the skill of disciplined, accurate listening. In reflection of feeling the counsellor mirrors the emotional tone and meaning of the client's communications by using vocal and bodily, as well as verbal, responding. The idea behind the concept of reflection is that counsellors are companions to their clients as the clients themselves clarify their own thinking, emotions, decisions and problems. Helping clients to help themselves is frequently better than offering them direct assistance.

To the beginning counsellor the notion of reflection may seem highly artificial. This gets combined with the need for many counsellor trainees to have to concentrate consciously on formulating their responses, thus detracting from their spontaneity and possibly adding to the feeling of artificiality. After an initial period of difficulty, though, most beginning counsellors work through their self-consciousness and doubts about the value of reflection and become much more proficient at it.

Even experienced counsellors may have problems making good

reflections. A good reflection most definitely does not entail the mechanical parroting of the last words the client has said. An example of such mechanical parroting is the story, probably apocryphal, about a well-known American counsellor who was counselling a suicidal client in his office near the top of a tall building.

Client: I feel terrible.
Counsellor: You feel terrible
Client: I feel really terrible.
Counsellor: You feel really terrible.
Client: For two cents I would jump out of that window there.
Counsellor: For two cents you would jump out of that window there.
Client: Here I go.
Counsellor: There you go.
Client: (Lands on the pavement below with a thud.)
Counsellor: Thud!

Many people falsely assume that, when they are 'listening', they have an accurate and clear grasp of what has just been said. This may be the case in simple conversations, but is likely to become less true as conversations become more complex and personally involving. A relatively straightforward, but not absolutely foolproof, approach to getting some way into another person's frame of reference is to start your responses with 'you' or 'your'. Using simple, clear English, work through Exercise 3.2. Some possible restatement responses are given at the end of the chapter, but there are usually several ways of making adequate restatements of the same client utterances.

Exercise 3.2   Reflection of content

This exercise may be done in a number of ways.

A   *On your own*
For each of the following client statements: (a) repeat the statement using 'you' or 'your' where the client uses 'I', 'me' or 'my'; and (b) again using 'you' or 'your', restate or paraphrase the content of the statement in clear, simple and, where appropriate, colloquial language.

B   *In pairs*
Alternate with one partner providing the repetition response and the other the restatement response for each client statement in the exercise. Then you counsel your partner for five minutes, focusing especially on reflecting the content of his or her statements in your responding. You and your partner reverse roles, then discuss, possibly also using audio feedback.

C   *In a training group*

The trainer gives group members time to formulate repetition and restatement responses to one client statement at a time. For each client statement, the trainer gets one group member to give the repetition response and then facilitates the sharing and discussion of all the group members' restatement responses, including his or her own version. The trainer may then demonstrate giving reflection of content responses in a brief counselling session with one of the group members. Afterwards the group may subdivide into pairs in which members counsel each other by giving reflection of content responses.

Example

Patient to clinical psychologist

Client: I used to be able to go out and have fun. Now I have to force myself to go out and don't really enjoy it any more. All the time I have a feeling of sadness and of not really being part of the group I am with.

Counsellor:

(a)   Repetition response. 'You used to be able to go out and have fun. Now you have to force yourself to go out and don't really enjoy it any more. All the time you have a feeling of sadness and of not really being a part of the group you are with.'

(b)   Restatement or paraphrase response: 'In the past you could really enjoy your social life. At the moment, however, you have lost your motivation and don't get much pleasure out of it. You always feel depressed and an outsider in company.'

Exercise

1.   Mother to social worker: 'My life is really going much better now I've got my health back. Before, having six children was too much for me, but now I want to have them all at home and I'm sure Bill and I can look after them.'

2.   Parent to bereavement counsellor: 'You know it's six months since Kevin was killed in an accident and I still find myself going into his room and having a quiet weep. I still miss him terribly.'

3.   Woman to women's counsellor: 'I want the agent who is responsible for the maintenance of my flat to arrange for the damp in my bedroom to be put right. It's three weeks since I asked and he still hasn't come. I'm sure he would have done something by now if it were a man making the request.'

4.   Patient to psychiatrist: 'I'm delighted with the progress that I've made. Previously just getting through the day was a real effort and I used to dread getting up in the morning. Now things don't upset me nearly so easily.'

Reflection of Feeling

Reflection of feeling may be viewed as *feeling with* the client's flow of emotions and experiencing. It does not mean being swamped or controlled by the client's emotions, but being sensitive and responsive to them. Beginning counsellors often have trouble with the notion of reflection of feeling, since they just talk about feelings rather than offer an expressive emotional companionship which goes some way to mirroring the client's feelings. Reflection of feeling requires accurate understanding of clients' vocal and bodily, as well as of their verbal, messages. While it overlaps with reflection of content, it differs both in its greater emphasis on 'feelings talk' and in the counsellor's added emotional expressiveness or matching of feelings. Needless to say, in this book I have the limitation of not being able to show vocal and bodily communication. Consequently, though I acknowledge that this is just part of any good reflection of feeling, the exercises here focus only on 'feelings talk'.

Being able to name and indicate the level of intensity of clients' feelings is an important part of the ability to make good reflections of feelings. In short, counsellors need to have a reasonably large vocabulary to describe emotions and the ability to use this vocabulary readily and flexibly. Exercise 3.3 is designed to explore and possibly expand your 'feelings talk' vocabulary. For each emotion you are asked to provide a range of adjectives which describe differing levels of intensity at which a person may experience that feeling. There are no single correct answers and much will depend on the way and the context in which the adjectives are used. A list of suggested adjectives is provided at the end of the chapter. This list is far from exhaustive and looking up the emotions in one or more dictionaries may help you to expand your vocabulary further, as well as making your use of 'feelings talk' words more precise.

Exercise 3.3   Exploring your 'feelings talk' vocabulary

This exercise may be done in a number of ways.

A   *On your own*
In the exercise below you are given a number of feelings, each of which can be stated in very strong, strong, moderate and mild ways. In the blank spaces, or on a piece of paper, write down at least one *adjective or*

expression to describe each level of intensity for each of the following feelings. By way of example some suggestions are provided for levels of intensity of anxiety.

B and C   *In pairs or in a training group*
For each emotion, independently formulate your answers and then discuss. Afterwards see if you can think of additional emotions which might be relevant to counselling and describe their levels of intensity.

Exercise

Level of intensity	Feeling			
	Anxiety	Fear	Happiness	Depression
very strong	panic-stricken			
strong	tense			
moderate	nervous			
mild	worried			

Level of intensity	Feeling			
	Sadness	Desire	Confusion	Confidence
very strong				
strong				
moderate				
mild				

Although the next exercise, Exercise 3.4, can convey the feeling nuances of neither the client's messages nor your responses, complete it as best you can. There are many different words and phrases which might be appropriate in responding to our hypothetical client. This is one of the lessons that counsellor trainees learn when, in a group setting, they each respond to the same client statement. In formulating your responses try to match, rather than to add to or subtract from, the level of intensity of the client's feelings. Some suggestions for words, phrases and responses are provided at the end of the chapter.

Exercise 3.4 Reflection of feeling

This exercise may be done in a number of ways.

A *On your own*
For each of the following client statements: (a) identify the words or phrases the client has used to describe how he or she feels; (b) suggest other words or phrases to describe how the client feels; and (c) formulate a response to the client focusing on and reflecting his or her feelings, starting with the words 'You feel . . .'. It may help to write out your answers.

B *In pairs*
Independently answer, and then together discuss your answers to, one client statement at a time. Then you counsel your partner for five minutes, focusing especially on reflecting his or her feelings in your responding. You and your partner reverse roles, then discuss, possibly also using audio feedback.

C *In a training group*
The trainer gives group members time to formulate answers to one client statement at a time and then facilitates the sharing and discussion of group members' answers, including his or her own versions.

  The trainer may then demonstrate giving reflection of feeling responses, where appropriate, in a brief counselling session with one of the group members. Afterwards the group may subdivide into pairs in which members counsel each other by giving reflection of feeling responses, again where appropriate.

Example
Old man to priest: 'I feel that I've not long to go now. I'm grateful that I've had such a good life. I've loved my family, who have meant more to me than anything in the world. While I don't want to die, I am not frightened any more of death.'

(a) Client's words and phrases to describe his feelings: 'not long to go', 'grateful', 'loved', 'have meant more to me', 'want to' and 'frightened'.

(b) Other words and phrases to describe how the client feels: 'time is running out', 'thankful', 'adored', 'most important of all to me', 'wish to', and 'afraid'.

(c) Possible response focusing on and reflecting the client's feelings: 'You feel that your time is nearly up. You are thankful for the blessings of life and especially for your family. The prospect of death, while unwelcome, no longer makes you afraid.'

Exercise
1. Immigrant to community-relations worker: 'I'm glad that we've come here,

since we're not nearly so poor as at home. I miss my homeland though. There I was accepted and respected and enjoyed the closeness of village life.'

2. Young male to youth counsellor: 'I wish that we could have a better club here. This town is very boring in the evenings and us young people need somewhere to go to meet each other and enjoy ourselves.'
3. Female to student counsellor: 'I had a terrific row with one of my lecturers in a laboratory class the other day. I felt that he was putting me down. I've noticed in the past that I quickly get very irritable with people in authority.'
4. Female to marriage counsellor: 'My husband seems to be losing his grip on his work as a painter and decorator. He does not get as much work as he used to and mopes round the house a lot. I'm getting fed up with living in such a depressing atmosphere.'

Reflection of Content and Feeling

Good empathic responses combine reflection of both content and feeling. In other words, they accurately pick up and reflect both the verbal messages and the emotional tone of the client's statement. Exercise 3.5 is on reflecting content and feeling. Though a standard format is used throughout the exercise, this is for didactic purposes and there are other ways of reflecting content and feeling, including of course the vocal and bodily communication of the counsellor. Some possible responses to Exercise 3.5 are provided at the end of the chapter.

Exercise 3.5 Reflection of content and feeling

This exercise may be done in a number of ways.

A *On your own*
   For each of the following client statements formulate a response which reflects both feeling and content using the standard format: 'You feel . . . because . . .'. It may help to write out your answer.
B *In pairs*
   Either formulate a response for each statement independently, then share and discuss, or formulate responses for all statements, then share and discuss.

C   *In a training group*
The trainer gives group members time to formulate the answer to one client statement at a time and then facilitates the sharing and discussion of group members' answers, including his or her own version.

Example
Man to unemployment counsellor: 'It's much more difficult than I thought it was going to be. I liked going to work and now the meaning seems to have gone out of my life. It's all very depressing'.

Possible response: 'You feel depressed and at a loose end because it is difficult losing your job and along with it your purpose in life.'

Exercise
1.   Girl to school counsellor: 'I hate being teased. I just hate it. I'm really no different from the other girls and yet they seem to enjoy ganging up on me. It makes me feel so angry and lonely.'
2.   Man to gay counsellor: 'I feel confused about what to do next. At times I think that it would be great to come out and end all the phoney game-playing. At other times I get nervous and feel that I can't take the risk.'
3.   Parent to pregnancy counsellor: 'It's so disappointing to think that my daughter has gone and got herself pregnant. She's had a good home and we have done our best for her.'
4.   Woman to medical counsellor: 'It was a great shock to me to learn that I have multiple sclerosis and that this is incurable. I still get anxious and depressed over it and can't really adjust to the news.'

Making a Succession of Empathic Responses

Perhaps especially in developmental counselling, but also in other kinds of interviewing, the counsellor may provide a series of empathic responses to help the client to explore more fully his or her self, problem area, decision, crisis or general life situation. The following excerpt from an interview with a female college student shows a series of empathic responses as required in Exercises 3.6 and 3.7. As you read the excerpt, remember that the counsellor does not know what the client is going to say next, but by means of empathic responding is helping her to tell her story in her own words and at her own pace. Furthermore, note that as the short transcript progresses the client is talking in a more self-referent or personal way and beginning to explore the impact of the marital break-up on her. Often it is the case that, when clients are responded to empathically, they shift from talking about more distant to talking about more personally relevant and emotionally tinged material.

Client: I went home last weekend and was surprised to find that my mother was in the process of buying another house.

Counsellor: You hadn't expected her to be planning to move.

Client: No. She has only been married to Jack, my stepfather, for just over a year and this means she's leaving him.

Counsellor: So your mother's house move means that her marriage is breaking up.

Client: Yeah . . . and he doesn't even know what she's doing and I feel sad about it.

Counsellor: You feel sorry that your stepfather doesn't know what is going on behind his back.

Client: I can see that they haven't been getting on too well together, but he's not a bad bloke and has put an awful lot of time and money into our present house.

Counsellor: On the one hand their relationship hasn't been good and yet, on the other hand, you don't dislike him and acknowledge the effort he has put into your house.

Client: I think it may be best for Mum to leave, but I wouldn't like him to feel that I had anything to do with persuading her. Also, I will miss not having a father-figure around.

Counsellor: Though the break-up may be the right thing for your mother, you don't want to be blamed for contributing to it. Also, it would be nice to still be able to have a father-figure around.

Throughout the above transcript, the counsellor is trying to stay sensitively and accurately in the client's frame of reference and to give her the message: 'Please go on. I am interested'. The above client found it relatively easy to talk superficially about herself when she came for counselling, but felt that she had no real identity of her own and was always craving other people's affection, not least through promiscuous sex which she found physically painful. As counselling progressed she began to feel a greater sense of confidence in her own worth and opinions.

An issue in practising empathic responding skills is whether it is better for trainee 'clients' to be themselves and discuss their own concerns or to role-play real clients whose problems they may have already come across. The main advantage of trainee 'clients' playing themselves is that their counsellors are more likely to get practice at responding to real feelings than they would in role-plays. Counsellor trainees would have to be very good actors indeed if they were able to role-play convincingly the depth and range of clients' feelings. Furthermore, by discussing their own concerns in the exercises, counsellor trainees may get more of a feel of being well or poorly counselled than if they were role-playing someone else's concerns. Disadvantages of trainee 'clients' being themselves include the fact that they may not present their counsellors with the kind or range of material that they might have come across in real counselling settings. Furthermore, there is the risk that some trainees may become so self-absorbed that they do not prepare themselves adequately for the needs of the clients with whom they may later be working.

Perhaps, however, it is not an either/or issue and trainees should be given the opportunity both to work on their own concerns and to role-play representative clients and issues from their present or future client populations. Exercise 3.6 allows trainee 'clients' to discuss their own concerns, while Exercise 3.7 encourages them to role-play clients. Added realism is brought into skills training if, from an early stage, trainees are given graduated exposure as counsellors to clients in a real-life rather than a role-play situation. Such practical work requires both careful screening of clients and close supervision of the trainees' interviews.

Exercise 3.6 Making a succession of empathic responses

This exercise may be done in pairs or in a training group.

A *In pairs*
You act as counsellor to your partner for 5, 10 or 15 minutes by using an opening remark, being attentive, using good body language, listening and making a succession of empathic responses. Your partner should explore either his or her style of personal communication, or counselling style, or a problem area or a decision he or she has to make. Furthermore, your partner should pause ever now and then to allow you to practise responding. You and your partner reverse roles, then discuss, possibly also using audio or video feedback. This exercise may be done for longer periods until one person is counselling for a complete interview of, say, 45 to 50 minutes. With these longer sessions you may not wish to reverse roles until you have had a break.

B *In a training group*
The trainer may start by demonstrating the exercise, with the trainer as a counsellor while one of the group members is a client. The group may then split into pairs to perform the exercise, either audio recording or video recording their sessions. The group then meets as a whole, with excerpts from the audio or video recordings being played back and commented on by the participants in the session, by the other group members and by the trainer.

This exercise should be done again and again to build up interview skills and confidence.

Exercise 3.7   Empathic responding to role-played clients

This exercise may be done in pairs or in a training group.

A   *In pairs*
Practise your empathic responding, with you and your partner each taking turns as counsellor and role-played 'client', by engaging in 5, 10 or 15-minute counselling sessions. Audio or video recording of these sessions may be helpful.

Either the 'client' should draw on his or her experience to present case material which is likely to be relevant to the counsellor's future work.

Or the 'client' should act a role based on *one* of the following vignettes, each drawn from a different setting.

1.   *Medical.* Susan, aged 68, is in hospital terminally ill with cancer. Her husband died two years ago and her only son lives 200 miles away and can only visit her occasionally. She says that the nurses insist on telling her that she is all right and will soon be out and about. She finds keeping up this pretence tiring and would like to talk to somebody in a less superficial way.

2.   *Marital.* Dave, a married man with three teenaged children, feels that he can no longer communicate with his wife. He is a teacher and recently has been seeing more and more of Liz, a staff colleague. He is feeling increasingly guilty about carrying on a relationship behind his wife's back and about the possibility that he may hurt his children. He would like to sort out his own feelings about the whole matter.

3.   *Occupational.* Anna, aged 28 and single, works as secretary to the managing director of a privately owned toy company. In the past year the company has been having financial problems, the result of which is that Anna has found herself having much more work and a less happy working environment. She has started having trouble sleeping at night and wonders whether the job is getting too much for her. Underlying her doubts about her job is a further doubt about whether or not she could find a more fulfilling career.

4.   *Educational.* Paul is a 15-year-old who will be sitting his 'O' levels in three months. He is finding it very hard to concentrate and says that he feels tense and depressed much of the time. He feels ashamed that he does not seem to be living up to his parents' expectations. They tell him that he is too much of a worrier and that he should be getting out and enjoying himself more. He wishes that he could have more friends.

B *In a training group*
   Trainers can ensure that trainees are exposed to the kinds of clients and client problems either that they are working with now or with which they may be faced in their future counselling work. Options for seeing that the trainees have practice at empathic responding with relevant case material include: (a) using experienced group members to role-play suitable clients, with the trainer acting as counsellor; (b) the trainer role-playing clients, with a group member acting as counsellor; and (c) the trainer providing typed handouts of vignettes or scripts on which the trainees can base their role-plays.

Advanced Empathic Responding

Advanced empathic responding expands or advances the client's level of awareness, yet still remains primarily in his or her frame of reference. Basic empathic responding matches the feeling and content of clients' disclosures and is largely neutral in terms of the depth of their previous and next statements, leaving decisions about direction and depth to the client. Advanced empathic responding, however, tries to reflect feelings and experiences at a slightly deeper and possibly more threatening level than the client's current disclosures. In a sense, the counsellor is 'forcing' the issue by making a response which offers the client the opportunity to go deeper into his or her experiencing. Consequently, since the chances of being wrong are greater, tentativeness or working *with* clients in such a way that they can correct faulty responding is even more important in advanced than in basic empathy. Factors which affect the timing of advanced empathic responding include: how well you know your client; how safe the client feels in the counselling relationship; and the level of emotional development and self-awareness of your client. Needless to say, the *how* or your response (your vocal and bodily communication) must be appropriate to the *what* of your response (the verbal content) in order to be received with minimal threat by the client.

One example of advanced empathy might be to make explicit *what a client is thinking*: 'You are giving a lot of reasons why you lost your job, but every now and then I get the impression that you may be blaming yourself as well'. Another example might be to make explicit *a theme*: 'You've brought up the issue of male intimacy a number of times and I'm wondering whether this isn't an important issue for you too'. A further example might be to make explicit *an underlying feeling*:

'Although you say that everything is all right and that you can get on without him, I catch a note of deep pain in your voice as though you are all choked up inside'. Advanced empathic responding may help the client to explore more personally relevant, emotionally tinged and threatening areas of his or her experiencing. However, if inaccurate, clumsily worded or badly timed, such responding can do more harm than good, as well as putting you at risk of losing your client.

Another way of viewing advanced empathy is that it consists of interventions which help clients to become aware of and realize their potentials rather than their current realities. These interventions may include not only deeper reflections, but also specific interventions which focus on the client's thinking difficulties and capacity for effective action. I discuss some of these interventions in Chapters 5 and 6. Perhaps focusing on clients' thinking and acting in such a way as to help them to realize their potentials might be better termed *additive* empathy in order to distinguish these activities from *advanced* empathy or responding in such a way as to reflect a deeper level of clients' thoughts, feelings and experiencing.

Client Perception of Empathic Responding

Person-centred counsellors consider it important not only that counsellors respond empathically but that their empathy is perceived by their clients. Two ways of exploring the extent to which clients perceive the empathy of their counsellors are from their behaviour in counselling and by asking them how they view their counsellors. There is some research evidence that clients vary in the depth of their self-exploration according to whether their counsellors are offering high, medium or low levels of empathy. Thus it might be inferred that, by engaging in different degrees of self-exploration, clients are perceiving the different levels of empathy of their counsellors, at least to some extent. Furthermore, there is again some research evidence that counsellors offering high levels of empathy are more likely to be successful with their clients on various measures of counselling outcome than those offering low levels of empathy,[2] though this research seems to apply particularly to person-centred counsellors.

A psychologist called Barrett-Lennard has devised a Relationship Inventory, the purpose of which is to ask clients how they see the relationship offered to them by their counsellors.[3] Again, this measure applies particularly to the work of person-centred counsellors. The reason I mention it here is that one of the Relationship Inventory's scales measures the client's perception of the counsellor's level of empathic understanding. The scale is made up of both positive and negative items. Some illustrative positive items are: 'He wants to understand how I see things'; 'He nearly always knows exactly what I mean'; 'He usually senses or realizes what I am feeling'; and 'He appreciates exactly how the things I experience feel to me'. Some illustrative negative items are: 'He may understand my words but he does not see the way I feel'; 'Sometimes he thinks that *I* feel a certain way, because that's the way *he* feels'; 'He does not realize how sensitive I am about some of the things we discuss'; and 'His response to me is usually so fixed and automatic that I don't really get through to him'.

Clients are likely to perceive their counsellors not only as the counsellors are, but also according to their own needs and wishes. Especially with more disturbed clients, there is a likelihood that their perception of their counsellors and of the counselling relationship will be distorted. This, however, does not invalidate the importance of empathic responding, since the better it is the greater is the likelihood of its being perceived, in some measure, by the client.

Evaluating your Empathic Responding

I conclude this chapter with an exercise aimed at getting you not to take your interviewing for granted but to develop the skills of evaluating yourself. Attempt to explore the ways in which your interviewing seems to be affecting the ways in which your clients are responding. In short, try to become as aware as you can of the interactive processes taking place in your counselling interviews. Relevant questions are: 'What was the client thinking and feeling?'; 'What was I thinking and feeling?'; and 'What was going on in the counselling interaction?'.

Exercise 3.8   Evaluating your empathic responding skills

This exercise may be done in a number of ways.

A *On your own*
   Assuming that you have one or more audio or video cassettes of you conducting counselling interviews, take three-minute excerpts from the beginning, middle and final thirds of one or more interviews and, for each excerpt, rate yourself on the following scale:

5 Very good empathic responding
4 Good empathic responding
3 Moderate empathic responding
2 Slight empathy in the responses
1 No empathy at all

You may also use this scale to rate single responses made by you after individual client statements and/or to give yourself an overall rating for an interview. Each rating should involve you in critcally thinking about your empathic responding strengths and weaknesses.

B *In pairs*
First one partner plays back three-minute excerpts from his or her interviewing as above. After each excerpt both of you make independent empathic responding ratings, then discuss them. This process is repeated with the second partner's interview excerpts. In conclusion, the partners might use their empathic responding skills as, in turn, they help the other partner in a self-assessment of his or her ability at empathic responding.

C *In a training group*
The trainer can get individual members to play back three-minute excerpts from their interviewing to the whole group. The trainer gives the group time to make independent empathic responding ratings and then facilitates discussion of their ratings. The trainer can show sensitivity to the interviewer by asking about his or her feelings about and reasons for any response, and also by attempting to ensure that any feedback from the group is constructive, identifying strengths as well as weaknesses. Another option is for the trainer to demonstrate the exercise and then to divide the group into threes or fours, with members' interview excerpts being rated and discussed in those smaller units. The trainer visits each subgroup in turn.

REFERENCES

1. Rogers, C.R. (1975) Empathic: an unappreciated way of being. *The Counseling Psychologist*, **5** (2), 2–10.
2. Truax, C.B. & Mitchell, K.M. (1971) Research on certain therapist interpersonal skills in relation to process and outcome. In Bergin, A.E. & Garfield S.L., (ed.), *Handbook of Psychotherapy and Behaviour Change*, pp. 299–344. New York: Wiley.
3. Barrett-Lennard, G.T. (1962) Dimensions of therapist response as causal factors in therapeutic change. *Psychological Monographs*, **76** (43, whole no. 562).

RESPONSES FOR EXERCISES

Exercise 3.1
1. (a) 1; patronizing, evaluating, irrelevant.

   (b) 1; judging, patronizing, inaccurate in terms of the client's feelings.
   (c) 4; good attempt at understanding the client's viewpoint.
2. (a) 2; slightly in internal frame of reference, implicitly advising, not responding specifically enough to the client as a person.
   (b) 3; first part of the response patronizing, second part possibly helpful.
   (c) 4; probably shows good understanding, assuming reassurance was what the client would like.
3. (a) 5; very good understanding.
   (b) 2; starts off well, then is leading.
   (c) 1; over-interpreting, advising.
4. (a) 2; sympathy, possibly, rather than empathy; may impede further exploration.
   (b) 2; slightly in internal frame of reference, judgemental.
   (c) 4; a good attempt at understanding.

The above ratings are the author's and are based on an assessment of verbal content only. You might infer different counsellor vocal and bodily communication to accompany any or all of the responses and thus differ in your ratings.

Exercise 3.2
Part (b): restatement responses. The following are intended only as suggestions. There is no single correct response to each statement.
1. 'Things are looking up now that you're feeling better. Being responsible for six kids used to be too much for you, but now you're keen for all of them to be living at home, since you're certain you and Bill can take care of them.'
2. 'You're telling me it's half a year ago that Kevin died in a mishap and yet you're aware that you keep moving to his part of the house and silently crying there. His absence is still a great loss for you.'
3. 'You would like the person whose job it is to take care of your apartment to see to it that the wet parts of the wall in your sleeping area are fixed. It's nearly a month since you made the request and he has yet to appear. You're certain that there would already have been action if someone of the opposite sex had asked.'
4. 'You're very pleased indeed with how much better you're feeling. Before, coping from getting up to going to bed was very laborious and each day you were apprehensive about rising. Nowadays you're much better able to handle situations which previously worried you.'

Exercise 3.3

Feeling	Very strong	Strong	Moderate	Mild
anxiety	panic-stricken	tense	nervous	worried
fear	terrified	frightened	fearful	uneasy
happiness	elated	joyful	happy	pleased
depression	suicidal	depressed	unhappy	low
sadness	griefstricken	distressed	sad	sorry
desire	craving	longing	desirous	wishful
confusion	chaotic	disorganized	bewildered	uncertain
confidence	bold	self-assured	secure	adequate

Exercise 3.4
There are no single correct responses other than for (a).
1. (a) 'glad', 'miss', 'accepted', 'respected', 'enjoyed', 'closeness'
    (b) 'happy', 'pine for', 'regarded with favour', 'honoured', 'had the pleasure of', 'intimacy'
    (c) 'You feel happy to have immigrated here, since financially you are much better off. However, you still feel a sense of loss for back home, where you used to enjoy acceptance, respect and the intimacy of village life.'
2. (a) 'wish', 'boring', 'enjoy ourselves'
    (b) 'would like to', 'dull', 'have some fun'
    (c) 'You feel you would really like a better club here, since this is a dull place in the evenings and needs a place for young people to get to know each other and have some fun.'
3. (a) 'terrific', 'putting me down', 'irritable'
    (b) 'heated', 'disparaging me', 'annoyed'
    (c) 'You felt that one of your lecturers was putting you down and you had a heated argument with him recently in class. You are aware that you can quickly feel very angry with authority figures.'
4. (a) 'losing his grip on', 'mopes', 'getting fed up', 'depressing'
    (b) 'going to pieces in', 'moves aimlessly', 'becoming exasperated', 'enervating'
    (c) 'You feel that your husband is no longer on top of his painting and decorating work, not getting so many jobs as before, and mopes round the house a lot. You feel exasperated with living in such an uninspiring environment.'

Exercise 3.5
Again, there are no single correct responses.
1. 'You feel extremely angry and lonely because you loathe being teased and yet, despite your being really no different from the other girls, they seem to take pleasure in ganging up on you.'
2. 'You feel confused about your next step because, on the one hand, there are times when you feel it would be great to be openly gay without all the phoney deceptions and yet, on the other hand, you have moments when you feel anxious about the risk.'
3. 'You feel disappointed because your daughter, despite your giving her a good home and doing your best for her, has gone and got pregnant.'
4. 'You still get feelings of anxiety and depression and can't really adjust to the news because it was a great blow to you to find out that you had multiple sclerosis and that this was incurable.'

4 The Initial Session and Beginning Skills

In this chapter I mainly discuss the initial session and the beginning skills connected with it. In Chapter 1 I said that counselling interviews could be categorized into five main groups: developmental, problem-focused, decision-making, crisis and supportive. I also proposed the notion of the counsellor as a decision-maker involved in role, treatment and responding decisions. The initial session, or possibly sessions, is the major, but by no means the only, time during counselling when treatment decisions are made. Indeed, one of the most important categories of treatment decision is the extent to which and the combinations in which the course of subsequent sessions should be developmental, problem-solving, decision-making and supportive. Crisis management presents some special initial session issues and I deal with these in Chapter 7. Since readers are likely to be working in many different contexts, with many differing levels of skill and knowledge of differing counselling methods, most of this chapter will focus on 'core' or central beginning skills which the counsellor is likely to need irrespective of context. Some of these skills are also relevant to those who use counselling skills in helping contacts.

THE INITIAL SESSION

One way of defining the initial session is the literal way of saying that it is the first session. However, the initial session is defined here as either the first session or the initial assessment period, which may last for more than one session during the counselling process.

Assessment

I use the term 'assessment' in preference to 'diagnosis', which is a more medical term with connotations of a classification scheme of psychiatric illness amenable to diagnosis, treatment and prognosis. The issue of assessment is one on which counsellors differ. Let me try to illustrate some of the issues by means of a case example.

> Tony, aged 21, comes to counselling in a state of great tension. During the initial session he frequently sighs and taps the counsellor's desk with the end of a pencil. He came for counselling after he was fired from a recent industrial training assignment because of complaints from his fellow workers that he was being too forward with some of the women at work. He talks about his difficulties in personal relationships, especially with women but with blokes as well. He started noticing his problems with women a couple of years ago. He reports difficulty in chatting them up and getting them to go out with him and states: 'With girls I go to pieces'. He reports being moody, very easily irritated, and getting very depressed to the point of thinking of suicide. He experiences much apathy and feels that he runs out of energy quicker than others.

One of the main issues regarding assessment is whether it does more harm than good. Four of the main criticisms of assessment are that it damages the counselling relationship, encourages dependency, is not based on any sound system of classification, and is unnecessary.

The 'damaging of the counselling relationship' argument is that what is curative in counselling is the counsellor's ability to offer a really good relationship based on a safe emotional climate in which clients can explore their own concerns. Assessment, which involves the counsellor in judging and evaluating, is an external frame of reference activity which is likely to block rather than facilitate the client's experiencing and self-exploration. For instance, Tony's concerns might be perceived as symptomatic of low self-esteem brought about by deficiencies in previous relationships. Consequently, what he needs is a good emotional experience and not just a set of counsellor techniques.

The 'encouragement of dependency' argument is that assessment puts the counsellor in the role of expert and that this diminishes clients' responsibility for their lives, since they expect change to come from outside rather than through their own efforts.

The argument that assessment is not based on any sound system of classification has two strands. The unitary-diagnosis strand is that a classification system for clients' concerns is redundant, since fundamentally all problems represent clients' inability to be in touch with their true selves or self-actualizing tendency. The other strand is that, even if classification is not entirely redundant, there are too many different classification systems, none of which is so soundly based as to merit allegiance.

The 'assessment is unnecessary' argument is that, whether counsellors assess or not, they end up conducting subsequent sessions in the same way, so why bother with assessment since it seems to be more for the sake of the counsellor's need for certainty than for the sake of the client?

There are a number of arguments for assessment. One argument is that clients have different concerns and are at different stages of psychological development, and that therefore assessment is necessary to ensure that they receive the most effective counselling help. For instance, without some form of assessment how does the counsellor know whether Tony needs developmental or some more problem-focused kind of interviewing, or possibly a developmental emphasis followed by more of a problem-focused emphasis? A second argument is that, with the growing sophistication of behavioural and cognitive or thinking-focused interventions, counsellors are in a much stronger position than they were previously to make effective interventions regarding specific areas of a client's functioning. A third argument is that counsellors who do not assess are not considering all the possible options, for example group work or referral elsewhere, which may be of benefit to their clients. A fourth argument is that counsellors do not have unlimited time and are under increasing pressure of accountability to demonstrate that they are a worthwhile expenditure to the agencies and institutions that employ them. If initial assessment leads to greater cost-effectiveness, then counsellors may be less likely to have their budgets cut and more likely to have them increased.

Probably the 'assessment versus no assessment debate' gets unnecessarily polarized. I consider that assessment is a desirable part of counselling and precludes neither a subsequent emphasis on a nurturant relationship nor an initial period in which the client is allowed to ventilate feelings and emotions. It is important that assessment takes place within the framework of a facilitative relationship and that great, but not exclusive, attention is paid to getting into the client's internal frame of reference. Assessment is best conducted *in collaboration with* clients and may illuminate rather than obscure their concerns, including the ways in which they are avoiding taking responsibility for their feelings, thoughts and actions. Additionally, sensitive assessment may improve rather than hinder the quality of the counselling relationship, since clients may feel that they and their concerns are more fully understood. A distinction may be made between global judgement of the client as a person and evaluations of patterns of living which are causing the client distress. Whereas the former are likely to be counter-productive, the latter may be perceived by clients as helpful if shared in an appropriate way. As with so much of counselling, the difference between good and bad is not so much *what* is being done but *how* it is being done. Assessment need not imply rigidity, and is best done with flexibility in regard to the varying concerns and communication patterns of different clients. Furthermore, much assessment takes place during later counselling as counsellor and client monitor progress and as differing goals emerge.

> At first the counsellor gave Tony the psychological space to tell in his own words why he had come for counselling. Then in collaboration with Tony he engaged in an exploration of his current pattern of living and background. As a result of this assessment, for a number of sessions Tony received a nurturing counselling relationship in which he could say what he really thought and felt and, also, learn to experience the counsellor as a safe person. As counselling progressed Tony was seen less frequently on an individual basis, but joined a counselling group composed of both sexes to help him work on his communication difficulties. In the later individual sessions, specific areas on which the counsellor helped Tony to work included clarifying and implementing his occupational self-concept and giving him insight into his self-defeating patterns of thought.

Objectives

The environmental context of the initial session will generate expectancies and constraints. For instance, developmental sessions may be more likely to take place in college counselling centres than in other settings, while careers-service settings emphasize decision-making interviews. Thus a number of the ideas presented here about initial sessions may have to be adapted according to your environment as well as to individual clients.

Initial sessions can be seen as having four interrelated objectives. First, the establishment of a *working alliance* in which rapport or a relationship base for future counselling work is established with the client. Such a relationship base involves clients perceiving themselves as accepted, respected and understood and perceiving their counsellors as trustworthy and competent. Second, the formulation of a *working model* or image of the client. This model is a set of hypotheses about the client's fears, areas of pain and ways of avoiding using his or her resources to best effect. It is built up during the initial session as the counsellor observes, listens, responds and explores. Furthermore, it may not be divulged to the client. Third, the setting of *working goals*, which are derived from the tentative model of the client and which take into account the client's particular needs and state of readiness. The detail in which these working goals are communicated to the client may be limited. Fourth, the making of some initial decisions about *working methods*, including whether the emphasis is to be on developmental, problem-focused or decision-making interviewing. Needless to say, the choice of working methods is related to the counsellor's theoretical orientation and range of skills.

Stages of the Initial Session

A tentative five-stage plan of the initial session is presented in Table 4.1, though counsellors may often need to be more flexible. Regarding initial sessions, a good distinction is that between *task* orientation and *person* orientation. A skilled counsellor conducts the task of collecting information and exploring concerns in the context of a good person-to-person relationship in which he or she remains sensitive to the client's feelings and anxieties. Again, I mention that the initial-session plan outlined in Table 4.1 may be too elaborate for some readers' needs, though certain elements of it are probably relevant. Furthermore, there is the problem for beginning counsellors of an assessment procedure which they may feel is beyond their skills and confidence both to conduct and also to follow through with different working methods according to clients' difficulties. This presents a problem in counsellor training where, on the one hand, it is desirable for trainees to work with real clients as soon as possible while, on the other hand, their skills and confidence need building up. Ways of handling this problem include: the screening of potential clients by trainers so that at first only clients within the trainees' range of competence are passed on; having trainees sit in on the assessment sessions of more experienced counsellors and then reversing this so that the more experienced counsellors sit in on the assessment sessions of trainees; trainees and experienced counsellors working together with clients whose difficulties are outside the trainees' skills; and close supervision, with trainees discussing with experienced supervisors audio-recordings of their initial sessions.

First there is the *introductions* stage of the initial session, the purpose of which can be summarized as meeting, greeting and seating. The counselling session starts at the moment of first contact with the client in the waiting area, and the initial impression that the counsellor makes on the client can influence the development of rapport and trust. When meeting clients in a waiting area, as well as calling out their names, it may be more friendly to go over to them and show them into the office rather than just stand at the door. They should be politely shown to a seat, possibly given permission to smoke if requested, and helped to feel at ease. At an appropriate moment, possibly even in the waiting area, there may be a greeting along the lines of: 'Hello, I'm . . ., a counsellor here'. The issue of what counsellors and clients call each other can be handled during the initial or subsequent sessions according to the wishes of both parties. From the initial moment of waiting-room contact counsellors observe and listen to their clients' verbal, vocal and bodily communication so that they can respond appropriately and also start formulating their working models.

The second stage is that of exploration of *presenting concerns*. Even in specialist counselling services clients may come to counselling with one or more of a variety of concerns. Table 4.2 lists some illustrative presenting concerns in four of the main settings in which counselling takes place, though many problems are presented in more than one

Table 4.1 *A five-stage plan of the initial counselling session(s)*

Stage	*Ilustrative counsellor tasks*
1. Introductions	Meeting, greeting, seating If necessary, establishing confidentiality or its limitations Starting the development of rapport and trust Basic data collection (?)

2. Presenting concerns	Facilitating client self-disclosure and self-talk
	Exploration of presenting concerns:
	  assisting client amplification and specification
	  engaging in clarification

3. Reconnaissance	Structuring Facilitating client self-disclosure and self-talk Broader exploration of client's mode of living, background, current stresses, self-concept, coping abilities, motivation and expectancies, etc. Assisting exploration Engaging in clarification
4. Contracting	Summarizing Structuring Formulating and discussing goals Presenting a treatment method or methods Handling questions Establishing a treatment 'contract'
5. Termination	Clarifying administrative details Arranging next appointment Parting

Table 4.2 *Illustrative presenting concerns by institutional or agency setting*

Institutional or agency setting	Presenting concerns
Medical	'I'm feeling depressed, lonely and very tense' 'I'm terrified of going out and mixing with people' 'Now I've had a severe heart attack, I must learn to live more sensibly' 'You don't expect that going blind will happen to you, but now I've got to adjust to it'
Educational	'I can't concentrate and keep putting off my work' 'I still feel dominated by my parents and don't know what I want out of life' 'Being an overseas student has been a big culture shock for me' 'I get very tense over exams and never seem to do myself justice'
Occupational	I'm undecided about my future career' 'I've just been made redundant and where do I go from here?' 'I'm finding increasing difficulty in keeping on top of the stress of my job' 'Now I'm planning for retirement I want some leisure interests'
Marital and family	'We seem to be in a continuous state of conflict and I just don't know what to do' 'I'm wondering whether to get divorced or not' 'Our sex life is no longer enjoyable' 'We have a problem child who is driving us to the end of our tether'

setting. The first counsellor task in the presenting-concerns stage is to give clients permission to talk about why they have come for counselling. Here the counsellor is likely to use opening comments like 'Tell me why you have come to see me', 'What brings you here?' and 'Put me in the picture about what is concerning you'. At first counsellors may just make it easy, mainly by means of empathic responding, for clients to talk about their presenting concern or concerns. The second counsellor task is to engage in mutual exploration of these concerns with the aim of amplifying and clarifying, usually by focusing on past and current manifestations of the concerns. Also, an important area to explore is the personal meanings that the presenting concerns have for the client. For example, a client who blushes may regard this as visible evidence to everyone that he or she is one of life's inadequates. I deal with some of the skills of exploring and clarifying problems in the next section of this chapter. The presenting problem is not necessarily the 'real' problem. It may be a problem about which it is relatively easy to talk. More threatening areas may emerge later in the initial or subsequent sessions.

The counsellor uses the material generated in the presenting-concerns stage to help construct his or her working model.

The third stage is that of *reconnaissance*, which is a continuation of the mutual exploration started in the presenting-concerns stage. This covers the client's background and in particular his or her current functioning in such areas as relationships, work, learning (if relevant), physiological functioning and current stresses. In some counselling contexts and for some client concerns and situations, the counsellor may decide to shorten or bypass the reconnaissance stage. For instance, in careers-counselling contexts the presenting concern, usually that of a decision to be made, is likely to be the only focus of the session, though often the motivation for career choices is more complex and involves more anxiety than is acknowledged. For other client concerns, such as anxiety about an imminent exam, it is perhaps best to take a problem-focused approach to the presenting concern immediately, leaving any reconnaissance until after the exams, if at all. Furthermore, for highly threatened and defensive clients the counsellor may decide that the reconnaissance stage should be handled without much probing, since the client feels insufficiently safe in the counselling relationship.

The fourth stage is that of *contracting*, or the process by which counsellor and client arrive at a formal or relatively informal agreement about treatment goals and methods. At the end of the reconnaissance stage, or possibly at the end of the presenting-concerns stage in problem-focused or decision-making counselling, the counsellor may summarize the major points of the client's concerns. This summary is the bridge between the exploratory work of the earlier stages, aimed at arriving at a working model, and the formulation and discussion of working goals. Depending on the counsellor's theoretical orientation and the concerns and needs of individual clients, these goals may be stated generally or more specifically.

Summarizing and goal-setting are part of the process of making decisions about working methods. Some counsellor decisions and considerations at this stage are presented in the treatment decision-making checklist presented in Table 4.3. The items on the checklist represent processes which take place either implicitly or explicitly in the counsellor's mind (or private domain). Only some of the results of such deliberations are likely to be shared with the client. If the client is prepared to proceed with the proposed methods a treatment 'contract' has been entered into by both parties. If not, further clarification and negotiation may be necessary or, alternatively, counsellor and client may agree to terminate the proceedings.

The fifth stage is that of *termination*. Tasks involved here include:

Table 4.3 *A counsellor treatment decision-making checklist for the initial session*

---

1. What are the client's expectations of counselling?
2. Can I be of benefit to this client?
3. Should I refer this client elsewhere?
4. How disturbed and out of touch with reality is this client?
5. Does the client present a risk to himself or herself, for example by being suicidal, or to someone else, by being extremely hostile?
6. To what degree does the client need a nurturing relationship mainly involving empathic responding?
7. To what degree and in what ways should my interventions specifically focus on altering the client's thinking and/or facilitating action?
8. Is group counselling indicated after, concurrently with or instead of individual counselling?
9. Would it be both possible and helpful if I worked to alter the client's environment?
10. Is the client on medication or, if not, is any medication indicated?
11. Should I discuss this client with another counsellor, or medical or other professional person?
12. In what way should I handle the discussion and presentation of working goals and methods?
13. To what extent is the client motivated to work on his or her concerns in collaboration with me?
14. How formal should my contract or agreement with the client be in regard to his, her or our behaviour in subsequent sessions?

---

bringing the interview to a close; if necessary, clarifying the issue of between-session contact; setting any homework assignments; dealing with outstanding administrative details, including arranging the next appointment; and parting. As with the initial meeting and greeting, parting from a client should be friendly and polite.

BEGINNING SKILLS

Some initial-session skills relate to the exploring and clarifying of client concerns. As implied in the earlier discussion on assessment, some counsellors would not see it as their job to explore clients' concerns for them, but to facilitate clients' *own* self-exploration. Good empathic responding is an important skill even for the counsellor who wishes to play a more active role in the exploration of client concerns. The counsellor can find out only as much as the client is willing to tell, and the amount and depth of client disclosures tend to be related to how safe and understood the client feels. Furthermore, good empathic responding is a discipline for counsellors to ensure that they listen properly to their clients' statements of their concerns.

Questioning

Paraphrasing Hamlet: 'To question or not to question, that is the question'. The arguments for and against questioning in counselling are similar to the arguments for and against assessment. Wrongly used, questions can lead to passive clients who implicitly or explicitly expect their counsellors to take responsibility for their lives. Furthermore, counsellors may put themselves in spurious positions of expertness and then not be able to 'deliver the goods'. Some common errors in questioning are listed below, though all of them are not necessarily errors all the time.

Too many questions

Here the client is likely to feel interrogated and on the defensive. For example: 'Did you talk to your husband?', 'What did he say?', 'How did you react?', 'Why did you react that way?'.

Closed questions

A distinction is sometimes made between open and closed questions. The closed question curtails or closes the client's options for responding whereas the open question leaves his or her options open. An example of a closed question is 'Do you want to come for counselling once a fortnight or not at all?', whereas an open question would be 'How do you feel about making future counselling appointments?'

Leading questions

Leading questions put pressure on the client to answer in a certain way. They are often in the counsellor's rather than the client's frame of reference. An example is 'Did you feel angry when she came round to see you?' as contrasted with the more open 'How do you feel when she came round to see you?'. At worst, leading questions may be totally unrelated to the client's current train of thought or even to his or her concerns.

Too probing questions

These questions are likely to cause the client anxiety because they are about material that he or she is neither ready nor willing to disclose. For instance, a clumsy counsellor might say to an obviously shy boy or girl: 'Do you masturbate and what are your masturbation fantasies?'.

Poorly timed questions

Timing is critical in the asking of good questions. For instance, a girl may be full of emotion as she relates having a row with her mother, when the counsellor says: 'And what was your contribution to causing the row?'. It is conceivable that when she had calmed down the girl might have been willing to explore the adequacy of her own behaviour in the situation, possibly without prompting from the counsellor.

'Why' questions

The risk of 'why' questions such as 'Why did you do it?' is that they lead to a search for intellectual explanations which are of little help to the counselling process. It is often better for the counsellor to ask 'how' questions, e.g. 'How did you behave in that situation?', if the client is to gain insight into his or her behaviour. For instance, a 'why' question might be 'Why don't you get on well with your boyfriend?', whereas a 'how' question would be 'How do you behave when things aren't going well with your boyfriend?'.

Exercise 4.1 is designed to help you to identify and experience questioning errors. I have excluded probing questions since they are fairly obvious and poorly timed questions, since good timing is often related to the development of trust over a number of sessions.

Exercise 4.1   Identifying and experiencing questioning errors

This exercise may be done in pairs or in a training group.

A   *In pairs*
   In order to (a) help you to become aware of when you are using questions in possibly incorrect ways, and (b) give you the experience of being on the receiving end of poor questioning, work through the following exercise with a partner. Use of an audio recorder may be helpful.

1. *Too many questions.* Using frequent questions, interrogate your partner about his or her counselling skills for two or five minutes, then reverse roles, then discuss.
2. *Closed questions.* You and your partner independently think of three issues about each other's counselling skills and write down a closed and an open question about each issue. Then counsel, with one partner asking each of the three questions first in closed and then in open form, then reverse roles, then discuss.
3. *Leading questions.* You and your partner independently think of three leading questions about each other's feelings about his or her counselling skills. Then counsel, with one partner asking each of the three leading questions and then asking how the 'client' partner feels about his or her counselling skills. After reversing roles, discuss.
4. *'Why' questions.* You and your partner independently think of a situation in your personal or work relationships in which you are experiencing difficulty. Then counsel, with one partner first asking 'Why are you having difficulty in that situation?' and then 'How are you behaving in the . . . situation in which you are having difficulty?'. After reversing roles, discuss.

B *In a training group*
The trainer gets two group members at a time to role-play a brief counselling excerpt involving one of the questioning errors. After each demonstration, the trainer facilitates a discussion in the group of the impact that such questioning might have on the group members if they were clients, including getting them to share their own experiences of being at the receiving end of inept questioning.

Another option is to let the group go through the pairs part of the exercise first and then hold a plenary sharing and discussion session.

Questions tend to receive much criticism in the counselling literature. Though the use of questions differs according to the theoretical orientation of the counsellor, below are five possibly beneficial ways, sometimes overlapping, in which questions might be used to explore and clarify client concerns. Needless to say, what is important is not only *what* questions are being asked, but also *how* they are being asked, i.e. what accompanying vocal and bodily communication is being used.

Obtaining specific information

In their initial assessments counsellors may require their clients to be more specific about their concerns. For instance, the statement 'I am a very heavy smoker' may be probed and broken down until a precise specification of the client's smoking behaviour is arrived at. This is the way behavioural counsellors tend to approach each problem area in a client's life. Some possible specification questions are: 'When did it start?'; 'In what situations does it happen?'; 'What precisely happens?'; 'What are the consequences?'; and 'How many times?'.

Asking for elaboration

In Table 2.3 I listed some continuation responses. Elaboration questions may be viewed as a form of continuation response in which clients are asked, or are given the opportunity, to expand on what they have already started talking about. On the whole, elaboration questions are more open than specification questions. Some possible elaboration questions or responses are: 'Would you care to elaborate?'; Would you tell me more?'; 'Can you give me an example?'; Would you care to explore that further?'; 'I don't quite understand . . . could you please clarify?'; 'Is there anything else you would like to say about that?'; and 'Is there more to it than that?'.

Focusing on feelings

Questions focusing on feelings are designed to elicit how clients feel about themselves, about others, about the counselling relationship, and about events and situations in their lives. In initial sessions it is often helpful to explore the personal meanings that the clients' concerns or problems have for them. Furthermore, since many clients are poor at listening to their own feelings, this may give them some useful practice at this. Below are some questions focusing on the client's feelings. Note that all the questions are either open or tentative, or both open and tentative. After all, the client should, but will not always, know his or her own feelings better than anyone else. Questions focusing on feelings include: 'How do you feel about that?'; 'I'm wondering what the emotional impact of that is on you'; 'How do you experience that?'; 'Would you care to describe your feelings?'; 'You seem to be feeling . . .'; 'I'm hearing that you're feeling . . .'; and 'You seem to have conflicting feelings. Is that true?'.

Exploring alternatives

Questions which help the client to focus on alternative ways of viewing themselves, others and situations in their lives may also sometimes help to clarify their concerns and problem areas.Here the counsellor is helping the client to formulate alternative ways of perceiving, thinking and acting. For example, exploring alternatives is always likely to be an important part of initial career decision-making interviews, though it can also be important in other kinds of interviews. The following are some questions that counsellors can use to help the client to explore alternatives: 'What are the options?'; 'Is there any other way of viewing the situation?'; 'Is there any other interpretation?'; 'Could you have behaved differently?'; 'Are there other ways in which you might approach the situation?'; 'Is that the only solution?'; and 'How do you think he/she views the matter?'.

Allocating counselling time

Another set of questions relevant to exploring and clarifying problems relates to checking with clients how much time they wish to spend on a concern or topic area and whether or not to move on to another area. Furthermore, the accuracy of the counsellor's view of the total picture needs to be checked with clients before asking them whether or not they agree to the formulation of working goals and methods. Such questions have obvious implications for allocating future counselling time. I have grouped all these questions under the broad heading of 'allocating counselling time' questions, and an example of each is provided in Table 4.4. Note how each question implies that the counsellor is *collaborating with* the client in the treatment decision-making process.

Table 4.4 *Some 'allocating counselling time' areas and questions*

Exploring	Would you like to explore that concern further?
Making a transition	'Can we now move on to looking at . . . area of your life?'
Summarizing	'Do you think that I have summarized your concerns accurately?'
Setting goals	'Do you agree that these are appropriate goals for our counselling work?'
Agreeing on methods	'Are you prepared to proceed along the lines we've just been discussing?'

As the above discussion suggests, I consider that questions are not of themselves bad, and some may even be absolutely necessary in counselling. Beginning counsellors often ask too many questions because that is the way they communicate outside counselling and they still lack confidence in their counselling skills. However, they can counteract this tendency and allow their clients more psychological space if, after each client statement, they make an empathic response, pause to see whether the client wishes to continue and, if not, then ask their question. Exercise 4.2 has been designed to help you develop your questioning skills and thus be able to use questions flexibly and constructively to facilitate your interviewing. In Exercise 4.2 I have not focused on allocating time questions since, to some extent, they will be covered later in this chapter.

Exercise 4.2   Developing your questioning skills

This exercise may be performed in pairs or in a training group.

A   *In pairs*
      With a partner work through at least two of the sections in the exercise plus the section on exploring and clarifying presenting concerns. Use of an audio-recorder may help you to monitor the impact of your questions on your 'client'.

B   *In a training group*
      The trainer gets two group members at a time to demonstrate in a brief counselling session one of the categories of questioning. After each demonstration the trainer facilitates a discussion of the impact that such questioning might have on the group members if they were clients, including getting them to share their own experiences of being at the receiving end of skilled questioning. The trainer then demonstrates, by acting as counsellor, the last section of the exercise, which involves exploring and clarifying presenting concerns. After a discussion of this counselling session the group subdivides to practise parts of the exercise, especially the last section.

Exercise
1.   Specification questions. Your partner presents to you a concern about his or her counselling style or personal behaviour. Spend a minimum of three minutes getting a more precise specification of his or her concern by using specification questions and empathic responding, then discuss. Afterwards reverse roles, then discuss.
2.   Elaboration questions. Your partner presents to you a concern about his or her counselling style or personal behaviour. Spend a minimum of three minutes getting your 'client' to elaborate the concern by using elaboration questions and empathic responding, then discuss. Afterwards reverse roles, then discuss.

3. Questions focusing on feelings. Your partner presents to you a concern about his or her counselling style or personal behaviour. Spend a minimum of three minutes helping your 'client's' exploration of his or her feelings about the concern by using 'focusing on feelings' questions and empathic responding, then discuss. Afterwards reverse roles, then discuss.
4. Questions exploring alternatives. Your partner presents a decision to be made or a problem area to be managed. Spend a minimum of three minutes helping your client to explore alternatives regarding the concern by using 'exploring alternatives' questions and empathic responding, then discuss. Afterwards reverse roles, then discuss.
5. Exploring and clarifying presenting concerns. Your partner presents a concern about his or her counselling style or personal behaviour. Spend a minimum of ten minutes exploring and clarifying his or her concern by using an appropriate mixture of empathic responding and of specification, elaboration, 'focusing on feelings', and 'exploring alternatives' questions, then discuss. Afterwards reverse roles, then discuss.

Making Transition Statements

In exploring and clarifying client concerns the counsellor may wish to change the subject by moving the content of the session from one topic area to another. Furthermore, as the initial session progresses, the counsellor may wish to move from one stage to another. These counsellor-initiated shifts of topic area and session stage may be done by means of transition statements. Such statements are likely to be made when counsellors consider that they have covered a topic area or session stage to their satisfaction or as fully as possible in the time available.

Transition statements must be made gently, yet firmly. Though they indicate that the counsellor considers that it is time to progress in the session, these statements may nevertheless be made in a way that allows the client to bring up any unfinished business before moving on. What is to be avoided in making transition statements is giving the client the feeling that they are under interrogation and that they are perceived by their counsellors more as objects than as people. In short, though transition statements are task-oriented, they are best made in a person-oriented emotional climate of collaboration and companionship.

Possible transition statements for moving from *one topic area to another* include: 'Well, we seem to have explored . . . area. Now let's move on to . . . area of your life'; 'I would also like to know something about your background and family'; 'I would also like to find out something about the work area of your life'; and 'I'm now wondering whether there are any current stresses in your life'.

Possible transition statements for moving from *one stage of the initial session to another include:*

(a) from the introductions to the presenting-concerns stage: 'Now would you care to tell me in your own words the reason or reasons that you have come for counselling';

(b) from the presenting-concerns to the reconnaissance stage: 'We seem to have explored your immediate problem and now I would like to get a broader picture of your current life situation and background';

(c) from the reconnaissance to the contracting stage: 'We have now discussed both your immediate problem and your life situation and now I would like to summarize what has been said so far and then discuss with you some ways in which we might work in future';

(d) from the contracting to the termination stage: 'Well, we're coming towards the end of the time we have available for this session. Before we do, I would like to spend a few moments discussing future arrangements'.

Exercise 4.3   Making transition statements

This exercise may be done in pairs or in a training group.

A   *In pairs*
Conduct the introductions, presenting-concerns and reconnaissance stages of an initial session with a partner who *either* presents a concern about his or her counselling style or personal behaviour *or* role-plays a client drawn from his or her experience. In this counselling session make sure you practise your transition statements in regard to both topic area and interview stage. At the end of your session get feedback from your partner on the quality of your transition statements. Afterwards reverse roles, though you may need a break between sessions.

B   *In a training group*
Here the trainer conducts the introductions, presenting-concerns and reconnaissance stages of an initial session with a trainee who either presents a personal concern or role-plays a client. As the trainer conducts the session, whenever he or she is about to make a transition statement he or she shares with the group his or her decision-making processes in regard to that statement. Thus the group not only learns how to make

transition statements but also obtains an insight into the kind of thinking that underlies them. After a discussion at the end of the demonstration session the trainer may subdivide the group and visit these subgroups as they practise making transition statements.

Summarizing

I mentioned earlier that a summary could be a bridging statement between the exploratory work of the initial session and that of goal setting and deciding on working methods. This is the use of summarizing on which I focus here. However, counsellors may also make summaries in later sessions, including the final one.

It is possible to look at the content of summaries on two broad dimensions: *reflection*, or responding from the client's frame of reference; and *feedback*, or responding more from the counsellor's frame of reference. Summaries which reflect content, feelings, and feelings and content are a form of basic empathic responding. However, counsellors may consider it important that they also give feedback about their views of their client's concerns. This may entail providing alternative frames of reference for viewing the concerns, making comments on the implications of the concerns, and possibly also identifying problems which the client has not overtly presented. Indeed, summaries can be presented in two parts, first reflection, then feedback, thus ensuring that the client's and the counsellor's viewpoints are both covered but kept disentangled.

Possible summary statements emphasizing *reflection* include: 'As I hear it, your major areas of difficulty appear to be . . . Would you agree with me?'; 'We've explored a number of areas now. Perhaps the time has come to summarize and to have a discussion about where we go from here. As well as a general problem of lack of confidence, you seem to have a number of more specific concerns . . . (mention main concerns). Additionally, you feel that your situation isn't being helped by some additional stresses in your life . . . (mention additional stresses). Do you think I've got the picture clearly?'; 'A theme running through a number of areas you have mentioned seems to be . . .'. Note that, as with most good empathic responses, the counsellor is checking for accuracy in each of these summary statements.

Though summaries can involve only reflection, they can never involve only feedback. The feedback part of a summary represents the counsellor's comments or contribution. This feedback is likely to follow as well as be in addition to reflection. Possible feedback statements include: 'In addition to the problem areas that you mentioned, it seems that . . . is also an area in which you are experiencing difficulty'; 'An implication for you of the difficulties you are experiencing seems to be . . .'; 'My own view is that often your behaviour seems to be hurting you more than anyone else and perhaps this is something we could work on'.

Exercise 4.4 Developing your summarizing skills

This exercise may be done in pairs or in a training group.

A *In pairs*
Conduct the introductions, presenting-concerns and reconnaissance stages of an initial session with a partner who *either* presents a concern regarding his or her counselling style or personal behaviour *or* role-plays a client drawn from his or her experience. In this counselling session make sure you practise summarizing. Opportunities for summarizing will occur at *the end of* the presenting-concerns and reconnaissance stages. Further opportunities for summarizing groupings of client statements will occur *during* these stages. Reserve putting feedback into your summary until the end of the reconnaissance stage. At the end of your session get feedback from your partner on the quality of your summaries. Afterwards reverse roles, though you may need a break between sessions.

B *In a training group*
Here the trainer conducts the introductions, presenting-concerns and reconnaissance stages of an initial session with a trainee who either presents a personal concern or role-plays a client. As the trainer conducts the session, whenever he or she is about to summarize he or she shares with the group his or her decision-making processes in regard to that particular summary. After a discussion at the end of the demonstration session, the trainer may subdivide the group and visit these subgroups as they practise summarizing.

Other Methods of Assessment

There are a number of ways other than the interview in which counsellors may collect assessment information for exploring and clarifying client concerns. For instance, the client may be asked to engage in

self-monitoring, keeping a written log or diary about a specific behaviour during a given period, say a week or a fortnight. Furthermore,
some counsellors get clients to fill in self-report questionnaires, for
example questionnaires that list situations which people find difficult
and which cause anxiety. Biographical information may be collected by
means of a questionnaire filled in either before or after the initial
session. Possibly the main use of such a questionnaire is in occupational
counselling where it may serve the purposes both of saving interview
time and of getting the client to think more deeply about the development of his or her occupational self-concept. Biographical-information
questionnaires are rarely used in conjunction with counselling on
emotional matters, though some counsellors may ask a client to write
out an autobiographical statement.

So far the discussion has centred on information supplied by the
client. Assessment information supplied by other people may come
from a number of sources. For instance, the counsellor may have
medical information available at the time of the first session or, as a
result of the initial session, may consider it appropriate for the client to
see a competent physician to check out some health or medication
matter. The counsellor may also wish to know about any psychological
or psychiatric treatment that the client has undergone or is undergoing.

Some clients can be observed in their natural settings. Counsellors
may themselves take their clients into situations that they find difficult,
for example eating in public, and observe how they behave. An indirect
form of observation in natural settings is collecting information from the
people with whom clients interact in their daily lives, for example
teachers, parents and marital partners. Many referral notes contain
some observations about the client's behaviour in his or her natural
setting. Assessment information may also be collected in simulated
settings. For example, marital partners can be asked to simulate a row
with each other and this may be audio- or video-recorded. Alternatively, the counsellor may enact with a client a role-play about a current
difficult personal relationship. Sometimes group counselling sessions,
including the initial one, are video-recorded, an assessment of the
playback being part of the immediate or a subsequent session.

Structuring

Structuring is a term used to describe the behaviours by which counsellors let their clients know their respective roles at various stages of the
counselling process. Structuring can be conveyed by bodily and vocal as

well as by verbal communication. All the transition statements from one session stage to the next might be viewed as a form of structuring. Perhaps the most important form of structuring comes at the contracting stage of the initial session and attempts to answer the implicit or explicit client question: 'What are you going to do to help me?'. Such a question poses a problem in a book like this because there is no definitive manner of structuring, since counsellors from different approaches structure in different ways. Let me illustrate this by indicating how person-centred and behavioural counsellors might differ in their approach to structuring.

The person-centred approach does not propose different forms of assesssment for different clients. Rather it posits a single diagnosis that all clients, because they have unthinkingly internalized others' values, need to be helped to become more in touch with themselves as the source of their values. Much structuring in person-centred interviews is more implicit than explicit. However, counsellors might make their views on their own and their clients' roles more explicit by statements such as:

> 'I see my role as more to support and help people as they make sense out of their own lives rather than to come up with ready-made solutions.'
> 'I'm afraid I cannot make your decision for you, since only you can do that, but I can help you to explore yourself in relation to the decision and I hope that that will be helpful.'
> 'Well, you've told me a lot about how your parents put pressure on you to be the sort of person they wanted you to be. I would like to create a climate of safety and freedom in which you can explore and get more in touch with the sort of person *you* want to be. It may feel a little strange at first, but rather than ask you questions, I will encourage you to talk about what is important to you so that you can gain confidence in and learn to trust yourself more than you do now.'

The behavioural approach to counselling rests on careful assessment of the client's problem behaviours, on specification of one or more goals for the counselling process in as precise terms as possible, and then on the selection of specific methods of treatment for each goal. Structuring in behavioural counselling is likely to involve presentation of a rationale for the behavioural approach in which the client's problems are viewed in learning terms, as well as agreeing on goals and stipulating working methods. The discussion on goal setting in Chapter 6 is much more in line with behavioural than with person-centred counselling.

Once the counsellor structures working goals and methods, the client may ask questions, for example, 'When am I likely to feel better?'. This is often hard to answer precisely, since counselling is not always successful with all clients and some of the success of counselling depends on factors outside the counsellor's control, for example how much effort the client makes and how helpful or detrimental his or her environment is in attaining counselling goals. Sometimes it is helpful to use your 'reflection of feelings' skills in responding to client questions; for instance, a question about counselling outcomes may be masking a desperate request for reassurance. Counsellors should be as realistic as possible in answering questions about the likelihood and timing of client changes, avoiding the twin errors of over-pessimism and over-optimism. Sometimes it may be appropriate to suggest to clients that they give counselling a try for a month or so and then assess whether they think continuing will be of benefit to them.

Since there are so many considerations affecting structuring, for example, the counsellor's theoretical orientation and the context in which the counselling occurs, perhaps it is best if I offer some guidelines which may have broad relevance for structuring. Below are some *guidelines regarding structuring*.

1. Be aware that much structuring may be done before the client comes for counselling by the publicity and image that the counsellor presents outside the counselling office.
2. Acknowledge that counselling is a new and strange experience for many clients and that care must be taken in making it more comprehensible and less threatening.
3. Avoid jargon.
4. Keep your structuring clear, simple and relatively brief: long, intellectual explanations are uncalled for and may impede progress by defocusing the session from the client's personal agenda.
5. Be consistent. Your suggested working methods should follow from your theoretical position and from any explanation you give to the client about his or her difficulties.
6. Make clear connections between the kind of counselling that is envisaged and the concerns that have brought the client for counselling.
7. Be realistic, both in regard to your own and to your client's strengths and limitations.
8. Be prepared to answer questions.
9. Acknowledge the client's feelings.
10. Check with the client the degree to which he or she is prepared to accept the kind of counselling approach you are suggesting.

Exercise 4.5 Developing your structuring skills

This exercise may be done in pairs or in a training group.

A *In pairs*

If possible, work with the partner you had for Exercise 4.4. Discuss with your partner any issues you should be taking into consideration regarding structuring within a counselling context in which you are currently or may in future be working. Then conduct a counselling session, which can be based on the 'client' with whom you worked in Exercise 4.4, but this time focus on providing the structuring for your continuing counselling contact. After discussion, reverse roles.

B *In a training group*

The trainer leads a discussion on issues in structuring, with special relevance to the present and/or future counselling roles of the trainees. The trainer may then demonstrate structuring with one of the group members, possibly the same person as in Exercise 4.4 acting as 'client'. In this demonstration the trainer not only structures but offers a commentary on his or her decision-making processes in regard to the timing and content of the structuring. After discussion of the demonstration session, the trainer may subdivide the group and visit these subgroups as they practise structuring.

Handling the Reluctant Client

Counsellors in a number of different settings may be faced with clients who have come not of their own volition, but because they have been referred by someone else. Some of these clients may find counselling congenial, especially if they see it as confidential and supportive of them, but others may see counselling as of little value, and some may even be covertly or overtly hostile. Silence and unwillingness to engage in real disclosure (talking, yet remaining psychologically silent) are two main ways of showing hostility. A number of clients may be reluctant to talk to counsellors because they perceive them as authority figures who are part of the establishment.

Some suggestions for counsellors in dealing with reluctant clients are as follows. First, it may be appropriate to let clients know whether their contact with you is confidential and, if not, indicate the limitations on confidentiality. Second, acknowledge empathically rather than deny the client's feelings of reluctance and engage in facilitating an exploration of these feelings. Third, discuss as clearly as possible what counselling consists of and, where possible, relate it to any concerns that the client may have. Fourth, be clear about the limits of your own responsibility to the client in order to avoid feelings of rejection which may infiltrate the emotional climate of the interview, for example through pressure for results or hostility towards the client. Fifth, sometimes you can give the reluctant client the option of coming to counselling on a trial basis before making a final decision about continuing. Even the best counsellors in settings involving many clients who are referred and who come reluctantly are likely to have some who stay reluctant and terminate counselling. Possibly as knowledge of counselling becomes more widespread, reluctance will be less of a problem, since both being in and being seen to be in counselling may pose less of a threat to a client's self-esteem.

Terminating the Initial Session

Beginning counsellor trainees can get quite anxious about how to terminate an initial session. The counsellor may have gone some way towards structuring the timing of termination by an opening remark like: 'Well, we've got 45 minutes together and I would very much like to know what is concerning you.' However, during the session it is the counsellor's responsibility to keep some track of the time and, if it has not finished sooner, to draw the session to its close at the end of the allotted time. Most experienced counsellors are fairly strict about not going over time. Reasons for this include: not wishing to keep later clients waiting; training clients to understand the limits of their interview time so that they can use it to best effect; preventing a professional contact from edging into a personal contact; and, for counsellors with private clients, not giving their counselling services away free. Nevertheless, there may be crises and emergencies which justify some deviation from the practice of ending on time.

Some counsellors pace their initial sessions so that the summarizing and structuring come towards the end of the allotted time, which makes for an easy progression into terminating the session. Where this is not the case the counsellor may make a statement which is a prelude to termination, along the lines of 'Well, we have about five minutes to go . . .' and possibly add a tentative question, for example '. . . I'm wondering whether there is anything further you would like to bring up before we finish?'. Alternatively, the counsellor can proceed straight into terminating the session and making arrangements for the next. Some beginning counsellors are not assertive enough in concluding their sessions. One manifestation of this is letting the session drift on beyond time. Another manifestation is terminating the session in a very diffident way which may be perceived by the client as lack of involvement. Arrangements for a subsequent session or sessions can be presented both positively and collaboratively to clients. For example, 'If you are agreeable, I would like to suggest that we fix an appointment for next week'. This kind of statement still leaves the client with the option to refuse.

Some practical considerations relevant to concluding an initial session with a client who will be seeing you again include the following.

1. Appointments book. You will need an appointments book in which the appointments can be filled in either by you or by a receptionist.
2. Appointments slip. It may be advisable to have some appointment slips made up that you can give to your clients so that they have a reminder of whom they are seeing, the date and time of their next appointment, and what to do if they cannot make the appointment.
3. Between-session contact. There may be some clients with whom you wish to raise the issue of between-session contact. For example, you might let very depressed people know how to contact you if they felt life was really getting on top of them.
4. Homework. You may need to check that the client is clear about any homework assignments to be completed before the next interview.
5. Further consultation. There may be some aspect of the client's concerns about which you would like a further opinion. For example, you may arrange for your client to see a doctor about some medical considerations.
6. Finance. If there is any payment of fees involved on the part of the client, details of this should be made clear.

Conducting an Initial Session

In this chapter I have suggested that there are some skills central to conducting initial sessions which tend to transcend the boundaries of different theoretical positions, counselling settings and clienteles. These skills include questioning, making transition statements, summarizing and structuring. The same skills are also relevant to subsequent sessions. Before you see your first client, it may be helpful for you to 'put it all together' and conduct a complete initial session. Exercise 4.6 is included for this purpose.

Exercise 4.6 Conducting an initial session

This is basically a pairs exercise, but it may also be done as part of a training group.

A *In pairs*
Conduct a complete initial session of, say, 45 minutes with a partner who *either* presents a concern about his or her counselling style or personal behaviour *or* who role-plays a client drawn from his or her experience. Go through all five stages of the initial session. Afterwards reverse roles, though you should take a break between sessions.

B *In a training group*
The trainer may wish to ensure that, before doing it themselves, trainees see one or more complete initial sessions performed by experienced counsellors. Ways of doing this include: presentations of video-recordings of initial sessions to the group; the trainer demonstrating a complete initial session and making arrangements for group members either to observe behind a one-way screen or actually sit in on the initial sessions of skilled counsellors. The trainees can then practise conducting initial sessions in pairs, with the trainer visiting each pair and discussing their progress with them.

---

5 Focusing on Thinking

An interviewer once asked comedian Woody Allen, 'How long have you been in psychoanalysis?' and Allen answered, 'Twenty-two years'. To the interviewer's next question, 'How's it going?', Allen replied, 'Slowly'. One of the reasons why many counsellors focus directly on their clients' thinking is to try to expedite the counselling process. There are many different kinds of client thinking difficulties. In this chapter I present some possible counselling interventions for altering clients' thinking in a number of the more common areas of difficulty. Some of these interventions overlap with each other. Furthermore, counsellors may use more than one intervention even when focusing on a single problem.

Counsellors who focus on clients' thinking difficulties often view thinking as a form of mental self-talk. People are viewed as being engaged during their waking hours in a more or less continuous process of self-verbalizing. Counsellors differ in the extent to which they consider that much of this verbalizing goes on beneath conscious awareness. Many counsellors who work with clients' thinking difficulties consider that their underlying verbalizations are often implicit in what they are explicitly saying.

It is hard to view thinking independently from feeling and action. For instance, people's thoughts are often the expression of feelings at varying levels of their awareness. Furthermore, it is possible to regulate one's feelings by the way in which one thinks about people and events. The connection between thinking and action is also two-way in that actions involve thoughts both before and during their execution. Also, changes in thinking can result from action, as indeed can changes in feelings. Thus even though Chapters 2 and 3 of this book focus more on helping clients to experience their feelings, and this chapter focuses more on altering their thinking and Chapter 6 more on developing their actions, none of these chapters should be viewed as watertight departments.

Broadly speaking, counsellors who focus on their clients' thinking difficulties may have one or more of the following objectives.

1. Eliminating or diminishing self-defeating patterns of thinking. The idea here is that humans learn various habits of thinking from their parents, significant others and the media. Some of these habits are more harmful than helpful to personal fulfilment.
2. Developing rational thinking skills. Clients may be helped to make decisions and to solve problems rationally.
3. Providing accurate information. Sometimes clients are unable to think effectively about a decision or a problem until they have appropriate information.
4. Developing self-control. Developing self-control, sometimes termed self-regulation, means that, through gaining a greater degree of control over their thinking, clients gain a greater degree of control over their feelings and actions.

WHEN TO FOCUS ON THINKING

There is no simple answer about when to focus on the way in which the client is thinking. Relevant considerations are likely to be the theoretical orientation of the counsellor, the level of vulnerability of the client, and the different client needs and reasons why clients come for counselling.

Theoretical Orientation of the Counsellor

Some counselling approaches (perhaps rational-emotive therapy[1] is the prime example) have as the central objective of their approach helping the client to become more rational. Consequently, the approach focuses on the way clients are thinking right from the initial session. Transactional analysis[2] is another approach which has a focus on thinking right from the start, since clients need to be taught the basic language or theoretical framework of the approach. By contrast, the person-centred approach tends to focus on patterns of thinking both later in the counselling process and also less directly. However, it could be argued that person-centred acceptance and understanding are two of the most important approaches to altering the ways in which clients think about themselves.

Level of Vulnerability of the Client

The notion of stages in counselling is connected with the *timing* of counselling interventions in relation to the state of *readiness* of clients. If highly vulnerable clients come for counselling, an early direct focus on their thinking difficulties may be inadvisable for the following reasons. First, they may need to use the early stage of counselling to discuss and discharge the feelings of hurt and pain which have brought them for counselling. Second, they may be so anxious and distorting information so badly that until they become less anxious and more realistic they may not have sufficient insight for exploring their thinking difficulties. Third, it is likely to take time for vulnerable clients to learn to trust their counsellor. Until a good relationship is established they may be too threatened to work on their own contribution to sustaining their distress. In other words, the timing of counsellor interventions focused on thinking is often related to the client's level of vulnerability.

Table 5.1 *A two-stage model of counselling*

Stage one: understanding and experiencing	Stage two: thinking and behaviour change
Counsellor Facilitates exploration Is responsive Is relatively passive	*Counsellor* Focuses on thinking and action Is more challenging and initiating Is more active
Client Engages in self-exploration Strives for self-understanding Develops insight Experiences self more fully	*Client* Focuses on areas of thinking difficulty Clarifies areas for action Develops and implements coping strategies

Table 5.1 briefly presents a two-stage model of counselling which takes into account the level of vulnerability of the client and which is perhaps most applicable to long-term developmental counselling. Moderately to severely disturbed clients may first need to feel accepted and

understood through their counsellors' offering a nurturing empathic relationship. Later they may receive a more active kind of counselling focused on altering specific areas of thinking difficulty and on changing behaviour outside counselling.

Different Client Needs

In Chapter 1 I suggested that there were five main kinds of counselling interviews relating to different client needs: developmental, problem-focused, decision-making, crisis and supportive interviews. The timing, nature and manner of counsellor interventions focused on thinking (more simply, their *when, what* and *how*) differ according to each kind of counselling interview. In the above section I mentioned some of the issues in focusing on thinking in developmental interviews. However, in large measure the same two stages apply both to problem-focused and to decision-making counselling, though the first stage will be shorter than in developmental counselling since there is not the same assumption of vulnerability.

Egan's three-stage problem-management model of helping illustrates this point.[3] In his first stage, that of initial problem clarification, the helper's behaviours are attending, listening, probing and understanding, whereas the client's behaviours are exploring the problem. His second and third stages are setting goals based on dynamic understanding, and designing and implementing action programmes. In other words, his first stage focuses on understanding and experiencing and his second and third stages on thinking and acting.

Decision-making counselling is more likely than problem-focused counselling to emphasize facilitating rational thinking rather than overcoming irrational thinking. Also, perhaps more than in other kinds of interviewing, the need for accurate information is a feature of decision-making counselling. Nevertheless, decision-making counselling also has the same two stages implicit in it. Initially it involves exploring clients' self-conceptions in areas pertinent to the decision, followed by clarifying and crystallizing the decision and then developing and implementing plans for action.

COUNSELLOR INTERVENTIONS FOR THINKING DIFFICULTIES

Counsellor interventions for thinking difficulties often entail helping clients to explore one or more specific areas in some depth. Such exploration may differ in speed, duration, extent and the amount of counsellor direction and participation. Sometimes focused exploration is introduced by the client who indicates a wish to work in a certain area, but on other occasions the counsellor may suggest that it might be fruitful to spend counselling time focusing on a certain problem in the client's life or on some aspect of his or her style of communicating and thinking.

Exploring Unrealistic and Formulating Realistic Standards

Many clients have standards which represent the internalization of others' thoughts and feelings about the way they should be rather than their own deeper feelings about the way they are, and clients make positive and negative assessments of themselves based on these standards. Standards can be beneficial so long as they help individuals to meet their real needs, but unrealistic standards can cause clients to be tyrannized by their 'shoulds', 'oughts' and 'musts'. Such unrealistic standards tend to engender negative emotions, for example anxiety, hostility and depression. Thus clients feel inadequate because they cannot live up to their unrealistic standards. Also, these unrealistic standards and negative emotions *sustain* their behaving in ways that are less rational than desirable.

A distinction is sometimes made between unrealistic standards and self-defeating verbalizations. The unrealistic standards represent an underlying theme, whereas the self-defeating verbalizations are the specific thoughts and statements emanating from the underlying standard. Below are some examples of unrealistic standards and self-defeating verbalizations contributing to negative emotions and actions.

> Val is a housewife in her early forties. *Her unrealistic standard is:* Everything must be perfect or I am less of a person. *Her self-defeating verbalization is:* 'Everything in the house has to be neat and tidy all the time.' *The negative consequences of this thinking include:* worry and anxiety that the house is not perfect; unreasonable demands on her family to be perfectly tidy; and hesitation about having friends round because they may notice that the house is not perfect.

> Simon is a family man with two children. *His unrealistic standard is:* I must always have approval or else I am less of a person. *His self-defeating verbalization is:* 'My children should overtly show appreciation for how hard I have to work to support them.' *The negative consequences of this thinking include:* hurt, self-pity and anger that his children are not the way he thinks they should be; lectures to the children on how they should be behaving towards him; and increased emotional and physical distance between the children and himself.

Jim is a young worker in his early twenties. *His unrealistic standards are*: You can always predict the future from the past; and I must always have approval or else I am less of a person. *His self-defeating verbalization is*: 'Once I start blushing I have got no control and other people will think I'm a weak, inadequate prat.' *The negative consequences of this thinking include*: depression and intense self-devaluation because of his blushing; and avoidance of social contact, which isolates him and further contributes to his depression.

Counsellor interventions in working with clients who have unrealistic standards fall into three interrelated areas: (a) teaching characteristics of unrealistic and realistic standards; (b) exploring unrealistic standards and self-defeating verbalizations; and (c) formulating realistic standards and helpful verbalizations.

Teaching characteristics of unrealistic and realistic standards

Counsellors may discuss with their clients both how to identify ineffective standards and also the characteristics of effective standards. Some of the main characteristics of unrealistic standards include:

1. Overgeneralization – making rules for *all* situations rather than allowing some flexibility for specific situations.
2. Perfectionism – making unrealistic demands on self, others and the environment.
3. Rating the person and not just the characteristic; for instance, Jim was saying not only that his blushing was bad but also that, because he blushed, *he* was bad.
4. Generation of negative or false emotions, including anxiety, hostility, self-pity, depression, pride and smugness.

It is important, however, that counsellors also indicate the characteristics of realistic standards, which include:

1. Being based on the individual's own needs and values.
2. Flexibility or, where appropriate, being amenable to change.
3. A functional rating of specific characteristics according to whether or not they are useful rather than leading to a global self-rating of oneself as a person.
4. Realism about the individual's resources.
5. Having an emphasis on coping with situations to the best of one's ability rather than being perfectionist in relation to them.
6. Being conducive to minimizing negative emotions and to engendering positive emotions.

Exploring unrealistic standards and self-defeating verbalizations

Counsellors can help their clients to identify unrealistic standards and self-defeating verbalizations in a number of ways. One approach is to heighten clients' awareness of the relationship between thinking and emotion and of the possibility of a greater degree of emotional self-control through learning to think more effectively. This can be done by discussing the area with clients. In fact, such a didactic discussion is central to the rational-emotive approach to counselling originated by Ellis.[4] In Ellis's ABC approach, A is the activating event and C represents the emotional and behavioural consequences of A. However, what happens at C is mediated by the individual's belief system pertaining to the activating event. If the belief system is rational (rB) then appropriate emotional and behavioural consequences will follow from A, but if the belief system is irrational (iB) then inappropriate emotional and behavioural consequences will follow. Ellis's ABC framework provides a simple way of introducing the idea of emotional regulation through controlling one's thinking.

Another approach is to facilitate clients' exploration of their unrealistic standards and self-defeating verbalizations. Here counsellors can help their clients to learn the danger signals, for example anxiety and depression, of ineffective thinking. Furthermore, counsellors can work collaboratively with clients to identify unrealistic standards, self-defeating verbalizations and their negative consequences in specific situations. Earlier I illustrated this kind of work when presenting vignettes of Val, Simon and Jim. It may help to use a flip-chart to visually reflect back to clients their own thinking. Common themes in clients' unrealistic standards are likely to include: perfectionism, excessive demands for approval, intolerance of mistakes by themselves, intolerance of human fallibility in others, a tendency to see the world in black and white terms, and the expectation that the world should always be the way they want it to be. Alongside their interview work, clients can do homework exercises in which they explore their standards and their consequences.

Exercise 5.1 Exploring unrealistic standards

This exercise may be done in a number of ways.

A *On your own*
   Either drawing on your experience with a client or on your own personal

life, analyse at least one situation in which the client or you could be acting more effectively by writing down, for each situation:
1. the unrealistic standard(s);
2. the self-defeating verbalization(s);
3. the negative consequences of 1 and 2 above;
4. any early warning or danger signals which might in future help the client or you to minimize the negative consequences.

B *In pairs*
Counsel your partner, who may either role-play a client or be him or herself, for so long as it takes you:
1. to discuss the relationship between thinking, feeling and acting;
2. to facilitate your partner's exploration of the standards, self-verbalizations and negative consequences of a specific situation in which the client or your partner is experiencing difficulty;
3. to feed back any further unrealistic standards and themes you have noticed in the interaction.

After a discussion and possibly a break, reverse roles.

C *In a training group*
The trainer acts as counsellor and demonstrates the exercise described in B above with one of the group members as a role-played or real client. The trainer uses a flip-chart to highlight aspects of the client's thinking. After the demonstration, the trainer facilitates a discussion about exploring standards and invites comments on the preceding counselling session. The trainer may then break the group into pairs to practise the exercise and, if possible, visits each pair.

Formulating realistic standards and helpful verbalizations

Formulating realistic standards and helpful verbalizations merges into and overlaps with exploring unrealistic standards, since it is those standards that are being discarded or reworded to become more realistic. Hence discussion of realistic standards inevitably involves discussion of unrealistic standards and vice versa. Earlier I mentioned some of the principles of realistic standards. I now provide a reformulation of Val's, Simon's and Jim's unrealistic standards and self-defeating verbalizations into more realistic and helpful versions.

Val
Unrealistic standard: Everything must be perfect or I am less of a person.
Realistic standard: It is unrealistic to expect perfection and counterproductive if I rate myself.
Self-defeating verbalization: 'Everything in the house has to be neat and tidy all the time.'

Helpful verbalization: 'While I prefer to keep a very tidy house, if I spend less time on tidiness this will not be disastrous and I can enjoy my family and friends more.'

Simon
Unrealistic standard: I must always have approval or else I am less of a person.
Realistic standard: Universal approval is not a necessity for me and I need not think less of myself for not getting it.
Self-defeating verbalization: 'My children should overtly show appreciation for how hard I have to work to support them.'
Helpful verbalization: 'While I would prefer my children to be more overtly appreciative, they have a right to their own feelings and if I demand appreciation from them this is likely to be counterproductive.'

Jim
Unrealistic standard: You can always predict the future from the past.
Realistic standard: Each anticipation about the future can be realistically judged on the available evidence.
Self-defeating verbalization: 'Once I start blushing I have got no control.'
Helpful verbalization: 'My blushing is inconvenient rather than a catastrophe and once it starts happening I can tell myself to keep calm and that I am capable of coping with the situation.'

A final comment on exploring standards is that, like many other thinking difficulties, unrealistic standards and self-defeating verbalizations have probably become well-established habits. Consequently they will need to be persistently challenged and reformulated both inside and outside counselling.

Exercise 5.2 Formulating realistic standards

This exercise may be done in a number of ways.

A *On your own*
   Either for each of the situations on which you were working in Exercise 5.1 *or* working with one or more new situations:
   1. formulate realistic standard(s);
   2. formulate helpful verbalization(s);
   3. suggest any changes in feelings or actions which might come about through your revised formulations.
B *In pairs*
   Either counsel your partner regarding the situation on which he or she was

working in Exercise 5.1 *or* allow your partner to present a new situation and together:
1. formulate realistic standard(s);
2. formulate helpful verbalization(s);
3. suggest any changes in feelings or actions which might come about through your revised formulations.

After a discussion and possibly a break, reverse roles.

C *In a training group*
The trainer works with the same 'client' as in Exercise 5.1 and demonstrates the exercise as described in B above, preferably also using a flip-chart on which to write the revised standards and verbalizations. After the demonstration, the trainer facilitates a discussion about formulating standards and invites comments on the preceding counselling session. The trainer may then break the group into pairs to practise the exercise and, if possible, visit each pair.

Exploring the Attribution of Responsibility

The term 'attribution' in social psychology refers to the ways and processes by which people attribute causes and meanings to their own behaviour, to others' behaviour and to environmental events. Another way of viewing attribution is in terms of making causal inferences about behaviour and events. Counsellors are invariably, either implicitly or explicitly, working with their clients on increasing the extent of their ability to make accurate causal inferences so that they may gain a greater degree of freedom to make choices in their lives. Since in counselling the area of attributing cause is so bound up with that of assuming responsibility, I have called this section 'exploring the attribution of responsibility'. Clients need to be able accurately to attribute responsibility for what has happened in the past, what is happening in the present, and what they might do in the future.

Below are two examples, one brief and one longer, of people whose misattributions of responsibility for their behaviour were sustaining their ineffectiveness.

> Jane and Peter were a married couple in their forties with two teenaged children both of whom were unhappy at home. Jane and Peter's marital relationship was characterized by much bitterness and mutual recrimination. Whenever their children indicated their unhappiness with the home situation to one of their parents, each parent started running down the other and blaming that person for being the sole cause of the deterioration of the emotional atmosphere in the home.

The second example is a happier one, since a change in attribution that took place during counselling had beneficial consequences outside counselling.

> Sammy, aged 16, came for counselling to a psychologist working in a residential school for delinquent boys. He had a long criminal record of breaking and entering, burglary and malicious damage. Sammy attributed the responsibility for his criminal behaviour to his father, whom he felt did not understand him, who was authoritarian and who used physical violence as punishment. In counselling he explored his relationship with his father and this helped him to understand his father's viewpoint, the stresses and dangers that he was under as a prison officer in Northern Ireland and the long hours he had to work to maintain the family's standard of living. Previously he had felt that his father had not devoted enough time to him. Sammy's increased understanding of his father and his growing ability to make the attribution that he, rather than his father, was responsible for his own behaviour led him to take the initiative to improve his relationship with his father. Gradually this initiative was reciprocated by his father, who took him on fishing trips and also found him employment as an apprentice painter and decorator, whereas previously he had said that he was washing his hands of him. Over a five-year follow-up, there was no recurrence of Sammy's criminal behaviour, which had been a huge embarrassment to his prison officer father.

Apart from ad hoc interventions during more general counselling interviews, counsellors can focus directly on clients' attributions of responsibility for what happens in their lives in the same three ways in which they can focus on unrealistic standards: by introducing and discussing the topic, by facilitating client self-exploration and by providing feedback. Possible themes in exploring the area of attribution include the following: the extent to which clients engage in blaming; the degree to which they are active or passive in meeting their needs; the degree to which they take responsibility for their thoughts and feelings as well as for their actions; and the extent of clients' responsibilities for their lives in the face of adverse family and/or social conditions.

Counsellors may draw to their clients' attention the way in which words can be used as camouflage for not assuming or attributing responsibility. For example, clients who make statements like 'It's all their fault' and 'They are always doing it to me' may be attributing responsibility to others as a protection against exploring their own responsibility for or contribution to creating and sustaining the situations about which they are complaining. In general, clients are more likely to attribute responsibility accurately if they use the personal pronoun 'I' rather than 'it' or 'they'. For instance, 'It happened to me' may be disclaiming responsibility in a situation where an accurate attribution of responsibility might be 'I allowed it to happen to me'.

Along the same lines, the use of verbs implying the possibility of choice is conducive to attributing responsibility more accurately. For example, 'I can't do something' might often be expressed more accurately as 'I won't do something'.

Counsellors can help their clients as they explore the accuracy of their attributions by examining specific situations. A good question for clients to ask themselves when exploring a difficult area is 'How is my behaviour helping me?'. Such a question assumes a degree of accurate attribution of responsibility and not seeing oneself as totally determined by external people and events. Counsellor feedback about the areas in which and methods by which clients misattribute responsibility for their lives has to be well timed and sensitively handled. The last thing that certain clients may be looking for from their counsellor is the suggestion that they may be contributing to their own and to other people's distress.

Exercise 5.3   Exploring the attribution of responsibility

This exercise may be done in a number of ways.

A   *On your own*
   Write down for one or more problem areas in your life:
   1. the ways in which you may be misattributing responsibility and hence behaving less effectively than you might;
   2. what might be more accurate attributions of responsibility;
   3. how attributing responsibility more accurately might change your behaviour in the situation.
   Draw on your experience to identify typical misattributions of responsibility in any counselling or work setting in which you are or have been.

B   *In pairs*
   Counsel your partner by:
   1. discussing the concept of attributing responsibility;
   2. facilitating your 'client's' exploration of possible misattributions of responsibility in any situation in his or her life, including giving feedback on any ways in which you perceive your client to be misattributing responsibility;
   3. together formulating more accurate attributions of responsibility;
   4. exploring how making his or her attributions more accurate might change his or her behaviour in the situation.
   Afterwards reverse roles.

C *In a training group*
The trainer can facilitate a discussion of attributing responsibility by presenting the concept, getting trainees to illustrate it from their personal and work experience, and illustrating it him or herself with examples pertinent to the counselling setting for which the group is being trained. The trainer may also break the group into pairs to practise along the lines of B above. Furthermore, the trainer might set as homework the part of the exercise in A above.

Exploring Anticipating Risk and Gain

People lead their lives into the future rather than into the past. However, past circumstances in clients' lives often colour their view of the future, making them more fearful of acting to meet their needs than might reasonably be considered necessary. Furthermore, many clients' sense of competence or anticipation of their competence to act successfully on their environments in order to meet their needs is lower than their actual competence might warrant. Sense of competence and anticipating risk and gain are closely related in that people who do not 'own' their competence are more likely to emphasize the risks of acting than those who do.

Counsellors can work with their clients in exploring not just why they are not acting (exploring risk) but also, and perhaps more important, what the benefits of acting in a particular situation (exploring gain) might be. An underlying question in exploring gain is 'What do you enjoy?' whereas a relevant question in exploring risk is 'What are you afraid of which is blocking you from getting what you enjoy?'. The term 'enjoyment' is used here as a more colloquial form of what psychologists might express as 'meeting your needs'. Many clients will be afraid of the consequences of failure, but a surprising number may be afraid of the consequences of success, for example handling the extra responsibility of a promotion at work. As one psychiatrist quipped, 'There is only one thing worse than not getting what you want and that is getting it'. An initial step for the counsellor is to get his or her clients to verbalize what they perceive as the gains and risks of certain courses of action. A subsequent step is for the counsellor to help clients to assess the realism of these perceptions. A further step, based on more realistic anticipations, is to explore appropriate ways of acting in the situation.

A final comment is that some clients, for instance delinquent boys and girls, may need help in inhibiting rather than disinhibiting some of their actions. Here, as well as exploring the risks and gains of delinquent behaviour, it may be helpful to explore alternative or substitute ways of meeting needs.

Exercise 5.4   Exploring anticipating risk and gain

This exercise may be done in a number of ways.

A *On your own*
Write down for one or more situations in which you seem afraid to act to meet your needs:
1. the risks of acting;
2. the gains from acting;
3. your assessment of the gains versus the risks;
4. what might be an appropriate course of action based on a realistic assessment of gain and risk.

B *In pairs*
Counsel your partner by:
1. discussing the concept of anticipating risk and gain;
2. helping your 'client' to explore and assess the gains and risks of acting in a situation in which currently he or she seems to be blocked from meeting his or her needs;
3. helping him or her to formulate an appropriate course of action based on a realistic assessment of gain and risk.

C *In a training group*
The trainer can facilitate a discussion of anticipating risk and gain by presenting the concept, getting trainees to illustrate it from their personal and work experience, and him or herself illustrating it with examples pertinent to the counselling setting for which the group is being trained. The trainer may also break the group into pairs to practise along the lines of B above. Furthermore, the trainer might set as homework the part of the exercise in A above.

Exploring Self-protective Thinking

There is a tendency among human beings to seek consistency in the ways in which they view themselves, others and the world. Furthermore, depending on their degree of disturbance, they are not only likely to be protective of their existing self-conceptions, but also not to be aware that they are protecting themselves. 'Defence mechanisms', 'defences' and 'security operations' are other terms for these self-protective thought processes.

Exploring clients' self-protective ways of thinking has to be sensitively handled, because these ways of thinking represent not only well-established habits, but also attempts by clients to avoid facing areas of themselves that they find frightening. Freud originally coined the term 'resistance' to describe all processes that oppose the work in psycho-analysis towards a client's recovery. Frequently there is ambivalence in clients about changing their behaviour, with part of them wanting change and another part wanting the security, albeit false, of the present. Clumsy counselling focusing on clients' self-protective ways of thinking may heighten their resistances to insight and so make matters worse rather than better.

The following are some of the many self-protective ways of thinking: introjection, projection, distortion, denial, misattribution and manipulation of feedback.

Introjection

Introjection means taking something from the environment and treating it as part of oneself. As such, the term 'introjection' often entails possessing unrealistic standards. The implication is that the introjected standards have been swallowed undigested rather than rationally considered and assimilated. Racial prejudice is an example.

Projection

Projection means taking something from oneself and treating it as part of the environment. Whereas with introjection the person internalizes something which is external, with projection the person externalizes something which is internal. Not surprisingly, people tend to project onto others aspects of themselves that they do not find particularly likeable. For instance, instead of acknowledging the extent of his or her aggressive impulses, selfishness or homosexual tendencies, a client may become very aware of such characteristics in others and actually attribute them incorrectly.

Distortion

'Distortion' is used here to incorporate all the ways in which people 'operate' on incoming information so as to maintain their picture of themselves. For instance, some clients minimize positive and maximize negative feedback whereas others do the reverse. Both, however, may share the same self-protective thought processes of distortion.

Denial

Denial involves totally warding off from conscious awareness something that the client regards as painful or threatening. An example is the 'perfect' mother who denies her aggressiveness towards her children. Existential counsellors emphasize that a denial of the finitude of death is widespread and that this curtails many people's capacity to live their lives as fully as they might. Avoidance is a common manifestation of denial, for example by remaining unaware that one is avoiding a difficult person or situation.

Misattribution

Misattribution, as used here, involves all the various ways in which people attribute causes in such a way as to block taking full personal responsibility for their lives. Blaming others needlessly is a prime example of misattribution. Both introjections and projections involve misattributions: introjection attributes to 'I' what should be attributed to 'him', 'her', or 'they', whereas projection attributes to 'him', 'her', or 'they', what should be attributed to 'I'.

Manipulation of feedback

A major self-protective way of thinking and behaving is to control the feedback that one receives from others so as to make it fit with one's self-image. One approach to relating to others is to engage in role-playing and game-playing which give them a false impression of how you really are. Another approach is to engage in 'aversive' communication so that others, who may possibly not be fully aware of what you are doing, feel too inhibited or threatened to give you much or any feedback which may clash with your self-conceptions. A simple example is the use of anger to inhibit negative feedback, though some of the feedback may then be relayed indirectly rather than directly. In other instances, self-protective individuals may be very successful in getting someone who sees them differently to deny the reality of their perceptions. Also, they may get allies who collude in putting pressure on people whose views are threatening. The politics of perception and of self-protection can be a veritable jungle in which the weaker, despite or rather because of the accuracy of their perceptions, may be psychologically hurt and damaged.

Exercise 5.5 Exploring self-protective thinking

This exercise may be done in a number of ways.

A *On your own*
   Make a written assessment for *each* of the self-protective ways of thinking listed here (introjection, projection, distortion, denial, misattribution, manipulation of feedback) of:
   1. the extent to which you perceive that you engage in this way of thinking;
   2. the specific areas or situations in your life that you handle in this way.
   Try to identify the main self-protective thought processes in any counselling or work setting of which you have experience.

B *In pairs*
   Counsel your partner and help your 'client' to explore the ways in which he or she engages in self-protective thinking. Try to get your 'client' to explore precisely *what* is being protected ('What are you afraid of?') as well as *how* it is being done ('How do you protect yourself from full awareness of what you are afraid of?'). Use the list of self-protective ways of thinking provided here as a guideline, not necessarily to be rigidly adhered to, for your 'client's' self-exploration. Afterwards reverse roles.

C *In a training group*
   The trainer can facilitate a discussion of self-protective thinking by presenting the concept, getting trainees to illustrate it from their personal and work experience, and him or herself illustrating it with examples pertinent to the counselling setting for which the group is being trained. The trainer may also break the group into pairs to practise along the lines of B above. Furthermore, the trainer might set as homework the part of the exercise in A above.

Exploring Alternative Frames of Reference

Clients are often locked into fairly rigid ways of perceiving themselves, others and situations. Sometimes, as in the case of a mother whose egotistical behaviour has damaged the emotional development of her children, it may be too threatening to explore alternatives to her present perception that she is the perfect mother who has the misfortune to have ungrateful children. In many other instances, however, clients may be ready to gain from exploring alternative frames of reference. Such situations could include exploration of alternative ways of perceiving: themselves and their own behaviour; other people and their behaviour, including a better understanding of others' frames of reference; the options open to them in a relationship, for example in resolving a conflict; possible solutions to any problems that need solving; and options in any decision to be made. The objectives of exploring alternative frames of reference may not only be to resolve a current situation more satisfactorily but also to help clients to acquire a greater degree of flexibility and choice about how they lead their lives in the future.

Counsellors can sometimes help their clients to 'loosen' their thinking about their lives in the following ways. First, they may discuss the concept of alternative frames of reference with them. This may include indicating to them that there may sometimes be many more possibilities in difficult areas of their lives than they currently acknowledge. Second, they may facilitate their clients' exploration of alternative frames of reference. Ways of doing this include: empathic responding; questioning, for example the kind of questions mentioned in Chapter 4 for exploring alternatives; suggesting alternatives to their clients; getting them to 'brainstorm', which involves generating as many alternatives as possible, regardless of their quality, in a relatively brief time; and use of role-play, for example to gain insight into another person's viewpoint or to try out a new role for themselves.

Exercise 5.6 Exploring alternative frames of reference

This exercise may be done in a number of ways.

A *On your own*
Pick a situation in your personal or work life in which you are having difficulty and write out:
1. as many different ways of behaving in the situation as you can think of in 10 to 15 minutes;

2. an assessment of whether any of these ideas might improve your effectiveness in the situation.

B   *In pairs*

Counsel your partner about a relationship, situation or decision in his or her counselling work or personal life where he or she is having difficulty by:

1. discussing the concept of alternative frames of reference;
2. facilitating his or her exploration of alternative frames of reference;
3. helping him or her to assess whether any of these ideas might improve his or her effectiveness in the area in question.

Afterwards reverse roles.

C   *In a training group*

The trainer can start by presenting some case material relevant to the counselling setting for which the group is being trained. This material should present the opportunity for generating and exploring alternative frames of reference. The trainer facilitates the group in generating as many ideas or solutions as possible and, afterwards, in assessing their merits. Other options include: the trainer demonstrating the exercise in B above with a group member as client; the trainer breaking the group into pairs to practise the exercise in B; and the trainer setting as homework the part of the exercise in A above.

Encouraging Specificity

In Chapter 4 I listed some questions that counsellors might use in the initial interview to get clients to be more specific about their concerns *in* counselling. Some clients may need assistance in thinking and communicating more specifically about their thoughts, feelings and concerns when they are *outside* counselling. Not only may they be confusing themselves, but they are likely to be confusing others as well if they think in vague and imprecise terms. Counsellors may help their clients to become more specific in a number of ways. For example, the counsellor's empathic responding can be clear and concise rather than vague and rambling. Furthermore, counsellors can help clients to clarify their concerns with skilled use of questions.

With some clients, however, the counsellor may have to focus directly on getting them to think and communicate more clearly and specifically. This might be achieved by making clients aware of how hard it may be for them to think through their difficulties when they are expressed in vague terms. Furthermore, it may be very difficult for those to whom they are relating to know what they are really thinking and feeling. Let me give three examples of vague and specific statements:

1. *Vague statement*: 'People seem to bother me these days.'
   Specific statement: 'I'm depressed and irritable because yesterday I had a row with Carla and Max over paying the electricity bill in the flat and it's still not resolved.'
2. *Vague statement*: 'I'm not feeling myself today.'
   Specific statement: 'I have been feeling very anxious and depressed today. I was so tense that I woke up at 4 a.m. and could not get back to sleep. I have not felt like eating anything and have been surviving on cups of tea. It feels as if there is a tight band of tension round my head. I have found myself crying three times today.'
3. *Vague statement*: 'I'm an irritable person.'
   Specific statement: 'When I get angry I get very tense, red in the face and start speaking loudly and aggressively without being too careful about whether I am really hurting someone or not. At least once a day I tell my two sons off for things like leaving their rooms untidy, bad table manners and watching too much television.'

Counsellors can help clients to explore whether they are thinking and communicating as clearly and speciically as desirable. Furthermore, they can help clients to reformulate vague into more specific statements of thoughts and feelings.

Exercise 5.7 Encouraging specificity

This exercise may be done in a number of ways.

A *On your own*
   Draw on your own personal and work experience to provide at least two examples of people thinking and communicating about their concerns in a vague way. Reformulate each vague statement into a specific statement.
B *In pairs*
   Counsel your partner for sufficient time to:
   1. present the concept of specificity;
   2. facilitate his or her exploration of how specifically and clearly he or she thinks and communicates in his or her personal and work relationships;
   3. identify any problems or concerns expressed in vague terms and help him or her to reformulate them into more specific terms.
   Afterwards reverse roles.

C *In a training group*
The trainer can facilitate a discussion of the concept of specificity and possibly illustrate it with some case material from the counselling setting for which the group is being trained. The group can be encouraged to draw on their personal and work experience to provide examples of people thinking about and communicating their concerns in a vague way. The group might work on reformulating some of these vague statements into more specific terms. Other options for the trainer include breaking the group down into pairs to do the part of the exercise in B above and/or setting as homework the part of the exercise in A above.

Challenging

Challenging, sometimes called confrontation, is a counsellor skill which aims to expand the client's awareness in some area. Another way of viewing challenging is that it means reflecting and/or focusing on discrepancies in thoughts, feelings and actions. The *how* of confrontations or challenges is just as important as their *what* or verbal content. Challenges can vary on such dimensions as: when they take place; whether they are gentle or forceful; whether they are brief or persistent; and the extent to which they deviate from the client's current frame of reference. Counsellors must remember that, though a good challenge may accelerate the counselling process, premature or clumsy challenges, especially with vulnerable clients, may retard the counselling process or cause clients to terminate counselling.

The following are some examples of counsellor challenges when focusing on and exploring aspects of their clients' thinking:

1. *Challenging in the area of standards*
   Client: 'I've decided not to ask Ruth out after all.'
   Counsellor: 'You were saying last week how badly you wanted to go out with her. It seems to me that you are saying that it is absolutely necessary for you to be accepted by all the girls you might ask out and that any form of rejection is such a catastrophe that you cannot handle it.'
2. *Challenging in the area of attributing responsibility*
   Client: 'I do my best to get on with my daughter and it's her fault that we don't get on.'
   Counsellor: 'You've already said that you're unwilling to make

much of an effort to get on with her unless she makes the first move. Therefore you seem to have some choice about how you behave in the relationship, since you're choosing not to make the first move.'

3. *Challenging in the area of anticipating risk and gain*
   Client: 'If I'm nice to my boss he may think that I'm apple-polishing, so I treat him fairly coolly.'
   Counsellor: 'On the other hand, you've said that you wish your boss would take more notice of your work and perhaps if you were more friendly that might help him to do this.'

4. *Challenging in the area of self-protective thinking*
   Client: 'Judy and Joan seem to feel pretty angry with the way we are being taught.'
   Counsellor: 'I'm wondering whether focusing on Judy and Joan's anger is a way of protecting yourself from acknowledging that you too feel angry with your teacher and are capable of angry feelings.'

5. *Challenging an existing frame of reference*
   Client: 'I think that they're a very uncooperative bunch.'
   Counsellor: 'Though you think that they're a very uncooperative bunch, they seem to be thinking and trying to communicate to you that you spend too much time on your own projects and not enough time on joint projects and on administration. Would you say that I've presented their viewpoint accurately?'

There are many other ways in which counsellors can challenge their clients. These include focusing on discrepancies: between the client's verbal utterances and bodily communication in counselling; between what the client is saying and what is being left unsaid about the counsellor–client relationship; between the client's past and present statements in counselling; and between the client's self-evaluation and the counsellor's own thoughts and feelings about the client. Challenges in counselling can go both ways, and some clients can be quite confronting and threatening to their counsellors. Where this happens counsellors must have the skills of responding to challenges. These skills include empathic responses which acknowledge rather than deny what the client is trying to communicate.

Confront your strengths.
Identify one you are not using fully.
see Egan ex. p. 93   *Focusing on Thinking* **113**

Exercise 5.8 Developing your challenging skills

This exercise may be done in a number of ways.

A *On your own*
Drawing either on your experience as a counsellor or on your personal life, write down a 'client' statement and relevant challenge for each of the following areas: standards, attributing responsibility, anticipating risk and gain, self-protective thinking and alternative frames of reference.

B *In pairs*
Counsel your partner, who discusses his or her counselling work and/or personal life for at least ten minutes. Where it seems appropriate, challenge the way your 'client' is thinking in one or more of the following areas: standards, attributing responsibility, anticipating risk and gain, self-protective thinking and alternative frames of reference. Afterwards reverse roles.

C *In a training group*
The trainer can facilitate a discussion of the concept of challenging and illustrate it with some case material from the counselling setting for which the group is being trained. The group can be encouraged to draw on their own personal and work experience to provide examples of helpful and harmful challenges. Other options for the trainer include: giving a demonstration interview in which challenges are used; breaking the group into pairs and getting them to practise challenging as in B above; and setting as homework the part of the exercise in A above.

Interpreting

Interpretations are explanations from the counsellor's frame of reference of client behaviours and thought processes. The kinds of interpretations that counsellors offer are likely to differ widely according to their theoretical orientation. For instance, whereas a psychoanalyst might focus on the interpretation of dreams within a Freudian framework, a transactional analyst might be interpreting an individual's social relationships in terms of the games that he or she is playing. Depending on the counsellor's theoretical orientation, information for interpretations may be obtained from: what the client is saying; how the client is behaving inside and outside counselling; dreams and slips of the tongue; and the counsellor–client relationship.

To some extent interpretations could involve offering an alternative frame of reference and, at worst, may involve persistent 'brainwashing' of clients so that they adopt their counsellor's way of thinking and language. A distinction is sometimes made between *shallow* and *deep* interpretations. Shallow interpretations are explanations which clients themselves are almost ready to recognize, whereas deep interpretations are explanations of what might be viewed as unconscious thought processes. The issue of the degree to which counsellors should interpret, if at all, is one which divides counsellors. Especially for beginning counsellors, shallow interpretations are likely to be preferable to deep ones. Incompetent interpretations may be 'red herrings' which unfocus and confuse clients rather than clarifying their thinking difficulties.

Interpreting is best performed in the context of a relationship in which the counsellor has had enough time to acquire some knowledge of the client's thought processes, interpersonal style and social context. Since this is not possible here, I have not included an exercise on interpreting.

Providing Information

Sometimes clients are unable to think clearly about their concerns unless they have the relevant information. This information can be presented in verbal or written form. Counsellors in different settings may need to have different kinds of information, either carried in their heads or readily available. Let me give three illustrations.

1. *Marital counsellors.* Their information needs are likely to include knowledge of: divorce laws and procedures; the legal advice and aid schemes; social security benefits; where clients can get specialized help for sexual dysfunctions; support groups for single parents; and availability of conciliation services.
2. *Student counsellors.* Their information needs are likely to include knowledge of: grants and financial aid; regulations regarding overseas students; claiming unemployment and social security benefits; the kinds of assessment operative in their institution; and a range of support groups and referral sources for specific students and student minority groups.
3. *Occupational counsellors.* Their information needs are likely to include knowledge of: interest, aptitude and achievement tests and measures; occupational trends; entry and training requirements for occupations; and sources of occupational information.

In providing information counsellors need to be sensitive to issues such as: whether or not to wait until their clients have requested the information; the degree to which they should be encouraging their clients to gather information for themselves; and their clients' thoughts and feelings on receiving the information. Counsellors also need to monitor the extent to which they allow their clients the safety and freedom to form their own views on whether or not and how to use the information.

Exercise 5.9 Providing information

This exercise may be done in a number of ways.

A *On your own*
  If you are working or planning to work as a counsellor in a particular setting, list all the main kinds of information that, for the sake of your clients, you should either know or have readily available.
B *In pairs*
  Together do the part of the exercise described in A above. Then you counsel your partner who, during the 10–15 minute session, makes some requests to you for information. Respond to these requests as appropriately as possible. Afterwards reverse roles. Then together discuss the issues involved in providing information in counselling.
C *In a training group*
  The trainer can facilitate a discussion, illustrated with case examples, on the use of information in the counselling setting for which the group is being trained. The trainer may then give a demonstration of how to respond to a client's requests for information. Afterwards, the group may break into pairs to practise responding to clients' requests for information.

REFERENCES

1. Ellis, A. (1977) The basic clinical theory of rational-emotive therapy. In Ellis, A. & Grieger, R. (ed.), *Handbook of Rational-emotive Therapy*, pp. 3–34. New York: Springer. Further Ellis references are to be found in Chapter 9.
2. Further mention of and some references to transactional analysis are to be found in Chapter 9.
3. Egan, G. (1982) *The Skilled Helper*. Monterey, California: Brooks/Cole.
4. See Note 1 above.

6 Facilitating Changes in Behaviour

All counselling aims to help clients to act more effectively to meet their needs. Thus empathic responding and focusing on thinking are both ways of facilitating action and behaviour change. In this chapter, however, I focus mainly on *direct* attempts by counsellors to help their clients to eliminate, change or acquire *specific* behaviours. My position is that the best approach to counselling emphasizes feeling, thinking and acting. However, if anything, Chapters 2 and 3, on listening and empathic responding, represent the client-centred or person-centred approach to counselling, whereas Chapter 5 represents the cognitive or thinking-focused approach. Though this chapter is broader than any single orientation, much of it might be viewed as behavioural counselling, where there is an emphasis both on the specification of precise goals and on the actions to be taken in order to achieve them. My approach to this chapter is to focus on: setting goals; facilitating acting through managing anxiety better; acquiring and developing specific behaviours and skills; and decision-making and problem-solving. Though the skills presented here are most relevant to problem-focused and decision-making interviews, where appropriate they could also be incorporated into counselling interviews which have a more developmental emphasis.

SETTING GOALS

Two statements that Freud was reported to have made about the goals of psychoanalysis were that it aimed to help patients 'to work and to love' and that its objective was 'to turn neurotic misery into ordinary human unhappiness'. Sometimes the goals of counselling are expressed as the enhancement of growth and the remedying of psychological pain. However, where the objective of the interview is that of a direct focus on changing specific behaviours, all the above statements of goals are too vague.

The first step in goal setting is to perform an assessment or behavioural analysis of the problem area or areas. Since behaviours always take place in environmental contexts, any relevant contextual variables will need to be assessed as well. Much of the discussion in Chapter 4, on issues involved in and methods of assessment, is relevant here. Counsellor skills in conducting assessments prior to setting goals include: empathic responding; appropriate use of questions, especially specification and elaboration questions; and making transitions and summaries. Ways in which assessment data can be collected include: what clients say and how they behave within counselling; self-report questionnaires; getting them to monitor behaviour on a homework basis; either the counsellor or someone else observing them in the setting in which the problem occurs; and simulating situations, for instance by role-play, which illustrate their problems.

The second step in goal setting is to formulate and state the goals to be attained as a result of counselling. The following are some desirable characteristics of goals for this kind of interviewing.

Goals Stated in Behavioural Terms

Clients may come to counselling stating their goals as feelings, for example 'I feel miserable and depressed' or 'I feel tense'. After an assessment in which, for example, the component behaviours of 'feeling miserable' are assessed, the goals can then be stated as specific behaviours, for example 'phoning up a friend once a day' or 'engaging in . . . activity that I enjoy twice a week', etc.

There are a number of points to observe here. First, behaviour modification can be conceived as not only altering observable external behaviours, but also altering covert internal processes such as thinking, and physiological or organismic states like anxiety and tension. Second, since behaviour always takes place in environmental contexts, it may be aspects of the environment that need changing, either by the client or for the client. Third, behaviour change ranges from weakening or elminating undesirable or maladaptive behaviours to initiating, becoming more comfortable with or strengthening desirable behaviours, or any combination of these. Fourth, counsellors may be, either concurrently or consecutively, working with clients on a number of different problem behaviours.

Specific and Measurable Goals

Statements of goals should be as specific and measurable as possible. For instance, a goal like 'I would like to overcome my weight problem' might be reformulated as 'On 1 July, six months from now, my goal is to weigh 160 lb (instead of my present 196 lb)'. The goal of weighing 160 lb would then be further broken down into the specific behaviours or sub-goals needed to attain the overall goal. Anxiety-reduction goals, for example reducing or eliminating examination anxiety, as contrasted with overt behavioural goals, are sometimes made measurable by asking the client to rate changes on a subjective anxiety scale ranging from 0 to 100. The top point of the scale, 100 subjective units of anxiety, represents the worst anxiety that the client can imagine experiencing in the situation, whereas 0 represents no anxiety at all. Various situations to do with examinations can be plotted between 0 and 100, depending on how anxiety-evoking they are. For a given student, 100 might be 'turning over the exam paper in the exam room', while 50 might be 'thinking about examinations when revising one week before the exam'. Goals that are specific and measurable enable counsellors and clients both to know what they want and to monitor their progress towards attaining it.

Helpful and Realistic Goals

In this context, goals are helpful if they are conducive to clients being better able to handle their problems. They need to be reviewed if they do not contribute in some substantial way to this aim. Goals are realistic if they acknowledge adequately client, counsellor and environmental constraints. It is pointless and probably counter-productive to formulate specific goals that are beyond the emotional resources and personal skills of clients. The fact that their standards and hence goals are unrealistic contributes to many clients' problems. For instance, counsellors may need to work with clients in exploring the realism of their levels of aspiration in regard to social, occupational or educational achievement. Furthermore, the level and range of skills of counsellors and their own value systems may also be placing constraints both on what goals are realistically attainable and on whether or not the counsellor is prepared to offer his or her services in their pursuit. Environmental constraints include time, money and the degree to which the environment is supportive and/or alterable. For instance, a client who is about to leave the district and yet has an impending public-speaking engagement about which he or she is terrified might have a different set of goals, focusing more on coping with the immediate situation, from those of a client with a longer time for counselling.

Goals Tailored to and Owned by the Client

Goal setting should be a collaborative process between counsellors and clients rather than a process in which counsellors impose their views on clients. This collaboration is important to maximize the chance of problems being clearly identified and goals being tailored in specific terms to these problems. Furthermore, clients' motivation to attain goals is likely to be much greater if they perceive that the goals are 'right' for them than if they do not. Lack of client motivation may be manifested in dropping out of or resisting counselling as well as in not completing homework assignments.

Once goals are stated, they may be perceived as forming part of an implicit, if not explicit, contract between counsellor and client in which both agree to cooperate to the best of their ability to attain them. Sometimes it may be helpful to write the goals down and to let clients have a copy of them as a reminder outside counselling. Some counsellors make out written contracts with their clients stating not only goals but also the client's and, possibly, the counsellor's obligations in trying to attain them. Sometimes such contracts are signed by both parties.

Where there are several goals, counsellors may need to work with their clients in ordering priorities. Two important considerations here are the degree to which specific behaviours are contributing to the client's distress and whether there are any time constraints, such as an impending exam. Goals are not immutable and the original goals may need to be reformulated as counselling progresses or as the client's circumstances change.

Exercise 6.1 Setting goals

This exercise may be done in a number of ways.

A *On your own*

Assess and analyse a problem drawn either from your own life or from your experience of a client. Write out goals for yourself/your client in relation to this problem which are:

1. stated in behavioural terms;
2. specific and measurable;
3. helpful and realistic;
4. tailored to and owned by you or tailored to and likely to be owned by your client.

B *In pairs*

Counsel your partner about a problem either drawn from his or her own life or role-played from his or her experience of a client. After you have clarified the problem in collaboration with your 'client', discuss the principles of setting goals and together formulate goals for subsequent counselling which are:

1. stated in behavioural terms;
2. specific and measurable;
3. helpful and realistic;
4. tailored to and owned by him or her.

Before concluding the session, discuss and formulate with your 'client' the kind of contract which might be most appropriate for subsequent counselling work. Afterwards reverse roles.

C *In a training group*

One option is for the trainer to give a demonstration interview on setting goals, using a group member as 'client'. Another option is for the trainer, after an introductory discussion, to set either of the exercises in A or B above as a homework exercise. The trainer then holds a plenary session in which group members present and receive feedback about the goals they have formulated.

MANAGING ANXIETY

Instructing Oneself with Coping Statements

People's capacity to act effectively is often inhibited by anxiety. Though the anxiety of some clients may be a fairly general characteristic of them as people (trait anxiety), much of the anxiety of other clients may be related to specific situations (state anxiety). One approach to helping clients with fears about specific situations is to train them to instruct themselves with coping statements instead of undermining their confidence with self-defeating verbalizations.

Below are a couple of examples of people contributing to their anxieties through self-defeating verbalizations.

> Mark, aged 20, was an assistant professional at a golf club. He was very keen to do well at his golf. Though he was able to make low scores in practice rounds, he consistently failed to do so in tournaments. When he played a bad shot in a tournament he would tell himself that this was dreadful and start worrying that now he would continue to play future holes badly and that his game might get out of control.

> Jane, aged 26, was a very bright student who was contemplating giving up her PhD in Biology because her Head of Department wanted her to conduct a seminar on her research findings. She kept telling herself that, if she did this, she might appear foolish in front of other people, not so much because of her research but because they would see that she was nervous about speaking in public and consequently would think less of her.

The reader may have noticed that both Mark and Jane's self-defeating verbalizations were based on unrealistic standards. In Mark's case one such standard was: the past is always a predictor of the future. In Jane's case an unrealistic standard was: I must always appear perfectly adequate and competent in front of other people.

Counsellors can train certain clients to confront and handle specific situations that they find stressful and anxiety-evoking in the following ways. First, they can help their clients to explore their standards relating to the stressful situation by such means as: discussing ways in which people's thoughts can affect their feelings and behaviour; identifying self-defeating verbalizations and their underlying unrealistic standards; and aiding the reformulation of more realistic standards and more helpful verbalizations. Second, and based on more realistic standards, counsellors can train their clients to instruct themselves with coping statements which calm them down and are task-oriented. These coping instructions replace the self-defeating verbalizations which are generating anxiety and impeding performance. Third, counsellors can support their clients as they practise their new skills in real-life situations.

Let me take Mark as an example. Mark's goal was to reduce his anxiety to the point where he could consistently score 76 or below in tournaments. His difficulties stemmed partly from the fact that he had allowed his life to become unbalanced in that his commitment to golf was pushing out most other things, including his social life. With all his emotional eggs in one basket, he was vulnerable. Part of counselling consisted of helping him to explore his life-style and standards and so identify his real needs. As a result of this he concluded that he would be a better golfer if he played slightly less golf, not more, since he was practising to the point of diminishing returns and, furthermore, this was curtailing his social life.

Along with exploring his more general life-style, the counsellor helped Mark to explore the self-defeating verbalizations and unrealistic standards he was bringing to the tournament and helped him to reformulate them. Below are a couple of illustrations.

> *Unrealistic standard*: I must never be seen to make mistakes.
> *Realistic standard*: To err is human, even if inconvenient.
> *Self-defeating verbalization*: 'If I make a mistake in a tournament that is terrible, since everyone will know that I have not got the mental toughness to be a good golfer.'
> *Helpful verbalization*: 'Golf is a game and my worth as a person is not determined by my success or lack of it as a golfer. Though I would strongly prefer to be a very good golfer, all I can do is to play as best I can.'

> *Unrealistic standard*: The past is always a predictor of the future.
> *Realistic standard*: The past is just one factor to take into account in predicting the future
> *Self-defeating verbalization*: 'Because I've played badly in tournaments in the past, I will always continue to play badly in them.'
> *Helpful verbalization*: 'My tournament performance in the past need not predict the future, since circumstances are now different. I am learning how to cope with my tournament anxiety and, when in difficulty, can now use my skills in instructing myself with coping statements.'

The counsellor then worked with Mark in formulating *coping statements for instructing himself* before, during and after the situation he found stressful.

For instance, the sorts of coping statements he could instruct himself in if he experienced anxiety *before* a tournament were:

> 'Keep calm and just think through how you can handle the situation.'
> 'Now, just keep your head and stay relaxed, since all you have to do is to cope as best you can.'

Along with these coping statements, he could challenge his self-defeating verbalizations and keep repeating to himself their more helpful reformulations.

The sort of coping statement he could instruct himself in if he experienced anxiety *during* a tournament was:

> 'OK. I've just played a bad shot and I'm feeling anxious. I know that I can reason my fears away and cope with this situation . . . Already I'm starting to feel some of the tension draining away . . . I know that I can cope with this situation . . . All that I have to do is just play one hole at a time and not worry about the ones before or after . . . Now slow down, keep calm

and just play as best you can . . . That's better; I'm becoming calmer and more in control.'

The idea here is that clients, instead of eroding their confidence by 'catastrophizing', learn to regulate their emotions through taking themselves through a self-instructional sequence. A good analogy might be that of a pilot coming in to land in very bad weather who is talked into a safe landing by a calm and competent air traffic controller. Clients, however, have to learn to instruct themselves into their own 'safe landings'.

Mark was given two additional tips about anxiety self-management *during* tournaments. The first was that it might be helpful for him to breathe more slowly and regularly once he started feeling tense, with if anything an emphasis on exhalation. This might contribute not only to calming him down mentally, but also to counteracting shallow and rapid breathing which is a physical manifestation of anxiety. The second tip was that, if he noticed he was experiencing tension in his body, he should tense and relax the muscle groups where he felt the tension. For instance, if he felt his hands and arms getting tense before he played a stroke, he could relatively surreptitiously tense the relevant muscle groups quite hard, hold for about five seconds, and then release the tension and focus on the feelings of relaxation as the tension ebbed away.

The sort of coping self-statements that Mark could instruct himself in *after* a tournament were:

> 'I acknowledge that I've had some success at controlling my anxiety.'
> 'I'm getting better at keeping my anxiety manageable now I've started to use my self-instructional skills.'

Mark, who received only two sessions of counselling, soon started to score better in tournaments and felt that his whole approach to golf and to life had improved. A possible side-effect was that he then passed his driving test after two previous unsuccessful attempts in which he had become too tense. This enabled him to buy a small car which made both his golfing and his social life easier.

Since clients have often had much experience in instructing themselves negatively, they will probably need to practise hard at reversing this tendency. It may be helpful for counsellors to make up homework cassettes for their clients on which they 'coach' them in instructing themselves with relevant coping statements. Some clients may prefer, or benefit more from, hearing their own voice rather than the counsellor's on the cassette.

Exercise 6.2 Instructing onself with coping statements

This exercise may be done in a number of ways.

A *On your own*
Either for a situation in your own life where you feel your performance is being lowered by debilitating anxiety or drawing on your experience of a situation in a client's life where his or her performance is being lowered by debilitating anxiety:
1. write down the unrealistic standards and negative self-verbalizations you consider relevant to the situation;
2. reformulate the standards and verbalizations in 1 above into realistic standards and helpful verbalizations;
3. write down one or more coping statements with which you or the client can instruct yourself for each of the following periods: before, during and after the situation.

B *In pairs*
Either counsel your partner about a situation in which he or she feels that his or her performance is being lowered by debilitating anxiety or get your partner to role-play a client with a specific situation that evokes such anxiety. Together with your 'client':
1. explore any unrealistic standards and negative self-verbalizations relevant to the situation;
2. reformulate the standards and verbalizations in 1 above into realistic standards and helpful verbalizations;
3. formulate one or more coping statements in which he or she can instruct him or herself for each of the following periods: before, during and after the situation;
4. if you have time, make up a cassette for your 'client' to use at home in which you coach him or her in instructing him or herself with coping statements.
Afterwards, reverse roles.

C *In a training group*
One option is for the trainer to work through in front of the group a personal situation in which he or she is or could be managing anxiety through instructing him or herself with coping statements. Another option is for the trainer to give a demonstration interview using a group member as a 'client'. A further option is for the trainer, after an introductory discussion and/or demonstration, to set either of the exercises in A or B above as a homework exercise. The trainer then holds a plenary session in which group members present and receive feedback about the coping statements they have formulated.

Use of Muscular Relaxation

In this book I focus on what might be termed the skills of verbal interviewing. Some counsellors, however, train their clients not only in how to instruct themselves with coping statements but also in how to use muscular relaxation. Though relaxation techniques are briefly mentioned here, you are advised to look elsewhere if you wish to develop your skills in this area.[1, 2, 3, 4]

Earlier I commented on advising Mark to tense and relax specific muscle groups, such as the arms, in which he experienced tension. In progressive muscular relaxation, the client progresses through a sequence of tensing and relaxing each of the main muscle groups in the body. Clients may be advised to practise and use their relaxation skills daily. Especially before going into a difficult situation clients could perform progressive muscular relaxation and then, when relaxed, instruct themselves with the kinds of coping statements that I suggested for before and during anxiety-evoking situations. Needless to say, clients need the ability to imagine their anxiety-evoking situations in order to be able to practise self-instructional statements without actually being in those situations.

Systematic desensitization is one of the most popular behavioural counselling techniques for anxiety reduction. This consists of three main elements: first, training in progressive muscular relaxation; second, the construction of one or more lists of hierarchies of situations or 'scenes' round a particular theme ranging from the least to the most anxiety-evoking, for example on a fear of examinations hierarchy, 'thinking about exams while revising at my desk three months before the exams' is the least anxiety-evoking scene, while the most anxiety-evoking scene is 'having to leave the exam room due to panic'; third, presentation by the counsellor to the client's imagination of progressively more anxiety-evoking scenes from the hierarchy. The assumption here is that presentation of 'scenes' when the client is relaxed inhibits the anxiety that is attached to them and that this reduction of anxiety is transferred into real life. Many counsellors who use systematic desensitization also train their clients to 'manage' the anxiety by means of self-instructional statements as the scenes are presented.

DEVELOPING SPECIFIC BEHAVIOURS

Behaviour Rehearsal and Assertive Training

Behaviour rehearsal is particularly helpful for certain clients who are deficient in interpersonal skills or who have the requisite skills but are inhibited from using them in specific situations. Role-playing is another term for behaviour rehearsal, the idea being that clients practise and become more proficient in their roles before enacting them.

Training clients to be more assertive is probably the main area in counselling in which behaviour rehearsal is used. Many counselling clients have difficulty in asserting themselves and, while some of them may require a more fundamental developmental counselling approach, others may gain from a direct focus on assertion. Below are some such examples.

> Sarah is a 27-year-old assistant solicitor who was promised a review of her salary six months after her firm's annual pay rises were announced, since at that time she had only just started her job. This review is now three months overdue and she feels embarrassed at raising the issue.
>
> Keith is a 39-year-old married man who is really fond of his family and yet whose relationships with them are not as happy as he would like. His family tell him that they find him too ready to find fault with them. Keith, however, feels inhibited about clearly showing the affection he feels for them.
>
> Tessa, aged 24, is a young married woman who feels that her husband's love-making is too focused on meeting his own needs and insufficiently focused on meeting hers. She would like to discuss this with him but is afraid that bringing up the subject might make him angry.

Training clients in assertiveness means helping them to express their thoughts and emotions to other people in appropriate ways. This is not just a matter of expressing negative emotions or 'standing up for one's rights' but, as in the case of Keith, may entail learning to express positive emotions. Sometimes a distinction is made between inhibited, assertive and aggressive behaviour.[5] In inhibited behaviour the individual is self-denying. In aggressive behaviour the individual engages in aversive communication in which his or her own needs may be met at the expense of another person. In assertive behaviour, the individual tries to make the interaction as mutually enhancing as the circumstances will allow. Both saying too little and 'coming on too strong' can indicate the same lack of confidence and skill in a given situation.

Counsellors and clients working in the area of assertion need to assess together the extent to which and the manner in which the client is behaving non-assertively or with inadequate or inappropriate assertion. The following questions are likely to be relevant to an initial assessment:[6]

1. Is the client's lack of assertion a general trait or does it relate only to one or to a few specific situations?
2. In *what* specific situations is the client failing to behave assertively? Examples here might include:
    (a) being too inhibited to ask someone to go out with you;
    (b) failing to ask someone to turn down a stereo that is too loud;
    (c) not saying what you are thinking in a group discussion;
    (d) not being prepared to give compliments;
    (e) having difficulty saying 'no' to requests for time and money.
3. With *whom* does the client fail to behave assertively?
    Possibilities here include: parents, marital partners, children, employers, friends, professional people, shop people, waiters, etc.
4. *How* does the client behave in situations where he or she lacks assertion?
    (a) What are the client's *feelings* and *physical reactions* in the situation and how intense are they?
    The client's *feelings* might include depression, anger, self-pity, confusion, helplessness and fear.
    The client's *physical reactions* might include blushing, feeling faint, nausea, heart pounding, etc.
    (b) What is the client *thinking* in the situation?
    This area may include thoughts about what others are thinking, about how inadequate the client is, and about how risky it is to be assertive.
    (c) How is the client *behaving* in the situation?
    Sometimes clients express opposition indirectly rather than directly, for example by non-cooperation and sulking. Some other behaviours which show lack of assertiveness include: avoiding the assertiveness situation altogether; silence or a low speaking voice; avoidance of eye contact; and not matching the facial expression with the underlying feeling, for example smiling yet feeling inwardly annoyed.
5. On what specific situations, if any, does the client wish to work? Here it is a matter of exploring the client's priorities and assessing his or her motivation for change.

Let me now use Sarah as an example of how counsellors use behaviour rehearsal in working with their clients to help them to become more assertive. The first stage in working with Sarah involved an assessment interview to decide on working goals and methods. By the end of the initial interview the counsellor and Sarah had collaboratively formulated Sarah's goal. This was, by the end of four weeks, to be able to go to the senior partner in her law firm and, in an appropriate way, ask for the salary review that she had been promised. As part of this discussion, the counsellor described the method of assertive training with particular relevance to Sarah's concern and tried to enlist her motivation for the approach. Some clients have reservations about being assertive, and client and counsellor should explore these together. Some of these reservations are connected with unrealistic standards: for instance, Sarah may have had the unrealistic standard 'I must be approved of by other people, especially those in authority, for everything I do.'

The second stage focused on clarifying and rehearsing appropriate ways of attaining Sarah's goal. Here counsellor and client worked together to generate and consider alternative 'scripts'. These involved not only looking at what Sarah might say but also exploring how her boss might react and then how she might reply. The counsellor was mindful of the fact that it was important to take Sarah's individual style of communication into account in formulating the 'scripts'. Also, attention was paid to how Sarah might instruct herself with relevant coping statements. Sarah and the counsellor then rehearsed a couple of 'scripts', with the counsellor role-playing the part of the senior partner. The rehearsals of the scenes were repeated until both Sarah and the counsellor felt comfortable with Sarah's performance. At one stage during this process Sarah and the counsellor reversed roles so that, by playing his part, she could gain greater insight into her senior partner's frame of reference. During this rehearsal period the counsellor coached Sarah not only in the verbal content of assertiveness, but also in appropriate vocal and bodily communication. Furthermore, Sarah was encouraged to do some homework involving imagining herself behaving appropriately when asking for the promised salary review.

The third stage entailed the counsellor supporting Sarah as she tried out the rehearsed behaviours in real life. It is important for clients to see these real-life try-outs as learning situations and not to be too disappointed if mistakes are made or if they do not automatically get what they want. In fact, Sarah had little trouble in her interview with her senior partner and her salary was raised. On other occasions, for example in long-standing relationships such as a marriage, interview time at this stage is likely to be spent in exploring how best to handle the other person's difficulties in adjusting to the client's new-found assertiveness. If the consequences of assertiveness have been negative, counsellor and client can review the appropriateness of the assertive behaviour and, where necessary, modify it.

Exercise 6.3 Assertive training

This exercise can be done in a number of ways.

A *On your own*
1. Write down as many situations in your life as you can in which you feel that you are not being assertive enough. Identify any recurring themes regarding:
    (a) the kinds of situations in which you find assertion difficult;
    (b) the kinds of people with whom you find assertion difficult;
    (c) your feelings, physical reactions, thoughts and behaviours in situations and/or with people where assertion is difficult for you.
2. For one or more of the situations identified in 1 above:
    (a) set yourself an appropriate assertiveness goal(s);
    (b) generate and write out at least two 'scripts' for handling each situation in an assertive way;
    (c) formulate some relevant coping statements for instructing yourself before, during and after the situation(s);
    (d) practise role-playing in your imagination, acting assertively in the situation(s);
    (e) if appropriate, try out one of your assertive behaviour 'scripts' in real life.
3. If you are working in a counselling setting, write down any recurring situations in which your client population finds assertion difficult. Are there any characteristic ways in which this lack of assertion manifests itself?

B *In pairs*
Counsel your partner and together conduct a review of the extent to which and manner in which your 'client' behaves assertively. Then counsel your 'client' in an area where he or she feels insufficiently assertive by:
(a) working together to formulate an appropriate assertiveness goal(s);
(b) exploring your 'clients' thoughts and feelings about being assertive in the situation;
(c) together generating at least two 'scripts' for handling the situation assertively;
(d) together formulating some relevant coping statements for 'client' self-instruction before, during and after the situation;
(e) rehearsing and coaching your 'client' in the appropriate enactment of one of the 'scripts';

(f)   discussing with your 'client' a plan for the enactment of the assertive behaviour in real life.
Afterwards reverse roles.
C   *In a training group*
One option is for the trainer to present case material from the counselling setting for which the group is being trained. For one or more of these cases, he or she takes the trainees through the assertive training procedures step by step. Another option is for the trainer to give a demonstration assertive training interview using one of the group members as 'client'. Other possibilities include: setting the part of the exercise in A above as a homework exercise and then holding a plenary sharing and discussion session; and letting the group work in pairs as in B above and then holding a plenary sharing and discussion session, possibly including the presentation of video-recordings of parts of the trainees' counselling sessions.

Using Modelling

Modelling or observational learning from demonstrations may be used both to inhibit anxiety and to develop specific skills. Some counsellors use modelling when trying to help clients to become less afraid of specific situations, such as contact with a dog or a cat. The feared activity is repeatedly demonstrated by the counsellor or another person so that clients can see that the consequences they fear do not occur. During this process the demonstrator may also engage in cognitive modelling that involves verbalizing appropriate self-instructions. Then the counsellor may jointly perform the feared activity with his or her client and, perhaps, bring the feared dog or cat closer and closer until the client holds it. The client may be encouraged to instruct himself or herself using coping statements. The counsellor's functions are those of anxiety inhibitor and guide. Ultimately, the counsellor withdraws from the situation and the client is encouraged to interact with the previously feared object on his or her own.

Modelling the skill can be an important part of the teaching of any communication skills, including those of counselling. Additionally, modelling can be used to teach decision-making and problem-solving skills. When using modelling, the counsellor must consider whether the modelled performance should be presented live, on film or video, or on audio tapes or cassettes. Another consideration is whether the presentation should be real or simulated.

The characteristics of the model may be important in helping the client to learn the behaviour. Clients are less likely to be receptive to the modelled performance if they do not identify with the model than if they perceive the model both in positive terms and as relevant to their own behaviour. Another consideration is whether to offer modelled presentations of the wrong as well as of the right behaviours, although the main emphasis must be on modelling the desired behaviours. Any modelling of negative behaviours must be clearly labelled as such and its utility in teaching the desired behaviours reviewed carefully.

When using modelling, whether for anxiety reduction or for developing social and other skills, it is desirable for clients to practise the demonstrated behaviour, including instructing themselves with relevant coping statements, as soon as they can. These practice sessions can be video-recorded or audio-recorded and played back to clients as appropriate. Alongside this, clients need the opportunity to discuss with their counsellors their thoughts and feelings about the modelled behaviour and their progress towards attaining it. A number of enactments may be necessary before the client either feels comfortable with or is skilled in implementing the modelled behaviour, which itself may need further presentations. Additionally, clients may require support as they practise their newly learned behaviour outside counselling.

Modelling may be used as part of broader methods of inhibiting anxiety or developing skills. For instance, in assertive training the counsellor may model the desired behaviours as he or she coaches the client in them. Additionally, the counsellor may encourage the client to learn from observing people who are skilled at the assertive behaviour outside counselling. Furthermore, modelling may be combined with the use of reinforcers or rewards, such as praise from the counsellor, as the client achieves a target behaviour. Last, but not least, there is a good deal of modelling involved in any counselling relationship as (we hope) counsellors model the skills of good personal relations, for example accurate listening and empathic responding.

Exercise 6.4 Using modelling

This exercise may be done in a number of ways.

A *On your own*
   Draw either on your personal experience or on your experience of a client in a counselling setting and, in relation to inhibiting an area of anxiety

and/or developing a skill, design a written programme emphasizing modelling involving:

1. a clear statement of goals;
2. a description of how the desired behaviour is to be modelled, including any relevant characteristics of the model;
3. the steps that you intend to take to practise or to allow the client to practise the modelled behaviour;
4. how you intend to monitor and provide feedback to yourself or to the 'client' on his or her performance and progress.

B   *In pairs*

Counsel your partner, who draws either on his or her personal experience or on his or her experience of a client in a counselling setting and, in relation to inhibiting an area of anxiety and/or developing a skill, design and implement, as far as possible, a programme emphasizing modelling involving:

1. a clear statement of goals;
2. modelling of the desired behaviour, possibly by you;
3. enactment by the 'client';
4. monitoring and providing feedback to the 'client' on his or her performance and progress.

Afterwards reverse roles.

C   *In a training group*

In many of the exercises in this book the trainer is encouraged to model the desired behaviours by giving demonstration interviews. In this exercise the trainer might give a demonstration of ways in which he or she might use modelling in counselling. A further option is for the trainer, after an introductory discussion and/or demonstration, to set either of the exercises in A or B above as a homework exercise. The trainer then holds a plenary session in which group members present and receive feedback about their programmes using modelling.

Using Rewards

Both counsellors and their clients can use reinforcement or reward to help develop specific behaviours. Some counsellors find such an approach very mechanical and will not use it. Other counsellors consider that the use of reward by the counsellor and/or the use of self-reward by the client can be helpful methods of altering specific behaviours. Furthermore, they do not consider such procedures unethical so long as goals and methods have been discussed and approved by both parties. The idea of using rewards is pertinent to counselling in at least three ways: identifying what clients find rewarding; use of rewards by the counsellor; and the control of behaviour by clients through self-reward.

Identifying rewards

In all uses of reward in counselling, it is important to find out what individual clients find rewarding. Note that I say 'individual clients' since, when it comes to rewards, individual preferences are important and one person's meat may be another person's poison. There are numerous ways of finding out what clients find rewarding, including: asking them; asking others about them, though here you must be sensitive to issues of confidentiality; making your own observations; getting them to observe and monitor their own behaviour; and getting them to fill out self-report questionnaires in which they check off their reactions to lists of items that people might find rewarding.

MacPhillamy and Lewinsohn's *Pleasant Events Schedule* is an example of a self-report questionnaire designed to help people to identify what they find rewarding.[7, 8] Those filling in the questionnaire rate each of its 320 items, which consist of events and activities generated after an extensive search of possible 'pleasing events', on a five-point scale of pleasantness. The idea behind the questionnaire is basically expressed in the old adage 'a little of what you fancy does you good'. Put another way, the authors of the questionnaire believe that one of the ways to control clients' depressive tendencies is to get them to identify and participate in more pleasant events and activities. Illustrative pleasant events include: being with happy people; thinking about friends; breathing clean air; listening to music; reading a good book; petting and necking; eating good meals; being seen as sexually attractive; seeing beautiful scenery; and visiting friends.

When working with children, pictures may be used instead of words to portray rewards. An example of this is the 'reinforcement menu' devised by Daley for finding effective rewards for eight-year-old to eleven-year-old mentally retarded children.[9] Twenty-two high-probability activities, such as talking, writing and colouring, were drawn in colour by an artist and enclosed in a single book or 'menu' with one activity per page. Children were encouraged to identify the activities in which they wanted to engage.

So far I have mainly been describing identifying what people find rewarding outside counselling. However, a possible view of the counselling process is to see the role of the counsellor as to control the interview by dispensing intentional and sometimes unintentional rewards. For example, counsellors may reward their clients' behaviours by means of such things as praise, attention, eye contact, smiling, empathic responding, warmth and genuiness.

Exercise 6.5 Identifying rewards

This exercise may be done in a number of ways.

A *On your own*
   1. List as many things, events and activities as you can think of that you find rewarding. Then note each item on your list using the following scale:

   Engaging in . . . is . . . for me.
extremely rewarding	4
very rewarding	3
moderately rewarding	2
slightly rewarding	1

   2. Write out a list of rewards which counsellors may intentionally or unintentionally use during counselling sessions. Then circle all items on your list that could also be rewards that clients use on their counsellors during counselling.

B *In pairs*
   1. Working with a partner, together spend the next 15 minutes writing down as many things as possible that people might find rewarding in their lives. Then independently rate each item for how rewarding engaging in it is to you, on the scale used in A above. Rate as 0 any item which you personally would not find rewarding.
   2. Again working with a partner, together use the next ten minutes to write down as many ways as you can think of that counsellors or clients may be intentionally or unintentionally using rewards on each other during counselling sessions. At the end of the ten minutes, discuss, giving your opinions of which are the most important ways.

C *In a training group*
   One option is for the trainer to do the parts of the exercise in B above as a whole group exercise from the start. Another option is for the trainer, after an initial discussion of what is required, first to let the group members do the parts of the exercise in B above in pairs, then to conduct a whole-group sharing and discussion session in which lists of 'rewards in life' and 'rewards in counselling' are compiled for the group as a whole.

Using rewards with clients

I have already implied that all the behaviours of the counsellor can be viewed in reward terms. In a well-known study, based on recordings of his interviewing, even Carl Rogers was found to be differentially rewarding by his behaviour certain categories of client utterances.[10] Rogers, however, more than most counsellors, is likely to allow his clients the freedom to acknowledge their own feelings and to develop their own lines of thought.

Here I focus on obvious attempts by the counsellor to use rewards with clients. For example, in careers counselling the counsellor may reward all attempts by the client to gather information relevant to a career decision. The rewards may include attention, praise and comments like 'good', 'well done' or 'that's helpful'. Another example is that of a counsellor and client who together have drawn up a list of sub-goals in increasing order of difficulty. For instance, sub-goals for a male client whose goal is to develop a close relationship with a member of the opposite sex might include: asking a woman out for coffee; taking a woman out to dinner; and holding hands with a woman. As the client reports back his progress the counsellor rewards the client with such comments as 'good' and 'well done' as each sub-goal is attained. In this use of reward the counsellor is encouraging performance by identifying target behaviours, drawing up a 'successive approximation' list of progressively more difficult sub-goals, each one coming nearer to the ultimate goal, and rewarding the client for attainment of a sub-goal. Counsellors need to ensure that the target behaviours are well learned so that they continue after counselling. One simple way of making the use of counsellor reward less mechanical than it sounds is for counsellors to use their empathic responding skills to help their clients to explore their thoughts and feelings as they progress towards attaining their goals.

Another example of the use of rewards by the counsellor is with clients who need active help in identifying and making contact with the people, activities and events that they themselves find rewarding. In the preceding section I mentioned the pleasant events or 'a little of what you fancy does you good' approach to depressed people. Here the counsellor may have to encourage and reward clients in the following areas: as they monitor the degree to which they engage in rewarding activities; as they formulate goals for greater participation in life; and as they take steps outside counselling that involve changing their behaviour.

Research on using rewards with animals has emphasized the importance of schedules of reward. Basically there are three main categories:

continuous reward, or rewarding people every time they perform a specific behaviour; never rewarding the performance of a behaviour; and intermittently rewarding the performance of a behaviour. Reward schedules are a fairly complex area of psychology. However, a simple point is that, if the client needs to be rewarded continuously by the counsellor in order to perform a behaviour, then performance of that behaviour is not going to continue when there is no counsellor to administer the reward. Often counsellors 'fade' from the scene by rewarding performance of a behaviour progressively less, in the hope that clients can get to the point where attainment of the desired behaviour brings its own rewards.

Exercise 6.6   Using rewards with clients

This exercise may be done in a number of ways.

A   *On your own*
   1. Write down the kinds of rewards that you consider ethical and helpful for counsellors to use with clients.
   2. Design a programme, involving the use of counsellor reward, for shaping a client's behaviour so that he or she may attain a real or hypothetical mutually agreed goal. Indicate when and how you would use counsellor reward.

B   *In pairs*
   1. Discuss with your partner the kinds of rewards that you consider ethical and helpful for counsellors to use with clients.
   2. Together with your partner design a programme, involving the use of counsellor reward, for shaping a client's behaviour so that he or she may attain a real or hypothetical mutually agreed goal. Indicate when and how you would use counsellor reward.

C   *In a training group*
   The trainer can present case material of treatment approaches to clients' difficulties involving the use of counsellor reward. If possible, these cases should be drawn from the counselling setting for which the group is being trained. Other options are for the trainer to facilitate a discussion on the use of rewards by counsellors and/or to give a demonstration interview focusing on the use of counsellor reward.

Using self-reward

Counsellors may also help their clients to learn the skills of self-control or self-reward. There are two main categories of rewards that people can control in order to achieve their specific behaviour-change goal. First, they can attempt to control the target behaviour *prior to* its execution. For instance, Robert may have a goal of losing 25 pounds over the next three months. One way in which he can control his food intake before eating is to ensure that food is put out of sight and out of reach. Furthermore, especially if he lives alone, he can control the kind and amount of food that comes into his house or flat. A second way in which Robert can control his eating is to give himself a reward after, say, every five pounds that he loses. Here the reward *follows* or *is contingent upon* performance of a desired behaviour or a series of desired behaviours that achieves a sub-goal. Essentially, training clients in self-reward involves teaching them how to: monitor their behaviour; set goals; establish appropriate rewards for their behaviour both before and after its execution; evaluate their performance; and, where appropriate, reward themselves for successful attainment of a goal or sub-goal.

Exercise 6.7   Using self-reward

This exercise may be done in a number of ways.

A   *On your own*
Design a self-reward programme for acquiring or altering a specific behaviour. Write down:
1. your goal;
2. how you intend to monitor your behaviour in order to establish its present level;
3. the steps in your programme towards achieving your goal, including specific instructions for how and when you intend to reward yourself;
4. the steps you intend to take to ensure that your behaviour change lasts once your goal has been achieved.
B   *In pairs*
Counsel a partner and together design a self-reward programme, based on the outline in A above, for helping him or her to acquire or alter a specific behaviour. Afterwards reverse roles.
C   *In a training group*
One option is for the trainer to present case material, drawn from a setting

relevant to the training group, on teaching clients to use self-reward. Another option is for the trainer to give a demonstration interview with a group member as 'client' in which together they design a self-reward programme. A further option is for the group, after an introductory discussion, to subdivide and do either the exercise in A or that in B above. The trainer then holds a plenary session in which group members' self-reward programmes are presented and discussed.

DECISION-MAKING, PROBLEM-SOLVING AND PLANNING

Counsellors can facilitate acting on the part of their clients not only by helping them to make individual decisions and solve single problems but also by helping them to acquire the processes of effective decision-making and problem-solving. A possible distinction between decision-making and problem-solving, albeit simplified, is that whereas the emphasis in decision-making is on the skills of rational thinking, problem-solving also encompasses clients' feelings and actions as well as their ability to cope with irrational thought processes. Here I first state the steps of a rational decision-making process prior to a fuller discussion of problem-solving. The steps in decision-making include: defining the area for the decision; generating alternative solutions; collecting information about the alternatives; examining the consequences of the alternatives; making the decision; and evaluating the adequacy of the decision in the light of feedback. These steps can be taught to clients, preferably with reference to an important decision that they are currently making.

Problem-solving, as used in this chapter, involves many of the considerations that I discussed in the previous chapter on focusing on thinking. It can be conceived of as consisting of six somewhat overlapping stages: orientation, analysis, decision-making, planning, action and evaluation.

Orientation

Orientation refers to a client's attitude to problems. Relevant orientation considerations are the degree to which the clients believe that: problems are a normal part of life; the best approach to problems is to try to solve them; it is important to be skilled at identifying problems as they arise rather than when they are full-blown; and it is often better to restrain impulsive behaviour and instead take a more systematic problem-solving approach.

Analysis

Having defined a problem, considerations relevant to an *analysis* of the problem include both self-examination and examination of the other considerations in the situation. The kinds of questions relevant in self-examination are: 'How am I contributing to generating and/or sustaining the problem?' and 'How realistic am I being in my thinking about the problem (relevant standards, attributions and anticipations)?'. Further matters to be considered include the way other people are thinking about the problem, including their standards, etc., and any other reality constraints, for example time and money.

Decision-making

The decision-making stage is closely related to the analysis stage, and here relevant questions include: 'What are the options open to me or to us?', 'How do I assess the consequences of the options?' and 'What decision or decisions do I wish to make?'.

Planning

The fourth stage is that of implementing a decision by means of planning. Such planning needs a clear statement of goals, which may focus on changing both *inner* events, for example personal thoughts, feelings and attitudes, and *outer* events, for example getting someone else to behave differently. An example from careers work might be that of Carol, who established the twin goals of altering her *inner* environment so that she did not restrict herself to traditional 'female' occupations and altering her *outer* environment by going for interviews for the best job available despite the stereotyping of occupations by gender. A good plan is based on a realistic time schedule and includes an outline of the steps to be taken to attain each of the goals. Depending on the theoretical orientation of the counsellor and on the wishes of the client, it may include provision for self-reward on attainment of goals and sub-goals. Clients' commitment to or motivation for implementing their plans may be improved if they are clear about the gains for themselves and others, if the plan is clearly written out, and if they have a verbal or written contract with another or with others.

Action

Plans are meant to be implemented and the next stage involves clients acting on their plans. The counsellor may need to support the client during the early stages of acting on plans, especially if they involve changes in well-established patterns of behaviour. It is not always easy to anticipate in the planning stage all the difficulties that may arise in the action stage. For instance, a male client who decides to try to achieve a better relationship with an alienated teenage daughter can only guess at his own and her reactions as he starts trying to repair the relationship. As well as using their empathic responding skills, counsellors may need to use challenges with clients, who may, if the going gets tough, be tempted to try to excuse themselves from not carrying through their plans. For example, if our client's daughter rejects his initial overtures, the counsellor may challenge the client's thoughts and feelings about giving up the attempt before giving it a proper try.

Evaluation

Plans need to be evaluated in the light of feedback. Earlier I stated that goals for planning may focus not only on changing outer events, such as overt behaviour, but also on changing inner events, such as the client's thoughts and feelings. The plan might include a section on how monitoring and evaluation of progress is to take place. Basically, the evaluation stage focuses on the question 'Is my plan realistic or does it need changing?'. Again, counsellors may need to support their clients as they evaluate feedback from the enactment of their plans and, if necessary, help them to revise or even to discard insufficiently successful plans. Just having the support of a counsellor during the stage of evaluating feedback may be enough to counteract many clients' tendencies to engage in self-protective distortions and denial of this feedback.

Many different counsellor skills are involved in facilitating problem-solving behaviour by clients. One such skill is that of providing a rationale for the importance of a problem-solving orientation. In addition to empathic responding, counsellor skills for the analysis and decision-making stages are mainly those of focusing on thinking, for example exploring standards and attributions and, where appropriate, challenging. A counsellor skill for the planning stage is that of encouraging specificity so that clients set out their proposed courses of action, both inner and outer, in a systematic way. Possible skills for the action stage include empathic responding and encouraging performance through appropriate use of counsellor-offered rewards, for example praise and interest. Counsellor skills which may be useful during the feedback stage include exploring self-protective thinking in instances where clients are having difficulty fully acknowledging the feedback they are getting and, where necessary, assisting clients in making revised plans.

Exercise 6.8   Developing problem-solving skills

This exercise may be done in a number of ways.

A   *On your own*
Take a problem-solving approach to any situation in your counselling work or personal life for which it seems appropriate. Assess your orientation to problem-solving and then write out:
1.   your analysis of the situation, including your own role in sustaining it;
2.   your decision-making options and your final decision;
3.   your plan for implementing your decision including, where necessary, changing your inner as well as your outer environment;
4.   how you intend to monitor and evaluate your progress.

B   *In pairs*
Counsel your partner and together take a problem-solving approach to any situation in his or her counselling work or personal life for which it seems appropriate. Discuss with him or her the importance of a problem-solving orientation. Then help your 'client' to analyse the situation, consider decision-making options, and come to a decision. At this stage you and your 'client' think through and write down a plan for implementing the decision including, where necessary, focusing on changing your 'client's' inner as well as outer environment. Include in the plan provision for monitoring and evaluating progress. Afterwards reverse roles.

C   *In a training group*
The trainer can illustrate a problem-solving approach to situations drawn from case material relevant to the interests of the training group. The trainer may give a demonstration interview of a problem-solving interview, possibly supplemented with a hand-out on how to write plans. Other options include getting the group to work either as individuals or as pairs

and holding a plenary sharing and discussion session focusing on examining their problem-solving plans.

POSTSCRIPT

In this chapter I have described a number of ways of facilitating acting. However, I do not mean to imply that clients never change their behaviour unless counsellors adopt these approaches. It is sufficient, in order for some clients to change, that they clarify and 'get more in touch with' their feelings about a person, activity or event. Other clients may be greatly helped by focusing on their thinking, and this may be enough to motivate action. In both these instances it may be assumed that the appropriate behaviour is latent in the client's repertoire. What is needed to make the desired behaviour manifest is a change of feeling and/or thinking. Nevertheless, for certain clients and indeed for many people outside counselling, systematic approaches aimed at changing and developing their behaviour have much to offer. Changes in feeling and thinking may precede, be concurrent with or follow these changes in clients' actions.

REFERENCES

1. Bernstein, D.A. & Borkovec, T.D. (1973) *Progressive Relaxation Training: A Manual For the Helping Professions*. Champaign, Illinois: Research Press.
2. Wolpe, J. (1973); *The Practice of Behaviour Therapy*. Oxford: Pergamon Press.
3. Goldfried, M.R. & Davison, G.C. (1976) *Clinical Behaviour Therapy*. New York: Holt, Rinehart and Winston.
4. Nelson-Jones, R. (1982) *The Theory and Practice of Counselling Psychology*. Eastbourne: Holt, Rinehart and Winston.
5. Alberti, R.E. & Emmons, M.L. (1974) *Your Perfect Right* (2nd edn). San Luis Obispo, California: Impact.
6. Bower, S.A. & Bower, G.H. (1979) *Asserting Your Self: A Practical Guide For Positive Change*. Reading, Massachusetts: Addison-Wesley.
7. MacPhillamy, D.J. & Lewinsohn, P.M. (1982) The Pleasant Events Schedule: studies on reliability, validity and scale intercorrelation, *Journal of Consulting and Clinical Psychology*, **50**, pp. 363–380. This article contains Form III–S of the schedule as an appendix.
8. Lewinsohn, P.M. (1976) *Your Personal Guide to Depression Control*. New York: Biomonitoring Applications, Inc.
9. Daley, M.F. (1969) The 'reinforcement menu': finding effective reinforcers. In Krumboltz, J.D. & Thoresen, C.E. (ed.), *Behavioural Counseling: Cases and Techniques*, pp. 42–45. New York: Holt, Rinehart and Winston.
10. Truax, C.B. (1966) Reinforcement and non-reinforcement in Rogerian psychotherapy. *Journal of Abnormal Psychology*, **71**, 1–9.

7 Further Considerations and Skills

In this chapter I deal with a number of further practical interview considerations and skills which, though important, did not fit easily into the preceding chapters. In this 'catch-all' chapter I cover: routine interview considerations and skills, for example making referrals, duration, frequency and number of sessions, and confidentiality; handling crises; counsellor self-disclosure; and medical considerations.

ROUTINE INTERVIEW CONSIDERATIONS AND SKILLS

Making Referrals

There are many different situations in which counsellors may think it is in their client's best interests to be referred elsewhere. For instance, as a result of assessment in an initial session, the counsellor may feel that the client needs either medical assistance or further information that he or she cannot provide. Furthermore, possibly the client would be best served by a different kind of counsellor who specializes in that client's particular problem, e.g. occupational choice, sexual, marital, spiritual, etc. It is important that counsellors have a good knowledge, preferably based on personal contact, of appropriate referral sources in their localities. Such referrals do not necessarily mean that the counsellor drops out of the picture altogether, but this is usually the case.

Sometimes it is apparent right at the start of an initial session that the client has come to the wrong person. On other occasions the question of referral may come at what would normally be the contracting stage of the initial session in which working goals and methods are discussed. The counsellor might make a summary ending: 'Based on what you have been telling me perhaps you should consider seeing . . . (nature of referral, e.g. an occupational counsellor). If you wish to pursue this further, I can probably recommend a suitable person.' This may be sufficient, but if the counsellor feels the need for further explanation, he or she might add: 'My reasons for suggesting this are . . . (state reasons)'. The manner in which counsellors raise the issue of referral in an initial session should be such as to allow their clients to explore the reasons for the suggestion. Furthermore, counsellors should allow their clients to feel that it is their decision whether to follow up any suggestion.

The matter of referring a client once the counselling relationship has had time to get established is likely to be far more emotionally tinged for both counsellors and clients than that of referral during an initial session. The reasons for such later referrals are numerous. For instance, counsellor and client may have reached an impasse which persists in remaining unresolved. Alternatively, either counsellor or client may consider that the client needs different skills from those that the counsellor has. A further reason is that either counsellor or client may be leaving the locality. Additionally, either party may feel that the other is difficult or awkward.

Counsellors need to explore carefully their motivation both for making referrals and, in some instances, for not making referrals. Referral of clients may generate in counsellors feelings that they are not good enough, have failed their clients in some way, and are abandoning them. However, sometimes counsellors feel relieved to have confronted an awkward situation that has been going on for some time. The kinds of feelings which might be, but not necessarily will be, generated in clients are those of rejection, abandonment, and not wanting to leave the security of an existing relationship to start with a new and strange counsellor.

It is important for referrals to be made skilfully. This increases the chances of positive results and also lessens the possibility of negative emotions being generated by the referral. Whatever the reasons for the referral, it is usually best that these are shared and discussed openly. Furthermore, it can be helpful if a referral is a joint decision rather than a unilateral decision on the part of the counsellor. Counsellors need to use their empathic responding skills to demonstrate an understanding of their clients' needs, perceptions of the counselling relationship, and feelings about being referred. Sometimes, for instance when they are leaving the locality, counsellors can prepare their clients for the referral and for the loss it entails.

Though the counsellor may phone or send an explanatory note to the person to whom the referral is being made, ultimately clients have to make contact for themselves. The issue of how much information to pass on at the time of referral involves not only the wishes and feelings of counsellor and client, but the practices of the institution in which they are working. Furthermore, people to whom the referrals are being made differ in the amount of information about clients that they like to have from referral sources. Sometimes counsellors may feel it appropriate to be available to support their clients during a transitional period to being with another counsellor, but this must be on the clear understanding that it is only a short-term offer. A final point is that, occasionally, counsellors are more in need of referral than their clients. For instance, certain clients or life situations may trigger off debilitating anxieties in counsellors, who may then need to refer themselves to a trusted colleague.

Exercise 7.1 Making referrals

This exercise may be done in a number of ways.

A *On your own*
1. Building a referral network. For your present or a future counselling role:
    (a) list all the categories of people to whom you might want to refer clients;
    (b) for each category assess whether you could pick up the phone and speak about a client to someone who is personally known to you;
    (c) state how you intend to remedy any deficiencies in your referral network.
2. Making a referral. For a situation that is relevant to your present or future counselling work, write out:
    (a) a statement or series of statements that you might make referring a client elsewhere;
    (b) the kinds of feelings that might be generated in your client and you during the process of making this referral.

B *In pairs*
1. Discuss how to go about building a referral network for any present or

future counselling roles that you may have. Cover each of the issues mentioned in A above, about building a referral network.

2. Identify the kinds of referral situations in which you are or may be involved in your counselling work. Ensuring that each of you gets a turn as counsellor, role-play making referrals in these situations.

C *In a training group*

The trainer can demonstrate with case material the kinds of referrals that may be necessary in the training group's present or future counselling work. The trainer may give one or more demonstrations of making referrals with group members role-playing clients. The trainer may break the group into pairs to discuss how to build a referral network and/or to practise making referrals. Afterwards there could be a plenary session in which group members share and discuss their experiences and views on making referrals.

Duration, Frequency and Number of Sessions

Perhaps it is most common for individual counselling sessions to be 45 to 50 minutes long, the so-called '50-minute hour', with the remaining ten minutes being left for such matters as writing up notes, resting and preparing for the next client. However, there are no hard and fast rules. Many considerations determine the length of sessions, including: the counsellor's workload; what is a financially viable length of time to see clients who are fee-paying; and the purposes of the session. Developmental sessions tend to be of a regular duration of around 45 minutes each, partly because a briefer session may be insufficient for clients to start exploring deeply and listening to themselves and partly because a much longer session might continue after client, counsellor or both have lost their momentum. Sometimes initial sessions are longer than 45–50 minutes because the counsellor is trying to complete an initial assessment, and sometimes subsequent sessions are shorter than 45–50 minutes because the counsellor has a specific task which can be accomplished in a briefer period, for example administering certain behavioural counselling techniques. Counsellors can adjust the duration of their sessions to suit both their clients and themselves. They are likely to be more productive if they avoid adhering rigidly to sessions of the same length for all their clients. However, when counsellors state that a session is going to be of a certain duration, there are reasons for adhering to it, including both encouraging clients to speak out within their allotted time and not keeping subsequent clients waiting.

Frequency of sessions can range from daily to weekly to bi-weekly to monthly to *ad hoc* arrangements when the client comes to see the counsellor only when in special need. Many of the considerations that determine length, like time and money, also determine frequency of sessions. Developmental sessions are often conducted on a once-a-week basis, though some counsellors prefer more frequent contact, especially with more vulnerable clients, in order to offer support and maintain the momentum of counselling work. Possibly there is a less fixed pattern for problem-focused and decision-making sessions, where counsellor and client negotiate the time of the next session at the end of their preceding appointment. It should, of course, be remembered that much of the work of counselling goes on between sessions as clients explore themselves further and try out changes in their behaviour. Also, some clients may be in counselling groups which meet between their individual sessions. Additionally, between sessions, counsellors are able to review their working goals and methods in relation to particular clients.

The number of sessions varies greatly according to such factors as client severity, counsellor availability, money, the purposes of the counselling contact, and the degree to which goals have been attained. Crisis interviews and supportive interviews may be for one or two sessions only, though sometimes they may develop into longer-term counselling. Decision-making counselling may last only for one session, but often involves two or three sessions, if not more. Problem-focused counselling may last for only one session, but perhaps four to eight sessions is more likely. Developmental counselling relationships may last for months, if not years, and sometimes involve 100 or more sessions.

Terminating Sessions and Relationships

In Chapter 4 I discussed terminating an initial session. Termination statements for *subsequent sessions* vary with the purposes of the interview. For a developmental interview along person-centred lines it may be sufficient to make statements like 'Well, I'm afraid that our time is drawing to a close' or 'It looks as though we're going to have to end now'. In all counselling sessions the assumption is that the ultimate responsibility for time-keeping rests with the counsellor rather than with the client. In problem-focused, decision-making and crisis interviewing, the session may end with a summary by the counsellor of the ground that has been covered during the session as well as mention of any homework assignments or other tasks to be completed before the next interview.

Decisions to terminate *counselling relationships* may be made either by counsellor or by client, or by both together. Ideally, such decisions are made because both client and counsellor believe that counselling goals have been attained. This state of affairs may be more apparent in problem-focused or decision-making relationships, where the goals are limited and specific, than in developmental counselling, where the goals are broader.

Some counselling relationships are based on a fixed-term 'contract' and so have termination built into them after a specific number of sessions or a specific time period. Two of the main reasons for fixed-term contracts are that they are considered by some to motivate clients and that they help the counsellor to share his or her time among more clients. Other counselling relationships may be based on an open-ended contract in which the limitations of the relationships regarding time and number of sessions have never been stated. This is especially likely to be the case for developmental counselling. If the counsellor feels that it is best to terminate such a relationship, for instance if further progress seems unlikely, this may be done gradually. Two approaches to this are: first, to prepare the client by discussing ending the counselling relationship a few times before it actually happens; and second, to 'fade' the relationship by seeing the client progressively less often.

In final counselling sessions it may be useful to review jointly what has been achieved during counselling. Also, the counsellor may wish to indicate his or her availability for any future contact with the client. Sometimes counsellor and client will discuss arrangements for further individual or group counselling with another counsellor.

Clients may themselves suggest termination or fail to attend subsequent sessions. It is always best to give the client the chance to offer an explanation for missing an appointment rather than to automatically assume that they are dropping out of counselling. Where clients do suggest terminating the counselling relationship, their reasons merit exploration. If after this the counsellor still feels that termination would be premature, this view should be shared with the client, along with the reasoning behind it. Clients who suggest termination can be threatening to their counsellors' self-esteem and sense of competence. Consequently counsellors need to listen to and, if necessary, contain their own emotions so that clients are given the freedom to make their own choices about whether or not to continue.

Confidentiality

Confidentiality is an issue which is very important to many clients. Clients often find it hard to talk about themselves and will be even more reticent if they do not feel that their disclosures are private. Related to this, client disclosures are often in very sensitive areas that would be threatening if disclosed outside counselling. Consequently, confidentiality is central to whether or not the client can trust or 'share faith' with the counsellor. Loss of confidentiality may come about both through the counsellor talking about the client with others in a way that identifies the client, and as a result of cassettes, transcripts and interview records falling into the wrong hands.

Confidentiality raises the question of to whom interview material is confidential. For instance, one option is for the counsellor alone to have the information. Another option is for this information also to be accessible to the counsellor's supervisor or supervision group and to the counselling agency in which the interviews take place. A further step is for the information to go beyond the counselling setting to people outside, for example parents, tutors, employers and the courts. This is probably the real dividing line concerning breach of confidentiality. If clients wanted people outside counselling to know about their disclosures they could have told them themselves.

Where counsellors are working in settings where there are significant limitations on confidentiality, this fact is best shared with the client right from the beginning. For instance, in respect of British courts, counsellors cannot claim privilege concerning matters that their clients have discussed with them. Also, in some school settings, the counsellor may be obliged to share his or her records with the headmaster or headmistress.

There may be other instances in which counsellors intentionally decide to breach confidentiality either in the client's best interest, for example to protect a suicidal client, or because they consider that they are unable to collude in an act which the client is contemplating, for example violence to another person. These can be difficult decisions and, even when made, there is the further matter of whether, when and how best to inform the client that confidentiality is about to be or has been breached. Sometimes clients themselves ask the counsellor to write a report to an outside person, for instance a note to a college tutor about a student's work difficulties. It can be helpful if such a note is compiled in conjunction with the client both as a check on its accuracy and so that the client knows precisely what is being said about him or her.

Keeping Records

Some counsellors take notes during their sessions, others make notes at the end of interviews, and still others scarcely bother at all. Person-centred counsellors who are trying to stay in their clients' frames of reference and facilitate their flow of experiencing tend to dislike the obtrusiveness of during-session note-taking and, if at all, make some notes at the end of the session. A major purpose of these notes is to help them to remember and so remain in their clients' frames of reference.

Counsellors who advocate note-taking and record-keeping do so for a number of reasons. I have already mentioned that it helps them to remember the client's frame of reference. Another reason is that notes are an aid in monitoring progress and seeing whether counsellor goals have been attained. Notes may help the counsellor to analyse the client's situation and to plan additional interventions. Additionally, they may be useful for the purposes of the counsellor's own supervision and for presentation at case discussions, though close monitoring of the counsellor's work is also likely to require listening to interview cassettes. Last, notes provide a permanent record which may be useful if the client returns for counselling or is referred elsewhere.

There are three main kinds of records pertaining to individual clients for which counsellors take notes. The notes themselves may be the record or the counsellor may edit and rewrite them into a more coherent form. The first kind of record is the *assessment record*, which is a written account of the presenting-concerns, reconnaissance and contracting (working goals and methods) stages of the initial session. This record should also contain information about how to contact the client between sessions. In making assessment and other records it is valuable to distinguish between information that the client provides and the counsellor's own observations.

Second, there is the *progress record*, which consists of the pertinent information discussed in each session, observations about client progress, any suggestions for homework before the next session, and any alterations in working goals and methods. If a behavioural counselling method like systematic desensitization is being used, each presentation of a hierarchy item will be separately recorded. Furthermore, any significant between-interview contact either with the client or with other people, professional or otherwise, concerning the client may be recorded in the progress record.

Third, there is the *termination record*, which summarizes what went on during counselling, specifies the extent to which goals were achieved, notes the reasons for termination, and lists any specific termination decisions made between client and counsellor, for example whether to continue in counselling with another counsellor. The termination record might also contain any observations about working with the client, for example his or her degree of motivation, that might be helpful for any subsequent counselling contact.

A fourth kind of record for which notes are pertinent, more focused on counsellor than on client needs, is a *statistical summary*, very often presented in the form of an annual report, of the work of an individual counsellor or counselling agency. Some counsellors make their records on cards and others on sheets of paper. At the front of each client's file there should be a summary card or sheet of paper on which the relevant statistical data are easily accessible. These data may include age, sex, marital status, nationality, nature of presenting concern(s), number of interviews and any further data that are specific to the requirements of a particular agency or institution. Counsellors are becoming more conscious of the need to provide statistical summaries of their work, accompanied by an explanatory text, as pressure mounts for them to become more accountable for their budgets.

Exercise 7.2   Keeping records

This exercise may be done in a number of ways.

A   *On your own*
  1. Regarding your present or future counselling work, write down what, if any, kinds of information you intend to collect for each of the following areas of record-keeping:
     (a)   assessment records;
     (b)   progress records;
     (c)   termination records;
     (d)   statistical summary (e.g. for an annual report).
  2. If you have access to actual or role-played clients, make up records for them and critically reflect on the usefulness of the information contained in these records.
B   *In pairs*
  Regarding your present or future counselling work, discuss with your partner what information, if any, you intend collecting for each of the following areas of record-keeping: assessment records, progress records, termination records and statistical summaries. Design and discuss the layout of any records you intend to keep.
C   *In a training group*
  The trainer can give examples, drawn from case material from the client

population for which the group is being trained, of record-keeping in each of the following areas: assessment records, progress records, termination records and statistical summaries. The trainer can encourage the group to keep records of their sessions with actual or role-played clients. The trainer may also hold a plenary session to share and discuss issues involved in and methods of record-keeping.

Use of Written, Audio and Visual Aids

Counsellors are often busy people who must constantly be alert for ways of saving their own time as well as increasing their impact on clients. Correctly and flexibly used, written, audio and visual aids can help to achieve this purpose. These categories are far from discrete: for instance a visual picture usually involves words and sometimes writing; written material involves a visual image; and audio material can be based on a written script. With this disclaimer, Table 7.1 lists some types and possible uses of *written aids* in conjunction with counselling. Use of such materials is likely to vary with the theoretical orientation of the counsellor: for example, behavioural counsellors will wish to monitor behaviour closely. It also varies with the objectives of counselling: for example, pre-interview questionnaires, tests, and hand-outs containing information are all likely to be emphasized in occupational counselling.

Table 7.2 lists some types and possible uses of *audio aids* in conjunction with counselling. The inventions of the tape recorder and of the lighter, more flexible cassette recorder have enabled counsellors to keep in touch with their clients outside the counselling room. The telephone seems to be useful especially for those who, at first counselling contact, wish to remain anonymous. A proportion of these people will later be prepared to a see a counsellor face-to-face. The radio is not mentioned in Table 7.2, since counsellors cannot rely on appropriate programmes for their clients being broadcast both in a way in which and when they could be useful.

Table 7.1   *Some types and possible uses of written aids in conjunction with counselling*

Category and type of aid	Illustrative uses
Information about clients	
Self-report questionnaires	Assessing assertiveness or engagement in pleasant events
Behaviour monitoring sheets	Analysis of the frequency, circumstances and consequences of behaviour

Pre-interview questionnaires	Saving interview time by previous collection of non-threatening material, for example a person's educational and work history
Autobiographical statements	Encouraging client self-exploration
Homework sheets and questionnaires	Accelerating the work of counselling by getting clients to focus on specific areas of their thinking and behaviour
Tests and measures	Collecting standardized information for and about clients in such areas as: interests and values; aptitude; mental ability; achievement; and personality
Information for clients	
Books	Teaching principles of a theoretical position, for example rational-emotive therapy or transactional analysis
Hand-outs	Providing occupational information, shortened version of principles of a theoretical position

Table 7.2 *Some types and possible uses of audio aids in conjunction with counselling*

Category and type of aid	Illustrative uses
For the client's benefit	
Telephone information	A way of giving information and suggestions, possibly pre-recorded, about how to handle specific problems, for example examination anxiety
Telephone counselling	Counselling the suicidal and despairing, counselling gays
Information cassettes	Information about specific occupations and jobs
Training cassettes	Training in skills such as relaxation
Self-instructional cassettes	Cassettes focused on helping clients to manage their own anxieties and develop their effective thinking skills
Cassette recordings of sessions	Allows both client and counsellor a further chance to explore the client's areas of concern and personal style
For the counsellor's benefit	
Cassette recordings of own sessions	Allows counsellor, possibly in conjunction with a supervisor or supervision group, to explore his or her interview style and treatment and responding decisions
Cassette recordings of others' sessions and approaches to counselling	Enables counsellor to learn from listening to the theoretical positions and practical skills of leading counsellors

Table 7.3 *Some types and possible uses of visual aids in conjunction with counselling*

Category and type of aid	Illustrative uses
Information about clients	
Video-recordings	Feeding back to clients how they relate in a group, showing marital partners their behaviour in conflicts
Blackboard or flip-chart	Giving clients a visual as well as a written analysis of their unrealistic ways of thinking and of more realistic formulations
Information for clients	
Real-life models	Modelling of feared behaviours to inhibit anxiety or of desired behaviours to develop social and other skills
Films and video-cassettes	Giving occupational information, illustrating social and other skills
Computer consoles	Giving occupational information, with some computer systems allowing the client to interact with the information by asking further questions
Information for counsellors	
Video-recordings of own interviews	Allows counsellor, possibly in conjunction with a supervisor or supervision group, to explore his or her bodily as well as vocal and verbal communication
Video recordings and films of others' interviews and approaches to counselling	Allows access to the verbal, vocal and bodily communication of leading counsellors

Table 7.3 shows some types and possible uses of *visual* aids in conjunction with counselling. Feeding back behaviour to clients in visual form may be a powerful way of confronting some of them with the discrepancy between their self-image and their actions. Counsellors need to help their clients to explore their thoughts and feelings in relation to this feedback so that they can use it constructively. I have already mentioned the importance of modelling or observational learning which, depending on the behaviour to be learned, may be heavily dependent on a visual model. For instance, though little may be lost by modelling thinking skills on audio-tape, the same cannot be said for modelling social skills. Occupational counselling is a field of counselling in which films, video-cassettes and audio-cassettes can be very useful ways of presenting information. Many attempts have been and are being made to utilize the potential for information-giving that computers and computer consoles have. This is a promising development in the application of audio-visual aids to counselling, Last, counsellors can develop their own skills by means of video-recordings and visually as

Exercise 7.3   Using written, audio and visual aids

This exercise may be done in a number of ways.

A   *On your own*
   With regard to your present or future counselling work and using Tables 7.1, 7.2 and 7.3 as guidelines, write down how, if at all, you might benificially use:
   1.   written aids;
   2.   audio aids;
   3.   visual aids.

B   *In pairs*
   Together you and your partner discuss, with regard to your present or future counselling work and using Tables 7.1, 7.2 and 7.3 as guidelines, how, if at all, you might beneficially use:
   1.   written aids;
   2.   audio aids;
   3.   visual aids.

C   *In a training group*
   The trainer may provide examples of the use of written aids, audio aids and visual aids in conjunction with counselling the client population for which the group is being trained. Another option is for the trainer to set either the individual or the pairs exercise and then hold a plenary sharing and discussion session on the use of written, audio and visual aids in counselling.

---

well as aurally monitor their interview behaviour. Furthermore, when it comes to learning about the counselling skills of leading practitioners from different counselling approaches, a picture may be 'worth a thousand words'.

HANDLING CRISES

Defining Crises

Crises may be defined as situations of excessive stress. Stress tends to have a negative connotation in our culture, though this is unjustified if one thinks of stress in terms of adjustive demands or, more colloquially, in terms of challenges in life. Each person has an optimal stress level or a particular level of stimulation at which he or she feels most comfortable. At this level the person may experience what Hans Selye, a noted writer on stress, has termed 'stress without distress'.[1] Beneath this level the person may feel insufficiently stimulated and bored. Above this level the person is likely to experience physiological and psychological distress. If the heightened stress is prolonged or perceived as extremely severe, clients may feel that their coping resources are inadequate to meet the adjustive demands being made on them. In such circumstances they are in a situation of excessive stress or a state of crisis.

This section, on handling crises, relates mainly to clients who are in a fairly acute state of crisis. At this stage clients may be experiencing heightened or maladaptive reactions in a number of different, though interrelated, areas:

1. *Bodily.* Bodily reactions may include hypertension and proneness to heart attacks, gastric or duodenal ulcers, etc. The weakest parts of different clients' bodies are most adversely affected by stress, though all parts are equally exposed to it. Further information on bodily reactions to stress is contained in Table 7.6, on disorders which may be psychosomatic.
2. *Feelings.* The feelings associated with excessive stress may include shock, depression, frustration, anger, anxiety, disorientation, and fears of insanity or nervous breakdown.
3. *Thoughts.* Some of the main thoughts associated with excessive stress are that clients are powerless to make a positive impact on their situations, that things are getting out of control, and despair or lack of hope for the future. The notion of excessive stress implies that clients' thought processes have become somewhat irrational and that they are thinking ineffectively, for example with 'tunnel vision', which involves focusing on only a few factors in a situation, or with the kinds of self-protective thinking I described in Chapter 5.
4. *Actions.* Avoidance and overactivity are perhaps the two main ways in which clients may be handling excessive stress. Their behaviour may range from rigid and repetitive attempts to deal with their problems to giving up and not making any effort. Violence, turned either outwards or inwards, is more possible at times of excessive stress than when clients' stress levels are lower.

Below are three examples of people who are finding that life is currently getting them down to the point where they are in a state of crisis.

Peter is a 57-year-old doctor who was divorced five years ago and whose only daughter lives with her husband in Australia. Recently Peter has been having problems with his partners in general practice. His personal isolation, personality clashes with his partners and heavy workload have contributed to his wondering aloud whether he has not already had the best out of life and if the remainder is worth living. He now sleeps badly, is off his food, and is increasingly withdrawing from social contact.

Janis is a 19-year-old hairdresser who recently broke up with her boyfriend. She said he found her too moody and irritable. Janis came from a home in which she felt she was repeatedly being 'put down' by her parents who, in turn, did not get on well with each other. She was never able to show any feelings of anger around them. She thinks that they will see her breaking up with her boyfriend as further evidence that she is a difficult person. She feels agitated, restless, tense and depressed.

Rob is a 52-year-old single steelworker who was made redundant a year ago and has remained unemployed ever since, despite looking hard for work. Recently his mother, with whom he lived, died. He feels that life has lost all meaning for him now that he has company neither at home nor at work. He says that he has been feeling depressed, disoriented and weepy.

It is very important to realize that crises, however large or small they may appear from an outsider's frame of reference, tend to seem overwhelming from the client's frame of reference. Some crises have been simmering in the background for some time and then erupt, whereas others are more clearly reacting to an immediate precipitating event, for example a bereavement or loss of employment. Perhaps many stressful situations only really turn into psychological crises at the point where clients feel that their efforts to adapt and cope are totally insufficient, at which stage they become most prone to despair, disorientation, breakdown and suicide.

There are numerous situations which may cause clients to feel that they are at the limit of their coping resources, though there are wide differences in people's ability to tolerate these various stressors. Resilience in the face of stress depends partly on personal resources, but may also be heavily influenced by the amount of family, social and community support available to clients. Table 7.4 lists many of the stressors which may cause clients to come or to be brought to counsellors' offices in a state of crisis. Whereas on some occasions one stressor may be enough to precipitate a crisis, on other occasions stressors may have a multiple, concurrent and/or cumulative impact. A common theme is that of changes which challenge the adequacy of clients' existing conceptions of themselves.

Table 7.4 *Illustrative stressors which may contribute to crises[a]*

Marriage and family	*Adverse social conditions*
Living in a state of continuous marital conflict	Poverty
Having a blazing row with a spouse/parent/child	Poor housing
Marital infidelity	Lack of social/community support
Problems in sex life	Being subjected to racial discrimination
Growing up feeling you are not being listened to	*Bodily harm*
Being financially dependent on parents	Drinking or drug abuse
Separation or divorce	Being mugged
Death in the family	Being raped
Serious illness in the family	Being battered by a spouse
Birth of a baby	Being diagnosed as having a severe or terminal illness
Financial problems	Being disfigured or disabled in an accident
Homosexual tendencies	Being in a war zone
Moving house	*Intrapersonal*
Occupational/educational	Loss of meaning in life
Threat of or actual redundancy	Feelings of guilt and worthlessness
Changing a job	Breakdown in self-protective thinking
Reorganization at work	Severe depression
Poor relations with a boss	Psychotic tendencies
Continuous office in-fighting	
Overwork	
Difficulty in controlling subordinates	
Lack of opportunity for mobility/promotion	
Retirement	
Impending examinations	
Failing an examination	
Public-speaking difficulties	

[a] There is overlap between the categories

Crisis Counselling

At times of crisis many people will have the support of family and friends. Others may not be so fortunate or may feel that, despite the support they are getting, they need the assistance of a professional counsellor who is not personally involved in their problems. Sometimes counselling itself may contribute to clients' crises. At worst this is because of incompetent and insensitive counselling. On other occasions, clients in counselling may feel under great stress as they start both acknowledging aspects of themselves that previously they have denied and trying out new behaviours. Crises for clients can be crises for counsellors too. Counsellors may feel under great pressure to relieve a client's distress and, at the same time, may feel threatened by the behaviour of a distressed person.

As indicated in the preceding section, there are many reasons why people may feel that their coping resources are being overwhelmed. Furthermore, there are considerable individual differences in the ways in which people react to excessive stress. Nevertheless, below I suggest some guidelines for conducting crisis counselling interviews.

Be prepared

Counsellors can relieve much of their own stress regarding client crises if they realize that, since these events are likely to be part of any working counsellor's life, they should be prepared. One means of preparation is to ensure that they have identified and can quickly mobilize a good support system, for example a competent physician or a bed in a psychiatric hospital (hopefully not for themselves!). Counsellors can also prepare themselves for crises if they think through the limits of their responsibility for clients. I consider that, so long as they have provided a sincere and competent service to the best of their abilities, counsellors have fulfilled their side of their 'contract'.

Act calmly

Even though it may seem a limitation on congruence if they do not really feel calm inside, it is important that counsellors act calmly and do not add their own anxieties to their client's agitation and distress. Responding in a warm, yet firm and measured way may both give the client the security of feeling that the counsellor is a strong person and help calm his or her heightened emotions.

Listen and observe

One of the main reasons that stressful situations become crises for many clients is that they feel that they have no-one they can turn to who will listen to and really understand their difficulties. Clients may become calmer and feel less isolated and despairing simply by being able to share their problems and air the related emotions. Catharsis is another word for this process of letting out bottled-up or pent-up feelings and emotions. Listening, observing and empathic responding help the counsellor to understand the client's subjective world as well as contributing to his or her feeling of being heard and accepted.

Assess client severity and risk

One area of assessing client severity concerns the degree to which they are in contact with reality. I mention some indications of severe disturbances in the section on medical considerations later in this chapter. Assessing client risk may also mean assessing the damage the client may do to other people. However, it is more likely to involve assessing the degree to which clients may damage themselves, including committing suicide. Though any suicide risk should be taken seriously, some of the factors which can help counsellors to assess its likelihood are:

1. Prior talk of suicide. A high proportion of suicidal people talk about the possibility before making an attempt.
2. Prior attempts at suicide. People with a previous history of suicide attempts may be more likely to try again.
3. Effectiveness of suicide plan. People with a well-thought-out and effectively lethal plan are more likely to succeed than those without such a plan.
4. Feelings of being overwhelmed by life's stresses. The potential for suicide is greater if people *feel* that they are under severe stress and unable to cope with it. They may have many related symptoms, for example being depressed and having insomnia, which are partly the results of and yet further contribute to their feelings of being unable to cope.
5. Lack of significant support. People who are isolated physically and/or emotionally from others and who have no other outlets for communication are more vulnerable to suicide than those who have more contact with others.
6. Demographic characteristics. The probability of suicide may be greater for males than females, for single or separated than for married people, and for those above rather than below 50. However, counsellors deal with individuals and should assess each case on its merits: for instance, despite the fact that the suicide risk is greater for those over 50, quite a few people in late adolescence and early adulthood commit suicide.

Assess client strengths and coping capacities

Counsellors can both assess and help their clients to explore and assess their strengths and coping resources. Often, in a crisis, clients are so overwhelmed by negative thinking that they allow themselves to get out of touch with their strengths. While not advocating superficial reassurance, the following counsellor remarks *may* be helpful with *some* clients in *some* situations: 'Well, we've explored your problems in some detail. I'm now wondering whether you feel that you have any strengths or resources for dealing with them?'; 'You've been telling me a lot about the negative aspects of your life. Can you tell me if there are some positive aspects as well?'; and 'As you talk you seem to be facing your problems very much on your own. I'm wondering whether there are any friends, relatives or other people who might be available to offer you some support?'.

Assist exploration and clarification of problem(s)

Clients in crises have often lost perspective on themselves and their problems. One of the reasons for this is that crises involve very intense feelings and, until some progress is made with relieving the intensity of these feelings, clients may lack the ability to be sufficiently rational about the factors generating these strong emotions. Counsellor skills during the work of exploring and clarifying problems are likely to include empathic responding, use of questions, summarizing and challenging those distortions in their clients' thinking that are making their lives seem hopeless.

Assist problem-solving and planning

For some clients the opportunity to talk with an understanding counsellor may give them enough confidence in their ability to cope with life for them to move out of the 'danger zone'. With other clients, the counsellor's role will include helping them to develop strategies for coping with their immediate distress and, if appropriate, for initiating ways of dealing with their longer-term problems. If the client is at any risk, plans for coping with the *immediate* situation should be formulated as specifically as possible and, indeed, the counsellor may feel some responsibility for seeing that they are implemented. For example:

> We have agreed that you will stay at your sister's for tonight and that we will meet again at 11 a.m. tomorrow. Do you think there is any reason why you cannot carry out this plan?

> I'm uneasy about your being on your own in such a distressed state. I know that Mr. Smith, the warden of your college, is keen to help students in difficulty. Would you mind if I phoned him to tell him about your situation?

As in these examples, assisting problem-solving and planning may involve the mobilization of additional resources who may be either professional helpers, for example doctors and chaplains, or friends and relatives. In some instances it may be better if the client takes the responsibility for making the contact, but not invariably. Counsellors should always assess what is in the best interests of their clients and, at a highly vulnerable time in their lives, should be prepared to act accordingly.

Be specific about your own availability

Part of the counselling plan with certain clients may be to give them the security of another appointment in the near future. However, counsellors also need to consider the matter of between-session contact. If such contact seems appropriate, they can say something along the lines of 'If you feel you need me in an emergency again, please don't hesitate to get in touch with me either here or at my home number, which is . . .'. In most instances clients will not get in touch until the next session, but they will appreciate the fact that the counsellor cared enough to be available if necessary. In other instances, counsellors either may be genuinely unavailable or may consider it more appropriate for clients to make any between-session contact with another person or agency. For instance, they might refer a client to a specific crisis service, such as the Samaritans.

Apparently the Chinese use two symbols for the concept of crisis: those of danger and of opportunity. Crises can be the impetus for certain clients to work on problems which have been simmering in the past, yet which have not really been confronted. This may release a tremendous amount of constructive energy. The pain of crises may be so acute that these clients both are forced to face the fact that all is not well and want to avoid any future pain of such magnitude. As counsellors work with the clients who have been in a crisis their old ways may increasingly appear to be more threatening than the risks of change. At best, a crisis can give counsellor and client the opportunity to form an effective counselling relationship which lays the basis for the client to develop the confidence and skills to prevent or to cope with future crises.[2]

Exercise 7.4   Crisis counselling

This exercise may be done in a number of ways.

A   *On your own*
  1. Identify crises in your past life and the people and behaviours that you found helpful in them.
  2. Write down, regarding your present or future counselling work, the kinds of stressors that bring, or may in future bring, clients in crisis to see you.
  3. How can you best prepare yourself to be effective in crisis counselling interviews?

B   *In pairs*
  1. Together identify, with regard to your present or future counselling work, the kinds of stressors that bring, or may in future bring, clients in crisis to see you.
  2. You counsel your partner, who role-plays a client in a crisis. As much as possible, pay attention to the following eight guidelines for working with clients in crisis: be prepared; remain calm; listen and observe; assess client severity and risk; assess client strengths and coping capacities; assist exploration and clarification of problem(s); assist problem-solving and planning; and be specific about your own availability. Afterwards reverse roles.

C   *In a training group*
  The trainer identifies the kinds of stressors and client behaviours in crises that are most common in the counselling setting for which the group is being trained. The trainer describes and may demonstrate crisis-counselling interventions with this client population, possibly getting group members to role-play clients in states of crisis. The trainer may set either the individual or pairs parts of this exercise and then hold a plenary sharing and discussion session.

COUNSELLOR SELF-DISCLOSURE

Counsellor self-disclosure refers to the ways in which counsellors let themselves be known to their clients. There are numerous ways in which counsellors may reveal themselves to their clients, for example by what they say, their vocal and bodily communication, the decor of their offices, their written communications, the way they handle themselves on the telephone, and the size of their bills. More specifically, in the counselling literature counsellor self-disclosure usually refers to counsellors talking about themselves.

Reasons For and Against Counselling Self-disclosure

You may think that clients go to counsellors to talk about themselves and their problems, and not to listen to their counsellors' own disclosures. Undoubtedly you are right, and there are risks in counsellor self-disclosure which I discuss later. However, I start positively by suggesting six reasons why appropriate disclosure on the part of counsellors may be beneficial.

Reasons for counsellor self-disclosure

1. Modelling a useful social skill. Many clients come from backgrounds where there has been relatively little open disclosure. In such closed emotional environments they either may not have learned how to or may have been afraid to talk about themselves in a personal way. Counsellor self-disclosure may be helpful in freeing clients to talk about themselves, both inside and outside counselling, in a more intimate way.
2. Counsellor genuineness. Previously I made a distinction between therapeutic and social conversations. The genuineness to which I refer here is therapeutic genuineness, focused on meeting the needs of the client, rather than social genuineness, which may be focused more on meeting the needs of both parties. Therapeutic genuineness may involve self-disclosure, with the counsellor being a real person in relation to the client and not hiding behind a façade of phoney expertness. However, this does not mean that the counsellor should not possess some expert skills. Appropriate counsellor disclosures may avoid counsellors appearing as wooden and disinterested.
3. Sharing experiences. Possibly the counsellor may have had some concerns similar to those of the client which it may be helpful to mention. An advantage of such sharing is that it may provide clients with new perspectives on their problems and on how to deal with them. It is very important that such sharing be non-possessive and conducted in ways that allow clients the freedom to accept or reject its relevance.
4. Sharing feelings. There are times when counsellors may consider it appropriate to share their feelings with the client. These may be feelings about the client as a person, about what the client is currently saying or doing, or avoiding saying or doing, or about the counselling relationship.

5. Sharing opinions. There are times when counsellors may feel that they have something useful to contribute to their clients' analyses of decisions and problems in their lives. Thus the counsellor may offer different perspectives on the ways in which the client is feeling, thinking and acting. Perhaps such sharing of opinions is less revealing of the counsellor than sharing personal experiences and reactions with the client. In sharing opinions the focus tends to be more on the client's life than on the counsellor's.

6. Being assertive. There may be occasions in counselling when the relationship may gain from the counsellor being firm and setting limits. Such occasions may include standing up to an aggressive client, not allowing counselling time to be persistently wasted, and ending sessions on time.

Reasons against counsellor self-disclosure

There are, however, grave dangers in inappropriate counsellor self-disclosure. Here I mention four of the main dangers.

1. Burdening the client. Clients usually have enough problems of their own without having to carry the burden of their counsellors' problems and difficulties. Furthermore, counsellors may have to be sensitive to the fact that, though clients may need their professional skills, not all their clients will be fascinated by them as people.

2. Seeming weak and unstable. Counsellors who inappropriately talk about themselves may appear to their clients to be less than well adjusted. Clients may ask themselves 'Why is he/she telling me this?' and perceive the reasons for the disclosure to be less positive than the counsellor's intention. Furthermore, vulnerable clients often need to perceive their counsellors as strong people and may become anxious about evidence to the contrary.

3. Counsellor domination. Too much counsellor disclosure can shift the focus of the interview from the client's concerns to those of the counsellor. In Chapter 3 I mentioned many kinds of counsellor responses that make for low empathy. Under the guise of self-disclosing in a helpful way, counsellors may often be less than helpful. Loughary and Ripley[3] mention four types of 'helpers' who use self-disclosure in a dominating way: the 'You think you've got a problem! Let me tell you about mine!' type; the 'Let me tell you what to do' type; the 'I understand because I once had the same problem myself' type; and the 'I'll take charge and deal with it' type.

4. Countertransference. Countertransference refers to negative and positive feelings, based on unresolved areas in their own lives, which arise in counsellors towards their clients. In other words, the counsellors' own needs may be distorting their perceptions of their clients' needs. For example, sometimes counsellors may be self-disclosing to meet their own rather than their clients' needs for intimacy. Kennedy rightly observes: 'Anything that smacks of "going well out of one's way" for a client may indicate that this problem is present. Counselors who observe themselves needlessly rearranging and extending appointments, or offering help for situations quite separate from the counseling, have firsthand evidence of emotional involvement'.[4] Some counsellors may, intentionally or unintentionally, use self-disclosure to manipulate clients to meet their own wishes for approval, affection or even sex. This highlights the importance of counsellors being aware of their motivation for self-disclosing and acting ethically.

Building Self-disclosure Skills

In the preceding section I emphasized that counsellor self-disclosures may be appropriate or inappropriate. It is difficult to lay down hard and fast rules for appropriateness because counsellors may self-disclose when conducting different kinds of interviews, from different theoretical positions, with different kinds of clients, and at different stages of their counselling relationships. Furthermore, counsellor self-disclosure itself is not a unitary concept. It can mean 'making comments about the sort of person I am', 'sharing experiences', 'sharing feelings', 'sharing opinions' and 'being assertive'. However, it is possible to suggest *some guidelines for appropriate self-disclosure*, including the following:

1. Be direct. If you are going to talk about yourself and your reactions, communicate them as clearly and honestly as you can.
2. Be sensitive to your client. Have sufficient awareness to realize when your disclosures may be helpful to your client and when they might be unwelcome or a burden. For example, intimate disclosures may be more appropriate later rather than earlier in a counselling relationship, if at all.
3. Be relevant. Do not slow down or defocus the interview by introducing extraneous material which has no relevance to the client's concerns.
4. Be non-possessive. Allow your clients to accept or reject the

relevance of your disclosures. Do not press them to think and feel things about you and your disclosures that meet your needs rather than theirs.

5. Be relatively brief. Remember that the focus of your interviews is on helping your clients rather than yourself, and that they may have only limited willingness and attention to hear about you.
6. Do not do it too often. By all means be expressive in your counselling, but do not talk about yourself too often. Counsellors who keep talking about themselves and their reactions run the risk of switching the focus of their interviews from their clients to themselves. Furthermore, they may raise doubts in their clients' minds about their stability and professional competence.

Sharing experiences and sharing feelings are two useful self-disclosure skills. Sharing experiences means sharing your own experiences of concerns similar to those of your clients in the hope that they may derive some personally relevant insights and knowledge from your disclosures. Below are a couple of examples.

Raymond is a 30-year-old man with a university degree who is going through a spell of unemployment. He seems to be doing a reasonably adequate job of looking for work but complains that much of the time he is bored and mopes around the house.
Counsellor self-disclosure. 'I went through a six-month period of unemployment some years ago. At first I felt apathetic and low, and wondered "Why bother to get out of bed?". Then I started increasingly to view my unemployment as an opportunity to do some of the things I couldn't do when employed and, strangely enough, the time started becoming very precious to me.'

Nicola is a 22-year-old nurse who is having problems in her marriage. She feels that her husband and mother-in-law keep picking on her and she finds herself getting increasingly angry.
Counsellor self-disclosure. 'Bill and I went through a difficult period when we were first married. I used to think he compared me adversely with both his mother and his previous girlfriends and I got more and more uptight and full of self-pity. It was some time before I realized that neither of us was prepared to make the first move to resolve our differences and that therefore I was contributing to my own unhappiness. I'm wondering whether you aren't doing the same thing.'

Exercise 7.5 Counsellor self-disclosure: sharing experiences

This exercise may be done in a number of ways.

A *On your own*

In respect of your present or future counselling work, identify some experiences of yours which it might be helpful to share with certain of your clients.

B *In pairs*

You counsel your partner, who discusses a personal concern or role-plays a client. During the course of a 5, 10 or 15-minute counselling session, try on one or more occasions to introduce an experience of yours which might help your 'client'. At the end of the session discuss with your partner the appropriateness of your attempts to share experiences. Afterwards reverse roles.

C *In a training group*

The trainer can illustrate with case material how the group might beneficially use their own experience to help clients in the counselling setting for which the group is being trained. The trainer may give a demonstration interview in which he or she engages in some sharing of experience. The trainer may also get the group to do either the individual or the pairs part of this exercise and then hold a plenary sharing and discussion session on talking to clients about your own experiences.

There are a number of areas in which counsellors can share their feelings with their clients, including the following.

1. Reacting to clients' disclosures. Counsellor comments might be: 'I'm delighted'; 'That's great'; 'That's terrible'; and 'I'm really sorry that you are going through such a bad patch'.

2. Reacting to clients as people. For example, the counsellor might say: 'I enjoy our time together'; 'I'm really concerned for you'; and 'You seem to feel that you are a pretty unattractive person, but I certainly don't think of you that way'.

3. Reacting to the counselling relationship. For example: 'I have to make an effort to keep listening when you start repeating yourself'; 'I feel that you are very tense in these long silences and wonder what is going through your mind'; 'I feel that we've had a good session today'; and 'I feel that we're at an impasse'.

Sharing feelings when reacting to clients' disclosures can be a good form of empathic responding which helps clients to feel the companionship involved in your understanding of what they are saying. Reacting to clients as people might appear judgemental, but the risk of this is lessened if your feelings are communicated as being subjective and personal reactions rather than objective and global judgements. Both reacting to clients as people and reacting to the counselling relationship may involve challenges to clients' existing views. Clearly the state of readiness of clients for such challenges must be taken into account. At best, sharing feelings can be a way of personalizing the counselling relationship in a way that strengthens clients. It is important, of course, that counsellors' vocal and bodily communications match the feelings that they are sharing.

Exercise 7.6 Counsellor self-disclosure: sharing feelings

This exercise may be done in a number of ways.

A *On your own*
   With respect to your present or future counselling work, write down the sorts of situations in which you feel it would be appropriate to share your feelings with clients. Then, for each situation, formulate a counsellor self-disclosure starting with the words 'I feel . . .'.

B *In pairs*
   You counsel a partner, who discusses a personal concern or role-plays a client. During the course of a 5, 10 or 15-minute counselling session, try on a few occasions to share your feelings with the 'client'. At the end of the session, discuss with your partner the impact of your attempts to share feelings. Afterwards reverse roles.

C *In a training group*
   The trainer may give some examples, taken from the counselling setting for which the group is being trained, of how sharing feelings can benefit counselling. The trainer may also provide poor or disastrous examples of sharing feelings. The trainer may give a demonstration interview in which he or she engages in some sharing of feelings. The trainer may also get the group to do either the individual or pairs part of this exercise and then hold a plenary sharing and discussion session on sharing feelings with clients.

MEDICAL CONSIDERATIONS

Though I do not favour a simplistic mind–body split, I use the term 'medical considerations' to indicate areas of counselling that require biological and medical as well as psychological knowledge. Many writers on counselling ignore the overlap areas between medicine and counselling. In general, counselling practitioners cannot afford such an omission. For counsellors, good relationships with a competent physician and with a psychiatrist can be important sources of additional knowledge and help. Also, counsellors may find themsleves working in conjunction with their clients' general practitioners: for example, where a client is on medication or where the counsellor wants to check whether their clients' presenting concerns have medical implications. In short, competent counsellors need some basic medical knowledge as well as access to trusted medical help.

There are numerous areas in which a medical opinion may be important. A client who has mental blockages may be brain damaged. For some clients, lowered interest in sex may have a medical rather than a psychological explanation. Here, however, I mention three areas where counsellors themselves may need basic medical knowledge. The first area is being able to identify severe disturbance. The second and third areas are being aware of psychosomatic symptoms and the use of medication in conjunction with counselling. Those of you who would like further information about medical considerations are referred to introductory psychiatry textbooks, for example those by Trethowan[5] and Willis.[6]

Severe Disturbance

One way of viewing severe disturbance is in terms of being out of touch with one's emotions, having considerable thinking difficulties and not being able to act in such a way as to attain significant personal goals, for example the attainment of any form of human intimacy. In this view, severe disturbance consists of having fairly common problems of living, but in a more serious form.

Another, yet overlapping, way of viewing severe disturbance is that of whether or not the client is psychotic or, in other words, significantly out of touch with reality. It is important that counsellors are aware of some of the main indicators of the psychoses (shown in Table 7.5) so that they may refer such clients for appropriate psychiatric assistance. The psychoses can be broken down into three main groups: schizophrenia, paranoia and manic depression.

Schizophrenia

Schizophrenia is better thought of as the disintegration rather than the splitting of personality. Its incidence is just under 1 per cent of the general population. Table 7.5 shows some prominent indicators of schizophrenia, though there are variations in the prevalence of each of these symptoms among the different categories of schizophrenia. Schizophrenia begins mainly in the teens and early twenties, though paranoid schizophrenia, characterized by delusions of persecution, is found in those aged 30 and over. A distinction is sometimes made between *process* schizophrenia, where the onset is gradual, and *reactive* schizophrenia, where the onset is rapid and in response to precipitating stresses. The prognosis for process schizophrenia tends to be unfavourable, whereas in the case of reactive schizophrenia the acute pattern may disappear within weeks, though sometimes this is the forerunner of a more chronic pattern.

Table 7.5   *Some indicators of schizophrenia, paranoia and manic depression*

Disorder	Indicators

Schizophrenia	Extreme emotional withdrawal
	Thought disorders, e.g. inability to focus coherently
	Speech disorders, e.g. personal language which does not communicate clearly
	Delusions (irrational fixed ideas)
	    of being persecuted
	    of being great
	    of being referred to and talked about
	Hallucinations (illusions)
	    most commonly auditory, e.g. 'hearing voices'
	Behavioural disturbances
	    lowered activity
	    bizarre mannerisms and postures
	    altered morals

Paranoia	Delusions of persecution
	Suspiciousness
	Selective perception of people and events to confirm suspicions
	Blame and hostility
	Possibly also
	    delusions of grandeur
	    delusions of a religious nature
	    delusions about being ill

Manic depression	*Depression* Pervasive lowered vitality and fatigue Pervasive negative self-image Ideas of guilt and unworthiness Suicidal ruminations Slowing of movement and speech Slowing of thought processes

Disorder	*Indicators*
	Sleep disturbance, especially early waking Loss of appetite and weight Decreased sexual interest
	Mania Elation and over-optimism Heightened activity Mental acceleration, flight of ideas Accelerated speech Heightened sexual interest Grand ideas and plans Decreased attention span Decreased judgement

Paranoia

The word 'paranoid' is now in everyday use to describe people with exaggerated fears that others are using and taking advantage of them. Paranoia is characterized by impaired contact with reality, involving such exaggerated fears in extreme form; it does not involve the severe disintegration of personality involved in paranoid schizophrenia. In other words, the delusional system or systems are relatively self-contained. A distinction is sometimes made between being in a *paranoid state*, a transient state of affairs brought on by unusual precipitating stresses, and *paranoia*, which develops slowly. This is similar to the reactive and process onset distinction mentioned for schizophrenia. Paranoid delusions are not restricted to persecutory ones, other delusions being manifested either on their own or in conjunction with persecutory delusions: 'I am being persecuted because I am so important'. You may have noticed that many of these psychotic delusions appear to be attempts by people to create their own reality in compensation for severe feelings of inadequacy.

Manic depression

There are three types of manic depressive reactions: the manic; the depressive; and the circular type characterized by alternations between mania and depression. Depressive are considerably more frequent than manic reactions; indeed the latter are often thought to be masking underlying depressive tendencies. Both manic and depressive reactions may run their course in three to nine months, with manic reactions taking the shorter and depressive the longer time.

On the surface, the manic reaction is the opposite of the depressive reaction, though it tends to be more acute and, unlike depression, never chronic or persisting over time. Whereas the depressive reaction is characterized by varying degrees of pessimism and underactivity, the manic reaction is characterized mainly by varying degrees of elation and overactivity.

Psychosomatic Disorders

Psychosomatic or psychophvsiologic disorders by definition suggest that a simplistic mind–body split is erroneous. Such disorders are caused and maintained primarily by psychological and emotional rather than by physical or organic factors. Table 7.6 lists disorders which *may* be, though are not necessarily, psychosomatic. I emphasize that there are also physical reasons for symptoms like asthma (for example allergies), and counsellors should not assume that they are always psychosomatic in origin. The more common psychosomatic disorders include peptic ulcers, migraine and tension headaches, asthma, high blood pressure and heart attacks. Psychosomatic disorders may be distinguished from hysterical or conversion symptoms, the latter being 'phoney' or imitative rather than actual physical disorders.

Table 7.6 *Disorders which may be psychosomatic*[7]

Affected area	Examples
Skin	Eczema, acne, hives
Musculoskeletal	Backaches, muscle cramps, tension headaches
Respiratory	Bronchial asthma, hyperventilation, recurring bronchitis
Cardiovascular	Hypertension, heart attacks, migraine headaches
Blood and lymphatic	Disturbances in the blood and lymphatic systems
Gastrointestinal	Peptic ulcers, chronic gastritis, mucous colitis
Genito-urinary	Disturbances in urination and menstruation
Endocrine	Hyperthyroidism, obesity, and some other endocrine disorders
Organs of special sense	Chronic conjunctivitis (pink-eye)
Disorders of other types	Disturbances in the nervous system in which emotional factors play a significant role, e.g. multiple sclerosis

Recognition by counsellors of possible psychosomatic pain and discomfort may make an important contribution to assessing accurately and empathizing with certain clients. This is an area where it is important for counsellors to collaborate with competent physicians, at least to see that, as far as possible, the symptoms are correctly identified. Since psychosomatic disorders are maintained primarily by psychological causes, counsellors are likely to be able to play an important part in their treatment.

Use of Medication

For a number of reasons counsellors working in medical and other settings are likely to need to be familiar with the more common psychotropic drugs, some of which are listed in Table 7.7. First, it may be difficult to make an accurate assessment of how clients are functioning unless the counsellor takes into account the effects of any drug that they are currently taking. Second, the counsellor may consider it advisable to refer a client to a physician if he or she feels that medication might be of benefit. Third, the counsellor may be working with a client who is on medication and may need to discuss with a physician the effects of the drug and the appropriate dosage, including the possibility of taking the client off the drug. Fourth, clients themselves may want to discuss their use of medication with the counsellor and, though counsellors should not go out of their depth, it may be reassuring if they are able to conduct an informed discussion.

All the drugs listed in Table 7.7 have possible toxic or side effects. For instance, even the minor tranquillizers can affect some people with drowsiness, lessened musclar coordination, lowered sex urge and dependency. A drug like lithium carbonate is highly toxic, and close medical monitoring is required. The levels of dosage, both amount and frequency, are considerations when physicians prescribe drugs and relevant when counsellors are working with clients who are on them. If counsellors need basic information about a drug they can ask a physician or, if they can obtain a copy, look it up in MIMS, which is a monthly index of proprietary preparations available for prescription in general practice.[8, 9]

Counsellors may need to explore their own and their clients' attitudes to the use of drugs. Some counsellors may have prejudices against virtually any use of drugs and also possibly against the medical profession. Other counsellors, like some clients, may treat medication as a crutch. Clients vary in their attitudes to taking drugs from viewing taking them as personal weakness to dependency on them. Though it may not always be possible, the objective of counselling is to help people to become psychologically self-reliant, and that includes taking as few psychotropic drugs as possible. However, that overall objective does not preclude being sympathetic to the taking of medication by clients, especially if they are severely disturbed or in a crisis which threatens to overwhelm their coping resources. As counselling progresses it may then become possible to wean the client off drugs, perhaps sometimes by smaller and less frequent dosages.

Table 7.7 *Some tranquillizing, hypnotic and anti-depressant drugs*

Category and illustrative drug(s)	Indication for use
Minor tranquillizers e.g. Librium,[a] *Valium*	Anxiety states
Major tranquillizers e.g. Largactil	Mania
Long-acting version given by intramuscular injection, e.g. Modecate	Schizophrenia
Hypnotics e.g. Mogadon	Insomnia
Anti-depressants Tricyclic, e.g. Tofranil, Triptizol	Endogenous depression
Monoamine oxidase inhibitors, e.g. Nardil (more toxic than tricyclics and usually used if the former are unsuccessful)	
Lithium carbonate Used to prevent recurrence of both frequency and severity in cyclic endogenous mood disturbance	Mania and depression

[a] The names of drugs are proprietary (i.e. the names used by the manufacturer)

REFERENCES

1. Selye, H. (1974) *Stress Without Distress*. Sevenoaks: Hodder & Stoughton.
2. Murgatroyd, S. & Wolfe, R. (1982) *Coping with Crisis: Understanding and Helping People in Need*. London: Harper and Row.
3. Loughary, J.W. & Ripley, T.M. (1979) *Helping Others to Help Themselves*. New York: McGraw Hill.
4. Kennedy, E. (1977) *On Becoming a Counsellor*. Dublin: Gill and Macmillan.
5. Trethowan, W.H. & Sims, A.C.P. (1983) *Psychiatry* (5th ed.). London: Baillière Tindall.
6. Willis, J. (1979) *Lecture Notes on Psychiatry* (5th ed.). Oxford: Blackwell Scientific.

7. Coleman, J.C. (1976) *Abnormal Psychology and Modern Life* (5th ed.). Glenview. Illinois: Scott Foresman.
8. MIMS, Haymarket Publishing, 38/42 Hampton Road, Teddington, Middlesex, TW11 0JE, published monthly.
9. Australian MIMS, 68 Alexandra Street, Crow Nest, Sydney, Australia.

8 Group Counselling and Life Skills Training

Broadly speaking there are two main methods, with some overlap, of working with groups of clients: group counselling and life skills training. Group counselling may be defined as the relationships, activities and skills of counselling groups of people together. Life skills training involves teaching a group of people any of a range of psychologically relevant skills. These skills are focused mainly on effective personal relations, on thinking and on occupational problems. Two different but interrelated models of how the counsellor can operate underlie these methods of group work. The assumption in group counselling is that the counsellor is a therapeutic *facilitator* focusing on the exploration of clients' thoughts, feelings and personal styles of relating. The assumption in life skills training is that the counsellor is an *educator* engaging in the transmission of knowledge and skills to clients who are trainees or learners. The two models of group, and indeed individual, counselling have been stated here in polarized form. There are, of course, intermediate positions, for example either engaging in group counselling with some didactic interventions or performing life skills training in such a way that the group is allowed to express and explore thoughts and feelings. I now look at each method in turn and conclude this chapter with a discussion about making role decisions.

GROUP COUNSELLING

Counsellors need to be familiar with group counselling for at least three reasons. First, they themselves may be leading or facilitating a counselling group. Second, they may wish to recommend clients to join counselling groups led by other people. Third, some of their clients may be having a group experience, possibly without the counsellor having initiated it, and bringing material from their group into the individual sessions. Before leading groups themselves, it is desirable that counsellors have a fair amount of experience both as group members and as co-leaders of groups. Group leader skills are in some large measure the outcome of experiential knowledge gained in groups. Good intentions and theoretical knowledge alone are insufficient and could even be damaging.

In practice, counselling groups are many and varied. They may be defined by: their theoretical orientation, e.g. person-centred, behavioural or gestalt; their focus on a problem area, e.g. public speaking or alcoholism; their clientele, e.g. mixed sex or women only; their objectives, e.g. remedial or 'personal growth'; their length, e.g. marathon; and a number of other factors. Couples counselling, involving one or two counsellors meeting both partners in a relationship, might also be considered a form of group counselling. However, if anything, when I discuss group counselling, it is the experiential encounter group aimed at the 'personal development' of members through a process of inter-member relationships to which I refer.

Deciding to Recommend Group Counselling

A treatment decision about its appropriateness always precedes a client's entry into group counselling. Below are some of the reasons why counsellors might consider group counselling a preferred method of treating certain clients; indeed, some counsellors consider groups to be a preferred method of treating all clients.

Potential advantages of group counselling

1. Economy of counsellor's time. This is the economies-of-scale argument whereby it is arguably cheaper to see eight clients together once a week for 1½ hours than each separately for 45 minutes, which totals six hours, i.e. four times as long.
2. Practice at personal relations. In group counselling, clients are likely to have to relate to a number of people who, in varying degrees, are expressing their thoughts, feelings and emotions, whereas in individual counselling they relate only to the counsellor,

who usually engages in a very limited form of disclosure. Practice at relating to a range of people, emotions and issues may help many counselling clients, since they tend to be deficient in their ability to send and receive communications from others.

3. Healing potential of other group members. A concept known as 'cohesiveness' is said to define the more successful counselling groups. Cohesiveness means both that the group members find participation in the group attractive and that they have a high investment in helping each other. Clients may find the disclosures, sharing of feelings and emotions, opportunity to cut beneath social masks, and caring and help offered by other members to be very therapeutic. Also, since clients are often shy, these relationships are something which are not readily available to them outside counselling. Sometimes groups are viewed as 'second-chance families' which provide emotional experiences that correct or remedy deficiencies in earlier relationships. At a less ambitious level, counselling groups provide much opportunity for members to learn from each other about personal relationships and different life-styles. Furthermore, counselling groups may lessen clients' feelings of isolation and tendencies towards self-denigration as they learn that they are not alone in having problems.

4. Participant–observer role of the counsellor. As a member of a group, albeit of rather different status than the other members, the counsellor has an excellent opportunity to listen to and observe its members as they develop or avoid developing relationships and intimacy with each other. Also, in couples counselling, clients' ability to relate to *the other* is a major part of the material used by the counsellor. The same applies to counselling with families. Where appropriate, the counsellor can draw clients' attention both to strengths and to self-protective ways of thinking and relating which create distance from others and dissonance within themselves. Observing and commenting on the way clients relate is not so easy in individual counselling, though in individual work counsellors and clients may discuss their relationship with each other.

5. Improved client motivation. There are two ways in which group counselling can improve clients' motivation. First, some clients may be much more motivated to attend counselling if in a group than as an individual, since they enjoy the companionship and opportunity for intimacy that groups provide. Second, clients may be motivated by other group members to change their behaviour. This may come about either by observing their behaviour or through direct encouragement from them.

Potential disadvantages of counselling groups

Despite the fact that group counselling has many advantages, it also has its share of problems and disadvantages, though these can be lessened by good group-counsellor skills.

1. High wastage rate. Groups which do not attain a state of at least moderate cohesiveness are likely to start losing many of their members. The risk of losing clients in group work, where clients are forced to relate to other group members who often are there precisely because they have communication difficulties, is probably far greater than that of losing them in individual work, where the client is likely to have a relatively safe relationship with the counsellor. For instance, in group counselling a client might be subject to considerable aggression from one or more of the other members. Though this could be a constructive learning experience for all concerned, it could also be beyond the coping resources of some clients and cause them to withdraw psychologically and possibly physically. Another reason why clients leave groups is that they feel that the group is just sitting around talking and not making any significant progress. There may also be practical reasons in a group of eight why its members leave, for example not being able to attend at the appointed time or leaving the district.

2. Pressure for conformity. All groups are likely to develop 'norms', or spoken or unspoken rules about how members should behave in the group. There is a risk that some of these norms may help members to avoid rather than deal with their problems. For instance, though groups tend to involve a high degree of personal disclosure, this is likely to be helpful only if it is genuine disclosure rather than self-protective pseudo-authenticity. Some clients may also be encouraged to conform outside the group by allowing themselves to become dependent on how group members advise them to behave instead of taking responsibility for their own lives.

3. Unethical leadership. Unethical leadership may take many forms. Some group leaders may be untrained for the task they are undertaking. Group leaders can also exploit clients emotionally and sexually. Furthermore, there is the opportunity for group counsellors to make a lot of money by charging excessive fees, though this is less likely outside the United States than inside, where both groups and fee-paying are more established. Additionally, group members may be inadequately protected by unethical leaders from being emotionally damaged within the group. Also, if they need fur-

ther psychological attention and support during or after the life of a group, this may not be available. A further possibility for unethical leadership is that of unnecessarily distancing members from those to whom they relate outside by fostering a dependency on the group.

Counsellors may decide that group counselling is desirable for a client *instead* of, *concurrently* with or *after* individual counselling. However, as a counsellor you may neither currently be running a group nor, if you are, have a vacancy available in your existing group or groups. In such circumstances you may wish to recommend a group to a client. Table 8.1 is a brief checklist of questions for assessing counselling groups. Some of this information may not be readily available, but all of it is relevant to a really informed decision about whether or not to recommend a particular group.

Table 8.1 *Checklist for assessing counselling groups*

1. What is the theoretical orientation and/or purpose of the group?
2. What are the methods that may be employed during its life?
3. What is the pertinent training and experience of the leader or leaders?
4. What are the size and criteria for membership of the group and is there a screening or selection process prior to entry?
5. When is the group likely to start? How long is each session? Over what period will the group sessions continue? Where will the group be held?
6. What, if any, is the fee for the group and are there any additional expenses that may be incurred?
7. To what extent is there a clear understanding or contract concerning the amounts and kinds of responsibility that are to be assumed by the leader and by the group members?

It is possible that increasingly counsellors and psychologists who conduct counselling groups will be required to become more overtly accountable and to provide the above kinds of information. In the mean time, counsellors are advised to make as much personal contact with potentially suitable referral sources in their localities as they can.

Exercise 8.1 Deciding on whether or not to recommend group counselling

This exercise may be done in a number of ways.

A *On your own*
   Assess the effectiveness in personal relations either of yourself or of a client known to you. Write down:

1.   what sort of counselling group, if any, you might consider joining yourself or recommending that your client join;
2.   what you see as the potential advantages of group counselling for your own or for your client's concerns;
3.   what you see as some of the potential problems and disadvantages of group counselling in your case or that of your client.

B   *In pairs*

Counsel your partner and together assess either his or her effectiveness in personal relations or the effectiveness of a role-played client. Then review with your 'client' whether individual or group counselling or some combination of the two might be beneficial for him or her. Afterwards reverse roles.

C   *In a training group*

The trainer may present and discuss cases, drawn from the setting for which the group is being trained, involving a decision on group counselling. In each case illustration the trainer should try to highlight the counsellor's decision-making processes. The trainer may give a demonstration interview involving assessing the relevance of group counselling for a group member 'client'. Another option is for the trainer to encourage group members to share and assess their own experiences of being in counselling groups. Assuming some previous exposure to groups, this option has the added advantages of being somewhat of a group experience in itself and of illustrating the variety of counselling groups. The trainer may also ask the trainees to do either the individual or the pairs exercise above (preferably the pairs exercise) followed by a plenary sharing and discussion session.

Preparatory Skills for Group Counselling

In the previous section I mentioned that groups can run into problems of attrition. Good preparation for any group you run is likely to increase its chances of success and decrease its chances of failure. It is very important that the group leader has clearly identified the kind of group that he or she wishes to run *before* any contact with clients about it. This involves making a series of planning decisions about the group, some of which are mentioned below.

Objectives

'What are my objectives in wishing to run a group?' For instance, you as leader may wish to run a person-centred experiential encounter group, a rational-emotive group focused on clients' thinking difficulties, or a behavioural counselling group aimed at reducing examination anxiety.

Number of counsellors

'Do I want to lead the group on my own or together with another counsellor?' When learning to be a group counsellor it may be helpful if your first group is co-led by a more experienced counsellor, both to ease your anxieties and so that you may observe him or her at work. Other reasons for having two counsellors include: it is more likely that each group member will relate well to at least one counsellor; two counsellors are likely to be able to observe more and consequently to give more feedback; it allows for differences in counsellor characteristics, for example gender; and it allows for differences in counsellor roles, for instance one might be more nurturing while the other might be more task-oriented and confronting. Reasons for not having two counsellors include extra expenditure of resources and the possibility of conflict between the counsellors about the aims and leadership style of the group. Needless to say, where counsellors are going to lead a group, both should share in its preparation.

Clientele

'What kinds of members do I wish to have in the group?' Sometimes group leaders run groups for a *homogeneous* clientele, for example single people, women, married couples, people with public-speaking difficulties, alcoholics, gays, etc. Other group leaders aspire to form *heterogeneous* groups composed of a range of different personalities and presenting concerns and of members of both sexes. The homogeneous versus heterogeneous distinction is imprecise since, for instance, even in a single-sex group there can be a range of different personal styles. Referring back to my earlier comment about the importance of group cohesiveness, this is something that, up to a point, can be planned for in group selection. Some considerations here are: each group might have a few members who are reasonably outgoing and who can act as catalysts; probably there should not be too wide discrepancies in the members' levels of psychological well-being; and compulsive monopolizers, extremely aggressive people and those likely to terminate early should be excluded.

Closed or open group

'Do I want the group, once under way, to be closed or am I prepared to admit new members during the life of the group?' *Closed* groups meet for a fixed time span, say six months or a year, and once started admit no new members. One of the stated reasons for this is that it allows members to develop a deep level of intimacy with each other without the possible disrupting effect of new members. *Open* groups may meet for either a fixed or an unspecified length of time. Members may leave when they feel ready to and others may join if this is deemed appropriate by the counsellor, possibly in consultation with existing group members.

Group size

'How big do I want the group to be?' There is a conventional wisdom in group counselling that seven is an ideal size for an interactional group, with from five to ten members being an acceptable size. Reasons for not going below five members include the large gap caused by anyone leaving and the fact that a very small group may not provide the desired range of personalities and opportunities for different kinds of inter-action. Large groups may get impersonal. Furthermore, they may inhibit shy members from participating at all. Also, large groups may split into subgroups. In some fixed groups, the counsellor may start with ten members to allow a few people to drop out without causing serious disruption.

Duration of group and frequency and length of sessions

'Over what period of time do I want the group to meet, how often, and how long should each session be?' Counselling groups with a develop-mental emphasis tend to meet for a minimum of six months and often last for a year or longer. Problem-focused groups are likely to be for shorter periods, say for six to ten sessions, on the assumption that this should be sufficient for most members to derive benefit from what may be as much an educational as a therapeutic process. Many groups meet once a week. However, some counsellors prefer to run developmental groups on a twice weekly basis so that the group does not lose momentum between sessions. Where the group has difficulty coming together, a counsellor might be prepared to hold the sessions bi-weekly or even monthly.

The length of each session for many counselling groups is from 90 minutes to two hours. Sessions of less than 90 minutes may not give enough time for all members to participate and for different themes to be developed. Sessions longer than two hours may be tiring for some participants and also difficult to spare time for on a regular basis. However, longer sessions, for example of three hours' duration, might be held if the group meets less frequently than once a week. Sometimes, either as part of a continuing group or as an event on its own, a 'marathon' group session will be held. This might entail six three-hour sessions spread over a couple of days, with breaks for eating and sleeping.

Location and physical setting

'Where is the group going to be held and is it a suitable location for attaining the group's objectives?' Leaders who run interactional groups need to have access to suitable premises for those purposes, though in the 'real world' compromises may have to be made. Ideally the room in which the group is held should have the following characteristics: quiet; privacy; pleasant decoration; reasonable size, e.g. neither too large nor too small; adequate heating (or cooling), lighting and ventilation; enough comfortable chairs so that the group may be seated in a circle; and guaranteed availability. Sometimes group members are formally seated round a table rather than in easy chairs and, on other occasions, they may be seated informally on cushions on the floor.

Contract

'What is the contract between the group members and me and how explicit do I intend to make it?' All groups operate within 'contracts' of varying degrees of explicitness. These contracts represent agreements about the behaviours that the group leader and group members may expect from each other. Some counsellors prefer to make details of the contract explicit either beforehand or at the start of the group, whereas others are prepared to regard the development of a contract as the group proceeds as a valuable part of the group experience. Contracts can take many forms, from being largely unstated, to being verbal, to being written and unsigned, to being written and signed by all parties concerned. Some issues that might be covered in a contract include: size of group; admission of new members; minimum attendance; contact with the counsellor between group sessions; any limitations on extra-group socializing; and confidentiality. Furthermore, certain contracts offer guidelines on desirable behaviours within a group, for example honesty about oneself and not interrupting others.

Advertising

'How am I going to obtain members for the group and make its availability known?' Sometimes counsellors run groups made up entirely of people who either have been or still are undergoing individual counselling with them. Letting colleagues know about their intention to form a group is another method of obtaining members. Once a counsellor is established as a group leader, a number of clients may come either self-referred or referred by others. Sometimes counsellors advertise their groups by such means as posters and hand-outs and insertions in appropriate newspapers, newsletters and journals, though there are issues of professional ethics where such advertising is concerned.

Exercise 8.2 Planning a counselling group

This exercise may be done in a number of ways.

A *On your own*
   Write out a plan for a counselling group to be run in an agency or setting of relevance to you. Make sure that you have thought through each of the following points: the objectives of the group; the number of counsellors involved; the clientele; admission of new members; group size; the duration of the group and the frequency and length of sessions; the location and physical setting; the nature of the contract; and how to obtain members for the group.

B *In pairs*
   Together with your partner write out a plan for a counselling group covering the points in section A of this exercise. Alternatively, each partner can plan his or her own group, then come together for sharing and discussion of their plans.

C *In a training group*
   The trainer may illustrate the planning of a group with case material drawn from the setting for which the group is being trained. Alternatively, the trainer and the group together can plan a counselling group. Another option is for the trainer to set either the individual or the pairs part of this

exercise and afterwards hold a plenary sharing and discussion session on planning counselling groups.

Intake interviewing

Intake interviews are individual interviews with prospective members prior to starting a group. Obviously groups composed on a 'first come, first served' basis or those made up from a counsellor's own clients may not need such interviews. Intake interviews are desirable for most counselling groups. First, they allow both counsellor and client to get to know each other, and this may reduce the likelihood of the client's leaving the group early. Joining a group can be a very threatening experience, especially for a shy and socially awkward person, and the importance of members feeling that they have a relationship with the counsellor should not be underestimated. Second, intake interviews enable the counsellor to implement his or her criteria for group selection both by enrolling suitable members and by excluding the unsuitable. Third, intake interviews enable the counsellor to explain the objectives and methods of the group and to answer questions. Some counsellors go beyond this to suggest ways in which clients can prepare themselves for the group either by reading, for example about the basic principles of the counselling approach being used, or by listening to audio cassettes or watching video cassettes, for example those illustrating desirable group-member behaviours in sending and receiving communications.

Exercise 8.3   Intake interviewing for a counselling group

This exercise can be done in pairs or in a training group.

A *In pairs*
   In Exercise 8.2 you probably planned a counselling group. Imagine that you advertised for members for the group and that your 'client' has come to you to ask about the feasibility of joining your group. Conduct an intake interview with your partner in which you: (1) help your 'client' to express and explore his or her reasons for wanting to join your group; (2) assess whether your client meets the criteria for inclusion; (3) if so, explain to your client the objectives and methods of the group you intend to run as

well as allowing ample time for answering any questions your client may have; and (4) check with your 'client' whether he or she still wishes to join your group and is clear about its objectives and administrative arrangements. Afterwards reverse roles.

B *In a training group*

The trainer may illustrate points about intake interviewing for counselling groups with case material drawn from the setting for which the group is being trained. The trainer may also conduct a demonstration intake interview using a group member as a role-played client. Another option is for the trainer to demonstrate, by means of an audio cassette or video cassette, an intake interview with a real client. Yet another option is for the trainer to set the pairs parts of this exercise and afterwards hold a plenary sharing and discussion on intake interviewing for counselling groups.

Leadership Skills in Group Counselling

There are wide variations in how group counsellors view and enact their roles, since virtually all theoretical positions in counselling have a group as well as an individual application. The amount of direction that the counsellor exercises is one of the most important dimensions on which group-leaders differ. A high level of direction indicates a teacher–learner or trainer–trainee relationship between counsellor and group members. At the other extreme, the counsellor may behave like one of the group members and offer no direction at all. In many interactional groups, however, there is a compromise in which the leader performs the role of an expert at the same time as, within limits, participating in the group as a member.

Many of the skills of group counselling are the same skills that are required for individual counselling, the difference being that they are adapted to the group setting. Skills such as empathic responding and structuring would fall into this category. There are, however, some skills that may be more likely to be used in group than in individual counselling, for example focusing on members' manner of relating, handling aggression and the use of exercises and games. Below I review some of the skills which you may require as a group counsellor.

Structuring

In Chapter 4 I described structuring as the process of letting clients know their own and the counsellor's role in the counselling process. One of the main results of an intake interview for a counselling group is to structure the client's expectations of the forthcoming experience. However, when the members get together for the first time the counsellor will probably want to make some opening remarks to the group as a whole. Since there are so many kinds of counselling groups, there is no uniform method of structuring. Furthermore, since members are often very anxious at the first session, they may not listen to the detail of the opening remarks, but rather be sensitive to their emotional impact. Further structuring may take place throughout the life of a group both by means of specific statements intended for that purpose and by means of counsellor body language and responses to specific client utterances.

Rogers tends to say very little when starting person-centred counselling groups or 'encounter groups'. He makes such opening remarks as: 'I suspect we shall know each other a great deal better at the end of these group sessions than we do now'; 'Here we are. We can make of this group experience exactly what we wish'; and 'I'm a little uneasy, but I feel somewhat reassured when I look around at you and realize that we're all in the same boat. Where do we start?'.[1] Rogers' opening comments are for groups in which the leader is intending to refrain from directing the group and instead wants the group members to share the responsibility for its development. Other group leaders may have more problem-focused agenda and make opening remarks which are more explicit about such matters as the group contract, desirable group-member behaviours and what will happen in subsequent sessions. Some group leaders start their groups by teaching the principles or language of the theoretical position from which they wish the group to operate.

Exercise 8.4 Structuring at the start of a counselling group

This exercise may be done in a number of ways.

A *On your own*
   In Exercise 8.2 you planned a counselling group and in Exercise 8.3 you conducted an intake interview for it. Imagine it is now two weeks later and your group is meeting for the first time. Formulate and write down a structuring statement to be made by you to all members at the beginning of your first group session together. Your statement should reflect the kind of group you planned in Exercise 8.2.

B   *In pairs*
   In Exercise 8.2 you planned a counselling group and in Exercise 8.3 you
   conducted an intake interview for it. Imagine it is now two weeks later and
   your group is meeting for the first time. Each of you should have the
   opportunity to be 'group leader' and to verbally make a structuring
   statement to all 'group members' at the beginning of your first group
   session together. When you are 'group leader' respond to any requests for
   clarification or questions that your 'group members' may have.

C   *In a training group*
   The trainer may discuss points about structuring in group work and also
   provide some audio-recorded or video-recorded illustrations, preferably
   drawn from the setting for which the group is being trained. Where
   possible the trainer should discuss the decisions involved in formulating
   and communicating the structuring statements made in the illustrations.
   The trainer may subdivide the group, ask the members to do the part of the
   exercise in B above, and afterwards hold a plenary sharing and discussion
   session on structuring at the start of group counselling.

Listening and empathic responding

One of the big differences between individual and group counselling is
that in group counselling much healing and learning can come from the
group members. Consequently much of the counsellor's behaviour will
be focused on creating an emotional climate in which the group
members can communicate with each other rather than on always
responding himself or herself. Group counsellors can show their
empathic understanding in a number of ways, including: the sensitivity
with which they make their opening remarks; their bodily communication; their capacity not to intervene unnecessarily; and by the quality of
their responses when they do choose to talk.

Four of the ways in which empathic responding may be different in
group from in individual work are as follows. First, the counsellor may
wish to respond empathically to communications between two or more
members. One way of doing this is to clarify what each member has
said. Another way is to summarize themes in the interaction. Second,
the counsellor may respond to the need of the group as a whole, for
example pleasure at having had a good session, frustration at lack of
progress, and resistance to dealing directly with issues, for instance fear
of being hurt, which may be at or just below the surface. Third, the
counsellor may need to respond empathically to the unspoken needs of

members who are not overtly participating and/or who may be feeling particularly vulnerable. Fourth, the counsellor may be trying, implicitly or explicitly, to allow and encourage the group members to respond empathically to each other.

Exercise 8.5 Empathic responding to members' communication in group counselling

This exercise may be done in a number of ways.

A *In threes*
You act as counsellor while your 'group members' either discuss an issue or relationship problem between them or role-play two partners discussing a problem in their relationship. Do not intervene after each statement. However, at appropriate moments, intervene by: empathically summarizing what *each* participant has been thinking and feeling; and empathically summarizing any themes in what the participants are *together* thinking and feeling. This session will probably need to last for at least 15 minutes. At the end discuss with your 'couple' how accurate and helpful they found your interventions. Afterwards, alternate roles.

B *In small groups*
The exercise in A above can also be performed in small groups in which the 'group members' interact with each other about their counselling skills, personal styles or any other topic(s) of their choice. If possible each person should have the opportunity to be group counsellor for this exercise.

C *In a training group*
The trainer may discuss points about using empathy in group work and also provide some audio-recorded or video-recorded illustrations, preferably drawn from the setting for which the group is being trained. The trainer may subdivide the group, ask the subgroups to practise along the lines of A or B above, and then hold a plenary sharing and discussion session on the use of empathic responding in group work.

Focusing on members' manner of relating

Earlier I mentioned that one of the advantages of groups, including counselling with couples and families, is that the counsellor is a participant–observer. Groups generate a considerable amount of material concerning members' ways of relating to other people, including the roles that they play to control others' reactions to them, for example playing helpless, being the clown. They also generate material about members' behaviour in groups, for instance their needs for power and control, or approval, and the degree to which they are socially facilitating. Furthermore, group processes, such as the forming of group norms or rules, subgrouping and scapegoating, may be observed. Groups also generate information about the thought processes which underlie members' personal styles, for example their self-standards, attributions, anticipations and defensive processes.

Often the other group members make valuable comments on the way another member is 'coming across' to them. Sometimes the counsellor may feel it advisable to reflect such comments as a way of emphasizing their importance. On other occasions counsellors themselves may provide feedback to individual clients about how they relate in the group, though the counsellor must be careful not to dominate the group. Such feedback might cover some of the following areas.

1. Amount of personal disclosure or the degree to which a member seems prepared to talk about himself or herself openly and honestly.

    'Bill, the group seem to be saying that they find you a very ambiguous person and do not really know you. They would like to get to know you better. What do you make of their feelings about you?'

2. The manner of expressing feelings or the extent to which and ways in which members show their feelings, including their impact on other group members.

    'Jane, at first when you started crying in these group sessions you seemed to elicit sympathy from the group. Now I detect a fair amount of impatience with you when you cry, as though you may often be seeking sympathy rather than dealing directly with your problems.'

3. Directness of communication or the degree to which a member is prepared to acknowledge his or her thoughts and feelings and to communicate them as such, possibly by making comments starting with phrases like 'I feel . . .' or 'I think . . .'.

    'Betty, I think that you seem to have the habit of disguising your own thoughts and feelings by asking questions of other people. You've just done this with Bill. Do you consider that that's a valid point? If so, you might try making more statements starting with "I".'

4. Vocal and bodily communication or the ways in which a member's non-verbal communication seems to be blocking or enhancing other people's ability to hear what he or she really wants to communicate to them.

'Keith, I felt that you were recounting a very painful experience then and yet every so often you smiled. The effect that this seemed to be having was to make it very hard for the group to know how vulnerable you really felt.'

5. Listening to, or the capacity of a member to listen to and, if necessary, respond empathically to and support other group members.

'Jim, did you notice that it really seemed to make a difference to Betty that you seemed able to understand and support her then? I think she very much appreciated that.'

6. Conflict resolution or the ways in which members handle differences between each other, including their ability to confront others and to handle confrontations themselves.

'Geoff, Diana seems to be saying that, every time she wishes to discuss your relationship, you change the subject and this makes her feel shut out and resentful. I've noticed in this group that you might have a tendency to avoid discussing difficult topics.'

Exercise 8.6   Focusing on members' manner of relating in group counselling

This exercise can be done *either* in threes or in a small group *or* as part of a training group.

A   *In threes or in a small group*
This part of the exercise needs three people, though it may be done with up to eight. You act as counsellor while your 'group members' interact with each other about their counselling skills, personal styles or any topic(s) of their choice. Do *not* intervene after each statement. However, at appropriate moments: (1) reflect comments, if any, from other group members about another member's manner of relating; (2) give constructive feedback to one or more members about their manner of relating, starting with such comments as 'I think . . .' and 'I consider . . .' rather than 'You are . . .' (as a guideline, these comments might focus on: amount of personal disclosure; manner of expressing feelings; directness of communication; vocal and bodily communication; listening; conflict resolution); and (3) give the person(s) about whom you have commented the opportunity to react to and explore the implications of your feedback, possibly with the help of the other 'group members'. Afterwards, if feasible, each of your 'group members' should have the opportunity to be group counsellor for this exercise. If the training group consists of from six to eight members, using two group counsellors at a time might be considered.

B *In a training group*

The trainer may discuss interventions for focusing on members' manner of relating in group counselling. The trainer may provide some audio-recorded or video-recorded illustrations of such interventions, preferably drawn from the setting for which the group is being trained. Where possible, the trainer should discuss the counsellor decisions involved in formulating and communicating the illustrated feedback. The trainer may ask the group to do the part of the exercise in A above and afterwards hold a sharing and discussion session focusing on members' manner of relating in group counselling.

Handling aggression

I mention the skill of handling aggression here because many beginning counsellors find this a potentially disturbing aspect of group work. It cannot be denied that counselling groups have the potential to be, and sometimes are, terribly destructive. Aggression in groups tends to manifest itself in two main ways: aggression between members and aggression directed towards the group leader. Aggression between group members may be handled in a number of ways. First, it may be allowed to run its course without any intervention from the counsellor. Second, the counsellor may encourage group members to 'own' their hostile feelings and to express them as 'I' messages, along the lines of 'I feel . . .' rather than as 'You' messages along the lines of 'You are . . . (followed by a derogatory statement)'. Third, the counsellor can endeavour to help group members to explore the feelings, thoughts and standards that underlie the anger. Fourth, the counsellor may support vulnerable group members until they are able to handle other people's aggression by themselves. This may include setting limits on another member's expression of anger. Protection of vulnerable individuals can demand a great deal of vigilance from the counsellor. I have already suggested that extremely hostile people might be excluded when forming a group. Fifth, in some instances, it may be appropriate to help members to identify the behaviour by which they may be setting themselves up as targets for attack.

Expressions of anger, especially when directed at the counsellor, can also be very threatening. It is helpful for counsellors to co-lead a counselling group until they feel confident enough to lead one on their own. A number of the points about coping with inter-member aggression are pertinent to the ways counsellors might choose to handle aggression directed at themselves, namely, not over-reacting to it, encouraging it to be expressed and responding to it by means of 'I' messages, and exploring the thoughts and feelings that underlie it. There is likely to be more need for counsellor assertiveness in group than in individual work. In interactional groups it is quite common for hostility to be one of the first *current* feelings that is expressed.

Exercise 8.7 Handling aggression in a counselling group

This exercise may be done in small groups or as part of a training group.

A   *In small groups*
Even though this exercise may seem artificial, it may help you to respond better if you are 'put on the spot' by other people's aggression when running a group.
Part one: aggression directed towards the leader. This part of the exercise requires a minimum of one other person and can be performed with up to seven other people. You act as counsellor while one or more of your 'group members' role-play being aggressive about the way you are running a hypothetical counselling group. Keep calm and practise hand-ling the situation as best you can, including: empathically responding to the anger; encouraging exploration of the thoughts and feelings under-lying the anger; and possibly encouraging others to send 'I' messages and yourself sending 'I' messages concerning your own thoughts and feelings in the situation.
Part two: inter-member aggression. This part of the exercise requires a minimum of two other people, though can be performed with up to seven people. You act as group counsellor while at least two of your 'group members' role-play engaging in a heated argument involving much 'putting down' of each other. Keep calm and practise handling the situation as best you can along the guidelines mentioned in part one of the exercise.
If feasible, each 'group member' should have the opportunity to be group counsellor for each part of the exercise.

B   *In a training group*
The trainer may discuss counsellor interventions for handling both aggres-sion directed towards the leader and inter-member aggression. The trainer may provide some audio-cassette or video-cassette illustrations of such interventions, preferably drawn from the setting for which the group is being trained. The trainer may get the group to do the parts of the exercise in A above and may also be a participant in/observer of/commentator on what is happening. If the group is subdivided for the parts of the exercise in A, the trainer may afterwards conduct a plenary sharing and discussion session focused on handling aggression in counselling groups.

Handling termination

In Chapters 4 and 7 I discussed handling the termination of individual counselling interviews and relationships. Here I briefly mention some points about the termination of group counselling relationships. In *open* groups the option for a member to terminate before the end of the group may be built into the initial 'contract'. Nevertheless, it may still be best for members' termination decisions within the life of these groups to be discussed and prepared for over a series of sessions rather than made and implemented abruptly. Handling the termination of *closed* groups at the end of their lives may involve the counsellor both in helping the group to work through its thoughts and feelings about the impending termination and, if necessary, working with individual members to find additional group and/or individual counselling experience. Counsellors may feel obliged to remain available to some of their former group members until they have managed to make suitable alternative arrangements for themselves.

LIFE SKILLS TRAINING

Life skills training aims to help people to acquire important life skills by means of structured programmes offered on a group basis. Sometimes life skills training is called 'personal and social education' or 'psychological education'. Much of the life skills training is focused on *communication* skills, for example empathic responding, self-disclosure or learning how best to reveal personal information, being assertive, managing sexuality, resolving conflicts, effective parenting, and public speaking. Other life skills training programmes focus on what might be termed *thinking* skills, for example anxiety management, coping with stress, decision-making and problem-solving. Still other programmes focus on *occupational* skills, for example making career decisions wisely, finding and being interviewed for a job, coping with unemployment, use of leisure time, and planning for retirement.

As mentioned at the start of the chapter, the counsellor's role in life skills training tends to be more one of educator than facilitator. One reason for this is that sometimes life skills training programmes are conducted with relatively large groups, say 20 to 30, as contrasted with five to ten for a counselling group. Indeed, sometimes such programmes are incorporated into educational curricula and are offered either by a counsellor or by a classroom teacher, or by a team of a counsellor and one or more teachers.

There are a number of reasons why counsellors are extending their roles to include life skills training. Many believe that too much of their effort in the past has been put into counselling a relatively few moderately to severely disturbed clients rather than into remedial, preventative, and/or developmental interventions for the majority. Perhaps this is especially the case for counsellors in secondary and higher education, who are under increasing pressure to become more accountable for the way in which they use their resources. Also, there is growing recognition that problems of living are widespread. Since there are not enough counsellors to meet all these needs, there is an increasing emphasis on running training programmes focused on specific skills that help people to help themselves.

Preparatory Skills for Life Skills Training

Like counselling groups, life skills training programmes need careful planning. Indeed, many of the same planning decisions needed in group counselling are relevant for life skills training. These include decisions about objectives, number of counsellors (or trainers), clientele, duration of the training programme, frequency and length of sessions, location and physical setting, and the nature of the contract.

Many life skills training programmes are of approximately six to ten 1½ to 2-hour sessions, though there are both shorter and longer programmes and sessions. Here, rather than repeating much of what I said about preparing for group counselling, I focus on some distinctive elements in the preparation and design of life skills training programmes.

Selecting training methods

There are many different options regarding methods or procedures if you find yourself needing to design a life skills training programme. Each method should be selected to help you and the group to achieve your training objectives as best you can, though you should be prepared to be flexible where necessary when actually running the programme.

Methods of presenting material include *lectures* and *lecturettes*. Whereas lectures may be cumbersome and encourage passivity on the part of the training group, well presented lecturettes may help to get points across which may then be followed by group activity. In Chapter

7 I listed *audio and visual aids* for counselling, and such aids are useful in life skills training both for presenting information and for feeding back to group members how they are performing. Live modelling of the skill in question by trainers is likely to be a particularly valuable visual aid. Also, a flip-chart is a very helpful visual aid in life skills training, not least because it can be used to collate and present the ideas of the group members themselves. Additionally, *written aids* may be used to collect and present material, for example hand-outs, books, self-report questionnaires and behaviour monitoring sheets.

Much of life skills training is likely to be conducted through *group activity*. Some of the disadvantages of having a large group of trainees can be minimized if the trainer is creative about subdividing the group into smaller units for various tasks. These smaller units may be twos, threes, fours, and so on. It is desirable if the area in which the skills training is taking place has the facility for subgroups to meet in some privacy. The two main forms of group activity are *skills practice* and *discussion*. One method of practising communication skills is to break the group down into threes and have two people either role-playing or engaging in a real interaction while the third acts as observer and discussant. Discussion groups are useful for trainees who wish to talk about and explore the concepts they are hearing about in their lecturettes and practising in their skills practice. Sometimes, however, trainees may want only to discuss the skill rather than practise it, and trainers need to be careful to keep a balance between the two.

Another important training method is the setting of *homework*. At first homework may focus on trainees becoming more aware of their own behaviour regarding the skill or skills being taught. Later, homework may be more focused on the trainees actually practising their newly acquired skill(s) in real-life settings. Homework may help to counteract one of the main criticisms of life skills training, which is that the skills do not last for long after the programme ends.

Selecting your own role

There are three main considerations in selecting your own role, though these are interrelated. The first is how much you want to direct the proceedings. Second, you will have to decide your method(s) in presenting the information required for others to learn the skill. Third, you must decide how best to use group activity. The way you make these decisions is likely to reflect your theoretical orientation, not just to counselling but probably also to teaching. Other considerations relevant to how you perform your role are: the nature of the skill or skills that you are trying to convey; the state of readiness and motivation of your trainees; and the amount of time that you have available.

Deciding how to evaluate your programme

It is inevitable that you will evaluate the outcomes of any life skills training programme that you run, if only informally in your own head. However, it may discipline your approach to defining and attaining your training objectives if you carefully consider criteria for and methods of evaluation right from the start of designing your programme. A further reason for this is that any rigorous evaluation of your training programme requires collection not just of outcome data, but also of baseline data to enable assessment of whether or not the programme has made any difference.

Trainer Skills in Life Skills Training

The skills of being an effective life skills trainer include those of counselling, teaching and consultancy. Since life skills training has experiential as well as intellectual objectives, *counselling* skills like empathic responding, creating an emotional climate in which it is safe to share personal thoughts and feelings, and confrontation are all likely to be necessary.

Teaching skills include: designing skills training programmes and curricula; implementing the programmes, especially in their more didactic aspects; and, possibly, evaluating outcomes. Ideas on designing life skills training programmes, in addition to those presented here, may be gained from such books as: Carkhuff's *Helping and Human Relations*, for rating scales of counsellor skills;[2] Ivey and Authier's *Microcounseling: Innovations in Interviewing, Counseling, Psychotherapy and Psychoeducation*, for ideas on microtraining involving breaking skills down into their component parts;[3] Egan's *You and Me: The Skills of Communicating and Relating to Others*, for a structured-exercise approach to communication skills training;[4] and Hopson and Scally's *Lifeskills Teaching*, for numerous ideas on working with groups in the school classroom.[5] Another source of ideas is the Pfeiffer and Jones' series *Structured Experiences for Human Relations Training*.[6]

Consultancy skills are likely to be necessary, since life skills training may be conducted in settings outside the counsellor's office. For instance, a school counsellor may need to enlist the support of, or possibly allay the anxieties of, people like parents, staff colleagues, the school head and the pupils themselves before being able to embark on a life skills training programme. Furthermore, once the programme is under way, the counsellor may be held answerable by these people for the impact of the programme, real or imagined, on the pupils. Last, but not least, the counsellor may wish to enlist the aid of one or more staff members as training assistants.

Exercise 8.8 is on designing your own life skills programme. Though perhaps it is not necessary to demonstrate the whole of Exercise 8.8, in Table 8.1 I show a possible outline for a life skills training programme for teaching empathic responding to 18 trainees for counselling roles in further and higher education. I stress that the trainer needs to work *with* the group and, where it seems in line with the overall training objective, should be flexible about considering varying the programme to meet their needs and wishes. For example, the speed at which trainees learn the concept or skill is highly relevant to how much time the group spends on any exercise. In the following programme, in addition to the eight weekly 1½-hour sessions, my contract with the trainees is that they do an equivalent amount of skills practice between sessions. Each trainee either is given Chapters 2 and 3 of this book, on 'observing and listening' and 'empathic responding', as a hand-out or purchases the whole book. Additionally, by the third session, trainees are required to have read the two articles by Rogers entitled 'The necessary and sufficient conditions of therapeutic personality change'[7] and 'Empathic: an unappreciated way of being'.[8]

Table 8.1 *An outline for a life skills training programme for empathic responding*

Each session is for 1½ hours each week, plus a minimum of 1½ hours' between-session homework.

Session	Objectives	Training methods
1	Creation of safe learning climate Initial understanding of concept	Introductions Exercise 2.1, Identifying the counsellor's frame of reference Lecturette on empathic responding Whole group discussion *Homework by next session* Exercise 2.4, Exploring your counselling attitude

Session	Objectives	Training methods
		Exercise 2.5, Listening to your reactions
		Exercise 2.6, Identifying your secrets
2	Increase trainee self-awareness Increase awareness of vocal and bodily communication	Whole group discussion of homework The group is subdivided into three groups of six for Exercise 2.7, Sharing your secrets Lecturette on vocal communication and bodily communication Discussion/feedback to trainer *Homework by next session* (in pairs) Exercise 2.2, Vocal communication Exercise 2.3, Bodily communication Exercise 2.8, Seating and body position
3	Increase awareness of vocal and bodily communication Develop disciplined listening skills	Whole group discussion of homework Lecturette on disciplined listening, opening comments and continuation responses Exercise 2.9, Developing your disciplined listening skills (in pairs) Discussion/feedback to trainer *Homework by next session* (in pairs) More practice of Exercise 2.9 Exercise 3.1, Assessing empathic responding
4	Increase knowledge of specific ways of avoiding low empathy Demonstration of high empathy	Whole group discussion of homework Film: Rogers counselling Gloria Discussion of film Discussion/feedback to trainer *Homework for next session* (in pairs) Exercise 3.2, Reflection of content Exercise 3.3, Exploring your 'feelings talk' vocabulary Listen to audio-cassette of experienced person-centred counsellor(s)
5	Knowledge about and skill at reflecting content and feeling in response to single statements	Whole group discussion of homework Lecturette on reflection Trainer models reflection of feeling and reflection of content and feeling Discussion/feedback to trainer *Homework for next session* (in pairs) Exercise 3.4, Reflection of feeling Exercise 3.5, Reflection of content and feeling
6	Ability to make a succession of empathic responses	Whole group discussion of homework Trainer models making a succession of empathic responses Trainees break into subgroups to practise making a succession of empathic responses Discussion/feedback to trainer *Homework for next session* (in pairs) Exercise 3.6, Making a succession of empathic responses (15-minute sessions)

Session	Objectives	Training methods
		Exercise 3.7, Empathic responding to role-played clients
		The above exercises should be video-recorded or audio-recorded
7	Further work on empathic responding and on the creation of an empathic emotional climate	Playback and discussion of homework
		Lecturette on evaluating empathic responding
		Discussion/feedback to trainer
		Homework for next session (in pairs)
		Exercise 3.6, Making a succession of empathic responses (30 to 45-minute sessions)
		Exercise 3.8, Evaluating your empathic responding skills
		Where possible, video-record or audio-record the above counselling sessions
8	Sharpen up empathic responding skills	Playback and discussion of homework
	Improved ability to monitor and evaluate own responding	Lecturette/discussion on improving your empathic responding in future
	Give trainees ideas about further development of their empathic responding skills	Discussion and evaluation of the empathic responding training programme
		Goodbyes (where appropriate)

I hope the outline in Table 8.1 is sufficient to demonstrate how you might answer the request in Exercise 8.8 for an outline of a life skills training programme, though of course it should not be imitated slavishly. You will, of course, need to adapt your programme to your clientele. For example, teaching empathic responding to counsellor trainees is different from teaching it to parents or marital partners: in fact, with these groups you might wish to use the term 'active listening' rather than 'empathic responding'.

Exercise 8.8 Designing a life skills training programme

This exercise may be done in a number of ways.

A *On your own or in a small group*
This exercise may be done either on your own or with up to three other people. Write down your decisions on a pad, a blackboard or a flip-chart. Design a life skills training programme for a skill that you, on your own or in conjunction with your group, think important. Assume that: you have eight 1½-hour sessions available; there are 18 to 20 people in your group;

the group meets once a week; and the programme will be conducted in an agency or setting of relevance to you. Make sure you cover the following points: the objectives of the programme; the number of trainers involved; the clientele; the location and physical setting; the nature of the contract; how to obtain trainees for the programme; your own role; how to evaluate the programme; and an outline listing specific objectives and training methods for each of the eight 1½-hour sessions, using the following headings – 'Session', 'Objectives' and 'Training methods'.

B *In a training group*

The trainer may present details of life skills training programmes of relevance to the setting for which the group is being trained. The trainer and the group may together select a life skill and design a programme for training people in it. Another option is for the trainer to subdivide the group and let each subgroup design a life skills training programme either for a life skill of their own choosing or for the same life skill. Afterwards the trainer conducts a plenary session in which the life skill training programmes are presented and discussed. The trainer may also wish to facilitate a discussion both of trainees' reactions to life skills training and of the research evidence concerning it.

ROLE DECISIONS

In this book I have now discussed three dimensions of the role of the counsellor: individual counselling, group counselling and life skills training. There are other possible dimensions of the role, for example time spent on administration, and consultancy focused on changing the systems which may be contributing to counselling problems. When there is more than one dimension to their role, counsellors are faced with the need to make role decisions about how best to allocate their time. Fig.

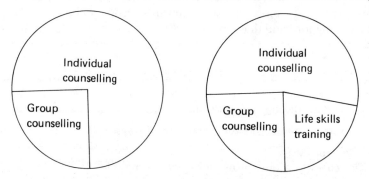

Figure 8.1   Examples of how two counsellors might distribute their time.

8.1 is a very simplified diagram of two different ways in which counsellors might distribute their time among individual counselling, group counselling and life skills training. The time distribution of Counsellor A is a fairly traditional one, with by far the major emphasis being on individual counselling and a lesser emphasis on group counselling. The time distribution of Counsellor B is one that is emerging in some settings, for example in education. Here there are pressures to help 'normals' to develop adequate life skills and consequently Counsellor B decides to spend less time on individual counselling. Counsellor B does, however, spend approximately the same amount of time as Counsellor A on group counselling, including doing group work with some clients who might be seen by Counsellor A on an individual basis.

With the emergence of a more complex role for counsellors, there is an increasing need for good role decisions. Counsellors must be clear both about their objectives in regard to their overall role and about the objectives of their specific interventions. Three aspects of such counsellor intervention are their clientele, their objectives and their method. The *clientele* for an intervention may be an individual, a group, or an institution or community. The *objectives* of an intervention may be remediation of moderate to severe psychological disturbance, preventing disturbance, or the personal development of 'normal people'. The *method* of an intervention may be counselling, education or consultancy. The different interventions that counsellors set out to make within a given time period should add up to a profile which reflects their objectives in regard to their overall role. Needless to say, in formulating their objectives and programmes, it is very important for counsellors to be sensitive to the expectations and wishes of the agency or institution in which they are working.

I have included Exercise 8.9, on making role decisions, because this is an important practical skill for the counsellor. However, I realize that this exercise is more oriented towards people who actually have counselling jobs and that, consequently, it may not be relevant for some of you.

Exercise 8.9 Making role decisions

This exercise may be done in a number of ways.

A *On your own*
   In regard to a present or future counselling role:
   1. Make out a table indicating:

(a) the possibe clienteles for your work;
(b) the kinds of objectives you might have for each clientele;
(c) the methods you might use with each clientele.
This part of the exercise is for 'loosening up', so try to get as many ideas down as possible. A format for your table is provided below.

Clienteles   *Objectives*   *Methods*

2. This part of the exercise is for 'tightening up'. Based on your clienteles/objectives/methods table, write out a new table in which you:
   (a) order priorities among the activities you might *realistically* do;
   (b) indicate what percentage of your time you might spend on each of these activities.

B *In pairs*
Either independently do the parts of the exercise in A above, then share and discuss, or jointly do them from the start.

C *In a training group*
The trainer may illustrate the processes and outcomes of role decisions, preferably using examples from the settings for which the group is being trained. The trainer and the group together may go through the parts of the exercise in A above, performing it as a group exercise. Another option is for the trainer first to allow the group to work independently, or in pairs and then to hold a plenary sharing and discussion session on making role decisions.

REFERENCES

1. Rogers, C.R. (1970) *Encounter Groups*. Harmondsworth: Penguin.
2. Carkhuff, R.R. (1969) *Helping and Human Relations: Volume One, Selection and Training*. New York: Holt, Rinehart and Winston.
3. Ivey, A.E. & Authier, J. (1978) *Microcounseling: Innovations in Interviewing, Counseling, Psychotherapy and Psychoeducation* (2nd ed.). Springfield, Illinois: Charles C. Thomas.
4. Egan, G. (1977) *You and Me: The Skills of Communicating and Relating to Others*. Belmont, California: Brooks/Cole.
5. Hopson, B. & Scally, M. (1981) *Lifeskills Teaching*. London: McGraw-Hill.
6. Pfeiffer, J. & Jones, J. (1969–77) *Structured Experiences for Human Relations Training*. Iowa City: University Associates Press. Vol. 1, 1969; Vol. 2, 1970; Vol. 3, 1971; Vol. 4, 1973; Vol. 5, 1975; and Vol. 6, 1977.
7. Rogers, C.R. (1957) The necessary and sufficient conditions of therapeutic personality change. *Journal of Consulting Psychology*, **21**, 95–104.
8. Rogers, C.R. (1975) Empathic: an unappreciated way of being. *The Counseling Psychologist*, **5**(2), 2–10.

9 Developing Your Counselling and Helping Potential

In the preceding chapters I provided a basic introduction to a range of different practical counselling skills. In this chapter I make some suggestions for those of you who wish to develop further your counselling and helping potential.

PRACTICAL, PERSONAL AND ACADEMIC DIMENSIONS

Counsellor training, even on a self-help basis, consists of three inter-related dimensions: practical, personal and academic. Consequently you may wish to explore ways of increasing your counselling and helping effectiveness by paying some attention to one or more of these dimensions. The *practical dimension* consists of a direct focus on counselling and helping skills, for example both skills training in laboratory settings prior to client contact and supervised work with clients on placements. However, counselling and helping relationships are not conducted just by technicians but by people. Therefore actual or prospective counsellors and helpers who experience difficulties in listening and communicating outside are likely to have similar difficul-ties inside their relationships with clients. Though good skills training may help with such difficulties, the time and attention that can be devoted to them in such practical training may be insufficient. A number of programmes for training counsellors and helpers include a separate *personal dimension* in which trainees can focus directly on their own problems of living and personal styles. All counsellors and helpers implicitly or explicitly operate from theoretical assumptions. Furthermore, some view what they do as an applied science in which it is very important to pay attention to research findings concerning the processes and outcomes of counselling. Thus the *academic dimension* of being an effective counsellor or helper includes knowledge of relevant theory and research. I now make some suggestions regarding the practical and personal dimensions. For those of you interested in doing further work on the academic dimension I have provided as an appendix a brief introduction to some of the theoretical literature underlying practical counselling skills.

The Practical Dimension

You may further develop your practical counselling skills through either self-help or training courses and workshops or supervised practical experience. In reality these different approaches to skills training often overlap. Also, you may do relevant reading in conjunction with each of these approaches.

Self-help

'Self-help' is a term which I use to encompass all activities which develop your practical skills without the aid of a counsellor trainer. There are a number of ways in which you can develop your skills of *empathic responding*. These come under the broad categories of observing others and practising or doing it yourself.

Ways of developing your skills of empathic responding by *observing others* include the following.

1. Listening to cassettes and tapes. Cassettes and tapes of interviews conducted by leading counsellors are available both in Britain and in the USA. One possibility is to listen to the whole session and focus on the counsellor, the client and the process. Another possibility is to rate the counsellor's level of empathy in regard to either single responses or three to four-minute groups of responses. Also, for breadth and for comparative purposes, you may wish to listen to the interviews of counsellors working within a number of different frameworks, for instance gestalt or transactional analysis.
2. Looking at video recordings and films. All the possibilities mentioned for audio cassettes are relevant for video cassettes, with the

added possibility of observing and rating bodily communication. Films are also valuable, but more difficult to screen and less flexible than video recordings for stopping and playing back.

3. Reading transcripts. Transcripts of interviews by leading counsellors are available, sometimes accompanying a cassette. Transcripts may be read in their entirety. Alternatively, you may wish to look at smaller segments or at individual counsellor responses and possibly rate them for empathic responding.

4. Being a client. Try to obtain the experience of being counselled by a highly empathic counsellor for at least one session, and more if possible. You may learn a lot about creating a safe emotional climate, the pacing of counselling interviews and the timing of individual responses.

Ways of developing your skills of empathic responding by *practising* them *yourself* include the following.

1. Composing an internal dialogue. Write out an internal dialogue in which you act as your own counsellor who is making empathic responses.

2. Responding to transcripts. Get a transcript of a session by someone like Rogers and go down the page covering up Rogers' responses, formulating your own, then checking Rogers' responses.

3. Responding to cassettes. Get an interview cassette of someone like Rogers and, immediately after a client statement, switch off the cassette and formulate your own response. Then listen to Rogers' response and compare it with your own. Focus on vocal as well as on verbal communication.

4. Co-counselling. Practise your counselling with a colleague on a co-counselling basis using audio or video feedback where appropriate.

5. Counselling real clients. Monitor your counselling of real clients by cassette recording your sessions and later playing them back and reviewing them.

6. Comparison with experienced counsellors. Have available a cassette recording of one of your sessions and one of the interview of an experienced counsellor. Listen alternatively to brief segments from each of the cassettes and review any significant differences.

7. Become part of a learning counselling skills self-help group. You may be able to form or become part of a learning counselling skills self-help group in which you work with, comment on and support each other as you develop your skills.

Many of the above suggestions, though they have been made in regard to empathic responding, are also relevant to developing your skills of conducting initial sessions, focusing on thinking and facilitating acting. For instance, if you obtain a catalogue from one of the suppliers of counselling interview cassettes, you may then be in a position to obtain a cassette of a leading counsellor who is focusing on a client's thinking difficulties. The addresses of some suppliers of interview cassettes etc. are provided at the end of the chapter.[1, 2]

Training courses and workshops

There are no hard and fast distinctions between training courses and workshops. If anything, however, training courses are spread out over a longer period, say two months or more, whereas workshops are relatively intense experiences lasting a day, a weekend, a week or possibly two weeks. Training courses may be full-time, half-time, day-release or a few hours a week. Workshops tend to, but do not necessarily, require full-time attendance. To illustrate the lack of a clear distinction between the two, sometimes workshops are called short courses.

   It may be possible to obtain details of training courses and workshops from national professional associations in counselling, in psychology and in other relevant areas. For instance, in Britain, the British Association for Counselling (BAC) publishes a list of courses entitled *Training in Counselling: a Directory.*[3] Furthermore, details of short courses, workshops and conferences are provided in BAC's quarterly *Newsletter* as well as in the British Psychological Society's monthly *Bulletin*. Table 9.1 lists the names and addresses of national counselling and psychology professional associations in Australia, Britain, Canada and the United States.

Table 9.1 *Names and addresses of national professional associations for counselling and for psychology in Australia, Britain, Canada and the United States*

Australia
Counselling: No national counselling association at time of writing.
Psychology: The Australian Psychological Society, National Science Centre, 191 Royal Parade, Parkville, Victoria, 3502

Britain
Counselling: British Association for Counselling, 37A Sheep Street, Rugby, Warks, CV21 3BX

Psychology:	The British Psychological Society, St Andrews House, 48 Princess Road East, Leicester LE1 7DR
Canada	
Counselling:	Canadian Guidance and Counselling Association/Société Canadienne D'Orientation et de Consultation, Faculty of Education, University of Ottawa, Ontario, K1H 6K9
Psychology:	Canadian Psychological Association/Société Canadienne de Psychologie, 588 King Edward Avenue, Ottawa, Ontario, K1N 7N8
United States	
Counselling:	American Personnel and Guidance Association, Two Skyline Place, Suite 400, 5203 Leesburg Pike, Falls Church, Virginia, 22041
Psychology:	American Psychological Association, 1200 Seventeenth Street, NW, Washington, DC, 20036

If you are interested in developing your skills in a particular approach to counselling, it may pay you to make inquiries about whether there is an agency to train people in the approach. For instance, training in facilitating person-centred groups and in transactional analysis has reached the stage where it is conducted on an international basis with local trainers. Additionally, if you are interested in developing your skills in a particular area of counselling, for example marital counselling or careers counselling, again it is advisable to make specific inquiries. In Britain, much of this information is available in BAC's training directory.[4]

Supervised practical experience

Supervised practical experience is an excellent way for you to develop your counselling skills. Some people may have ready access to suitable clients, whereas for others access to clients may be a major stumbling block to adequate supervision. Counsellor training courses of reasonable duration are remiss if they do not attempt to ensure that their trainees, when ready, have enough clients and also that they are well supported and supervised, especially when first assuming responsibility for clients. In settings where the focus is on helping contacts rather than on counselling interviews, for example nurses in hospitals, the more experienced can help the less experienced to develop their counselling skills. For many reasons, however, even experienced counsellors may find it beneficial to spend some time with a supervisor. These reasons include: guarding against falling into bad habits; updating their knowledge and skills; obtaining assistance with difficult clients; and, if necessary, receiving personal and/or professional support.

Much of the value of supervised practical experience depends on the quality of supervision. Indeed, Robert Carkhuff has both suggested and produced evidence to support his position that the level of skills of the counsellor trainer is perhaps the most critical element determining the effectiveness of practical skills training.[5] Of all methods of supervising counselling trainees' practical work, I consider listening to and commenting on cassette recordings of their interviews to be by far the most effective. Clients' permission for cassette recording can usually be obtained so long as they are assured that the material will be treated as confidential and 'scrubbed clean' in the reasonably near future. Without this cassette evidence, the supervisor is unable to focus on *how* the trainee responds to the client. Consequently, the very important area of responding decisions is largely lost to supervision. Other possible elements in supervision include focusing on: trainees' reasons underlying their treatment decisions; their own feelings towards their clients and about their interviewing; and understanding and being effective within the institutional or agency context in which they are working.

Opinions differ about whether counselling supervision is best done with just one person at a time, or in twos, threes or even larger numbers. Reasons for keeping supervision on an individual basis include the facts that listening to cassette recordings is very time-consuming and that trainees may be prepared to explore themselves in relation to their counselling more deeply on a one-to-one basis. Reasons for supervising groups of two, three or more include making it possible for trainees both to comment on other people's counselling and to learn from each other. Also, there are the obvious reasons of economy and practicability if there is a shortage of supervisors.

Practical skills reading

There are a number of introductory books on how to counsel, but most of them are stronger on discussion of issues than on any systematic attempt to build the reader's counselling skills. A good and easily readable discussion of many of the issues that the counsellor is likely to face is contained in Kennedy's *On Becoming a Counsellor*,[6] which is written more for the voluntary than for the professional counsellor. Another book which is strong on discussion of issues, but this time geared more towards training professional counsellors, is Zaro and her colleagues' *A Guide for Beginning Psychotherapists*.[7]

Introductory books mainly on empathic responding include Patterson's *Relationship Counseling and Psychotherapy*[8] and Gordon's *Parent Effectiveness Training.*[9] Gordon's book, though written at a more introductory level than Patterson's, is more specific about developing the skill of empathic responding. The first volume of Carkhuff's *Helping and Human Relations*[10] provides a more advanced introduction to the skills of empathic responding, along with other skills, for example confrontation and counsellor self-disclosure. Carkhuff's book includes a number of exercises which can be used in counsellor training. Other books containing exercises are Gilmore's *The Counselor-in-Training*[11] and Hackney and Corimer's *Counseling Strategies and Objectives.*[12]

In 1982 a second edition of Egan's *The Skilled Helper*[13] was published. In it Egan presents what he terms a 'problem management' model or framework for helping, consisting of three stages: (1) problem exploration and clarification; (2) developing new perspectives and setting goals; and (3) action. Empathic responding is especially important in the first stage of his model. Egan has also produced a training manual entitled *Exercises in Helping Skills.*[14] This book is a series of exercises with little of its own text, since it was written to accompany the text of *The Skilled Helper.* Brammer's *The Helping Relationship*[15] is a further introductory book on counselling, though only one of its seven chapters is devoted to empathic responding.

Rogers' *Encounter Groups*[16] provides an inexpensive and good introduction to group counselling. A longer and more advanced treatment of the subject is provided in Yalom's *The Theory and Practice of Group Psychotherapy.*[17] Some suggestions for further reading about life skills training are to be found at the end of Chapter 8.

Counselling textbooks provide an easy way of reading about the different approaches to practical skills and to counselling problems. In addition to general chapters on such matters as goals, initial interviewing and empathic responding, the practice part of my textbook *The Theory and Practice of Counselling Psychology*[18] contains chapters devoted to more specific problems, for example: thinking difficulties; personal, marital and sexual relationship concerns; and occupational concerns. Other counselling textbooks include Hansen and his colleagues' *Counseling: Theory and Process,*[19] and Brammer and Shostrom's *Therapeutic Psychology,*[20] and Ivey and Authier's *Microcounseling: Innovations in Interviewing, Counseling, Psychotherapy and Psychoeducation.*[21] A series of surveys of research on counselling processes and outcomes is to be found in Garfield and Bergin's edited volume entitled *Handbook of Psychotherapy and Behavior Change.*[22]

Counselling journals are a means of keeping abreast of developments in practical counselling skills. Journals specifically about counselling include: the *British Journal of Guidance and Counselling*, published by the Careers Research and Advisory Centre;[23] *Marriage Guidance*, published by the National Marriage Guidance Council;[24] BAC's journal *Counselling*; the American Personnel and Guidance Association's *Personnel and Guidance Journal*; and the Canadian Guidance and Counselling Association's *Canadian Counsellor*. The American Psychological Association publishes two counselling psychology journals: *The Counseling Psychologist*, geared to the continuing education of practitioners, and the *Journal of Counseling Psychology*, which publishes research papers. There are numerous other journals which have papers relevant to the practical skills of counselling, without having counselling as a primary focus. Some of these are psychological journals and some are journals of other groups, for example prison officers and social workers.

The Personal Dimension

Another way in which you can develop yourself as a counsellor is to pay attention to your personal effectiveness. An assumption here is that all people, not just moderately to severely disturbed clients, have to work on being effective in their lives. The old adage 'Physician heal thyself' also applies to helpers and to counsellors. However, this means making a sincere effort to change and not just going through the motions. There is a risk in counsellor training programmes that trainees get too involved in self-exploration and in analysing their relationships with other members of the group. Consequently they lose sight of the main objective of their training, which is to enable them to be competent providers of counselling services. Four approaches to your personal development are self-help, individual counselling, group counselling and life skills training.

Self-help

Effective living is a continuous process of psychological self-help. Much of the knowledge and skills you acquire in learning about counselling can be applied to helping yourself. For example, you can consciously try to become better at learning to listen to your own feelings. Furthermore, your skills of focusing on clients' faulty habits of thinking can easily be transferred to exploring your own difficulties and disciplining yourself to think more realistically. Also, if you are experiencing problems in acting effectively, you should have some insight into ways of changing your behaviour. Sometimes the notion of self-help is extended to include knowing how to utilize resources in the environment, be they friends, relatives or even other counsellors, on an *ad hoc* basis. Further suggestions for self-help include engaging in regular co-counselling with a suitable person and becoming a member of a self-help group.

Individual counselling

Some counselling approaches, for example psychoanalysis, make the experience of being a client undergoing a particular counselling approach a mandatory part of training. This is partly to improve the personal effectiveness of trainees and partly to help them understand the application of the approach for 'professional' purposes. In developing yourself as a counsellor or helper you may wish to undergo developmental, problem-focused or decision-making counselling from a competent professional.

In a number of countries, terms like 'psychotherapist' and 'counselling psychologist' are used in addition to the term 'counsellor'. Counselling psychologists are people with recognized psychological qualifications who perform counselling. The terms 'counselling' and 'psychotherapy' are often used interchangeably. Attempts to differentiate the two terms are never wholly successful and, if anything, they denote differing emphases rather than separate skills. For example, psychotherapists, probably more than counsellors, work with moderately to severely disturbed clients in medical settings. Indeed, many psychotherapists are psychiatrists, who are doctors with psychological as well as medical training. At the time of writing there is no legal registration of psychotherapists in Britain and the accreditation of counsellors and counselling psychologists is still in its early days. Even where there is accreditation, the message to anyone choosing a counsellor for themselves is *caveat emptor* or 'buyer beware'. Also, make sure you get a counsellor who you feel offers you the prospect of an effective working relationship, however well qualified he or she seems on paper.

Group counselling

As with individual counselling, participation as a client in group counselling may help both your personal effectiveness and your counselling skills. There are usually numerous opportunities for those living in large cities to become members of counselling groups. However, people living in small towns and rural areas are likely to find such opportunities much more limited. In Chapter 8 I discussed some of the advantages and disadvantages of group counselling. Also, I mentioned some criteria for assessing counselling groups. Both those sections are as relevant when considering group counselling for yourself as they are when making decisions in regard to your clients. The appendix, on different theoretical orientations, is pertinent to groups as well as to individual counselling, since each counselling approach is usually offered in group as well as in individual form.

Life skills training

North America seems to be far more advanced than Europe both in the literature on and in the provision of life skills training. There may be some opportunities in your area for learning life skills, for example assertiveness, by means of a structured group experience. In the remainder of the twentieth century this is likely to be a burgeoning area in the provision of counselling services as the 'psychological education' movement gains ground outside the United States.

Exercise 9.1 Developing your practical counselling skills

This exercise may be done in a number of ways.

A *On your own*
   Design a plan for developing your practical counselling skills. Write down as specifically as possible:
   1. your goals;
   2. the methods you intend to use to achieve your goals, for example details of self-help, training courses and workshops, supervised practical experience, practical skills reading and personal development;
   3. a realistic time schedule for achieving each sub-goal;
   4. how you intend to monitor and evaluate your progress.

B *In pairs*
   Either do the part of the exercise in A above independently, then discuss, or do it jointly. Another option is for you to act as counsellor and first facilitate your partner's exploration regarding developing his or her practical counselling skills and then help him or her to design and write down a

plan to achieve his or her goals. Afterwards reverse roles.

C *In a training group*

The trainer illustrates with examples how people in the area of counselling for which the group is being trained go about developing their practical counselling skills. The trainer may self-disclose about his or her own professional development in the skills area. The trainer may conduct a demonstration interview in which he or she facilitates a group member's exploration regarding developing his or her practical counselling skills and formulation of a plan to achieve his or her goals. Another option is for the trainer to ask the group to do the independent or pairs parts of this exercise and, afterwards, to hold a plenary sharing and discussion session about the development of practical skills during the training course and/or after it is finished.

CONCLUDING COMMENT

I hope that reading and being involved with this book has helped you to attain some of your professional and, possibly, personal goals. Being a skilled counsellor or helper can be very satisfying. There is not only the satisfaction that comes from good performance of the skills in themselves but the added satisfaction of seeing clients change, grow and become more fulfilled. In the first chapter I emphasized that the objective of counselling and, by implication, of helping is to help people to help themselves. However, the spread of practical counselling skills is relevant not only to the quality of professional and voluntary counselling and helping, but also the quality of everyday life. Many of these practical counselling skills, perhaps with minor modifications, are also among the basic skills of happy and fulfilled living.

REFERENCES

1. Films, tapes and cassettes are available on hire from the British Association for Counselling, 37A Sheep Street, Rugby, Warks, CV21 3BX (Telephone 0788 78328/9).
2. An American source for tapes and cassettes is the American Academy of Psychotherapists, 1040 Woodcock Road, Orlando, Florida 32803.
3. Ackroyd, A. (ed.) (1981) *Training in Counselling: a Directory*. Rugby: British Association for Counselling.
4. Ackroyd, A. (ed.) (1981) *Training in Counselling: A Directory*. Rugby: British Association for Counselling.

5. Carkhuff, R.R. (1969) Critical variables in effective counselor training. *Journal of Counseling Psychology*, **16**, 238–245.
6. Kennedy, E. (1979) *On Becoming a Counsellor*. Dublin: Gill and Macmillan.
7. Zaro, J.S., Barach, R., Nedelman, D.J. & Dreiblatt, I.S. (1977) *A Guide for Beginning Psychotherapists*. Cambridge: Cambridge University Press.
8. Patterson, C.H. (1974) *Relationship Counseling and Psychotherapy*. New York: Harper and Row.
9. Gordon, T. (1970) *Parent Effectiveness Training*. New York: Wyden.
10. Carkhuff, R.R. (1969) *Helping and Human Relations: Volume One – Selection and Training*. New York: Holt, Rinehart and Winston.
11. Gilmore, S.K. (1973) *The Counselor-In-Training*. Englewood Cliffs, NJ: Prentice-Hall.
12. Hackney, H. & Corimer, L.S. (1979) *Counseling Strategies and Objectives* (2nd ed.). Englewood Cliffs, NJ: Prentice-Hall.
13. Egan, G. (1982) *The Skilled Helper* (2nd ed.). Monterey, Carlifornia: Brooks/Cole.
14. Egan, G. (1982) *Exercises in Helping Skills*. Monterey, California: Brooks/Cole.
15. Brammer, L.M. (1979) *The Helping Relationship* (2nd ed.). Englewood Cliffs, NJ: Prentice-Hall.
16. Rogers, C.R. (1970) *Encounter Groups*. Harmondsworth: Penguin.
17. Yalom, I.D. (1975) *The Theory and Practice of Group Psychotherapy*. New York: Basic Books.
18. Nelson-Jones, R. (1982) *The Theory and Practice of Counselling Psychology*. Eastbourne: Holt, Rinehart and Winston.
19. Hansen, J.C., Stevic, R.R. & Warner, R.W. (1977) *Counseling: Theory and Process* (2nd ed.). Boston: Allyn and Bacon.
20. Brammer, L.M. & Shostrom, E. (1982) *Therapeutic Psychology: An Approach to Actualization Counseling and Psychotherapy* (4th ed.). Englewood Cliffs, NJ: Prentice-Hall.
21. Ivey, A.E. & Authier, J. (1978) *Microcounseling: Innovations in Interviewing, Counseling, Psychotherapy and Psychoeducation* (2nd ed.). Springfield, Illinois: Charles C. Thomas.
22. Garfield, S.L. & Bergin A.E. (1978) *Handbook of Psychotherapy and Behavior Change* (2nd ed.). New York: Wiley.
23. The Careers Research and Advisory Centre's address is Bateman Street, Cambridge, CB2 1LZ.
24. The National Marriage Guidance Council's address is Herbert Gray College, Little Church Street, Rugby, Warks.

Appendix
Theories underlying Practical Counselling Skills

Counsellors and others who use practical counselling skills are always operating from implicit if not explicit models of human behaviour or of 'what makes people tick'. Some of the more well-known and sophisticated of these models are labelled psychological theories. As well as attempting to understand the principles of human behaviour, each psychological theory tends to use its own language. These differences in language can be confusing to experienced as well as to beginning counsellors since, sometimes, the same or a similar concept appears in one or more different theories, each time in different terms. Consequently some differences between theories are more apparent than real.

Regarding counselling, the distinction between academic and practical can be very misleading. For example, every 'practical' counselling method is based on an 'academic' theory. Furthermore, without adequate knowledge of the relevant theory or theories underlying their practice, counsellors may be much less effective. In short, they may be making interventions in counselling without really knowing why. Additionally, it can be helpful to understand not only the theoretical basis but also the research evidence supporting any counselling method under consideration.

You may develop your theoretical knowledge in the same ways as you can develop your practical skills: by self-help and by attending training courses and workshops. The suggestions in Chapter 9 on how to find out about practical skills training courses apply equally to finding out about courses to increase your theoretical knowledge. In fact many, if not most, courses concurrently focus on both practical and theoretical dimensions, so that the learnings in one area can support those in the other and vice versa.

In the remainder of this appendix I give an introduction to eight theoretical and practical approaches to counselling. Also I provide a short bibliography on each position. Before reading about the different approaches, you may wish to complete Exercise A.1, which explores your theoretical preferences.

Exercise A.1   Exploring your theoretical preferences

This exercise may be done on your own or as part of a training group.

A   *On your own*
   For each of the following questions, give 2 marks to your first preference, 1 mark to your second preference, and 0 marks to the other answers. Answer all questions and do not rate any two preferences as equal.

   Questions
   1. People are motivated by:
       (a)   their instincts
       (b)   their belief systems
       (c)   their drive to actualize their potential
       (d)   their environments
   2. People are psychologically disturbed when they:
       (a)   are sexually repressed
       (b)   think in self-defeating ways
       (c)   are out of touch with their true feelings
       (d)   have maladaptive habits
   3. The best way to understand people is:
       (a)   to understand the way they see things
       (b)   to know what rewards are controlling their behaviour
       (c)   to understand the ways in which they think
       (d)   to explore their unconscious
   4. Human nature basically:
       (a)   is good and prosocial
       (b)   has destructive and aggressive tendencies
       (c)   is neither good nor bad
       (d)   has biological tendencies towards irrationality
   5. Counsellors can best help their clients by:
       (a)   designing programmes to modify specific behaviours
       (b)   offering an understanding and caring relationship
       (c)   interpreting their dreams
       (d)   teaching them how to think effectively

6. People function psychologically well when they:
   (a) are capable of acknowledging their true feelings
   (b) are rational
   (c) are relatively free from defences against anxiety
   (d) behave in adaptive ways
   Look at the end of the chapter to see the meaning of your marks.

B *In a training group*
The trainer may get the group to answer all the items independently. He or she then gets them to make up their theoretical preferences profile. Afterwards, the trainer may go through the questionnaire discussing with the trainees the possible implications for their counselling practice of the way they have answered the questions. The trainer may also make suggestions for further reading.

DIFFERENT THEORETICAL POSITIONS

You may learn about counselling theories either from primary sources, written by the theorists themselves, or from secondary sources, written by others. Some books are a combination of primary and secondary sources: for example, Corsini's *Current Psychotherapies*[1] consists of 13 chapters, each presented and written by an advocate of a different theoretical position, including some of the original theorists. Reviews of different counselling theories are presented in some secondary source textbooks, for example Hall and Lindzey's *Theories of Personality*,[2] Hansen and colleagues' *Counseling: Theory and Process*[3] and my own *The Theory and Practice of Counselling Psychology*.[4] However, the following review of different theoretical positions emphasizes primary sources.

Person-centred

Person-centred or client-centred theory emphasizes the importance of people's subjective self-concept, which consists of the ways in which they perceive and define themselves. However, often people acquire self-conceptions that are based on others' opinions and values, yet treated as if they were the individual's own. Once people acquire false self-conceptions they have a tendency to deny and distort discrepant information and feedback, thus sustaining their difficulties. The major emphasis of the person-centred approach to counselling is on helping clients to become more in touch with their real selves or 'actualizing tendency' by means of a safe and trusting counselling relationship characterized by the core counsellor-offered conditions of accurate empathy, non-possessive warmth or respect, and genuineness.

The founder of the person-centred approach is Carl Rogers (born 1902). Two good introductory books are his *On Becoming a Person*[5] and his more recent *A Way of Being*.[6] Other books by Rogers include: *Counselling and Psychotherapy*,[7] his seminal work on his approach; *Client-centred Therapy*,[8] a co-written book containing a statement by him of his theory of personality and behaviour; *Encounter Groups*,[9] about group counselling; *Freedom to Learn*,[10] about personal development in educational systems; *Becoming Partners: Marriage and Its Alternatives*,[11] about fulfilment in different kinds of partner relationships; and *Carl Rogers on Personal Power*,[12] about the political implications of his theory. The fullest statement of his theoretical position is to be found in an edited publication entitled *Psychology: A Study of Science*.[13]

Gestalt

Gestalt means form, shape, pattern or configuration. Life is characterized by a continuous process of imbalance in the person, no sooner one gestalt being completed than another begins. The gestalt approach focuses on the ways in which people form, or fail to form, strong gestalts at the contact boundary between person and environment. There are a number of contact boundary disturbances which contribute to neurosis. Gestalt counselling and therapy consists of the application of a number of techniques focused on making clients aware of *how* they are blocking good contact with their own senses and with the environment. Gestalt techniques include skilful frustration, drama and fantasy work, dreamwork and various games focused on awareness. The counsellor's role is much more directive in gestalt counselling and therapy than in the person-centred approach.

Fritz Perls (1893–1970) was the originator of the gestalt approach. A good starting point is his *The Gestalt Approach and Eyewitness to Therapy*,[14] which is a not too difficult overview, published posthumously, of gestalt theory and practice. *Gestalt Therapy Verbatim*[15] is another good introduction to his work. The fundamental, if somewhat outdated, statement of his position is *Gestalt Therapy*,[16] a book co-written with Ralph Hefferline and Paul Goodman.

Existential

'Existence' means literally 'to stand out'. Being or *dasein* (being there) means standing out or affirming one's unique existence. Death or biological extinction is the ultimate form of non-being, and a realistic awareness of death is considered a prerequisite to a full appreciation of life. There are also many relative threats to being which the individual needs to confront, including the contingencies of fate, suffering, meaninglessness, isolation and existential guilt. The existential counsellors believe that people are answerable for what they make of their lives, including both their actions and their attitudes. There is no single existential approach or single pre-eminent existential theorist. Existential counselling places great emphasis on the person-to-person quality of the relationship between counsellor and client. Within the relationship, existentialist counsellors help their clients to explore and overcome the ways in which they avoid a real sense of being. Existential counselling goals include *dasein* or experiencing one's existence as real, being aware of the conditions of existence, assuming responsibility for defining one's existence, the capacity for intimacy and the attainment of meaning.

Yalom's *Existential Psychotherapy*[17] is a sound and fairly comprehensive survey of the approach. Frankl's books, *Man's Search for Meaning*,[18] *The Doctor and the Soul*[19] and *Psychotherapy and Existentialism*,[20] describe the approach he has labelled 'logotherapy', emphasizing people's need for meaning in their lives. May and Bugental are two other prominent existential counsellors. May's books include *Man's Search for Himself*,[21] and *The Meaning of Anxiety*,[22] and Bugental's include *Psychotherapy and Process: The Fundamentals of an Existential Humanistic Approach*[23] and *The Search for Authenticity*.[24]

Transactional Analysis

Transactional analysis involves looking at people's relationships and behaviour in terms of ego states, which are patterns of feeling, thinking and behaviour. Each person has three ego states, Parent, Adult and Child, which represent parental and cultural influences, reality-oriented data processing, and childlike wishes and impulses, respectively. The practice of transactional analysis has four main subdivisions: structural analysis of ego states; transactional analysis, or analysis of single social transactions involving a statement and a response; game analysis, which entails exploration of more complex social interactions, invariably involving some destructive ulterior motivation; and script analysis, or analysis of the preconscious life plans by which people structure their time and have their destinies determined.

Eric Berne (1910–1970) was the prime originator of transactional analysis. His most systematic book, *Transactional Analysis in Psychotherapy*,[25] was published in 1961. Berne's ideas on analysing people's psychological games were elaborated in *Games People Play*,[26] and his ideas on script analysis were developed in *What Do You Say After You Say Hello?*,[27] published posthumously. Another reference on script analysis is *Scripts People Live*[28] by Steiner, who was an associate of Berne's. An introductory secondary source is Woollams and Brown's *The Total Handbook of Transactional Analysis*.[29]

Rational-emotive

Rational-emotive therapy (RET) emphasizes how people create and sustain their emotional disturbance through irrational thinking and self-talk. Though the culture, parents and the media foster irrationality, this is sustained by the individual's continually reindoctrinating himself or herself. RET posits an ABC framework, with A the activating event, B the belief or beliefs about the activating event, and C the consequence. Whether or not the consequences (C) are appropriate to the activating event (A) depends on the degree to which the person's beliefs about the activating event are rational (rB) or irrational (iB). Changing irrational beliefs involves D, detecting and disputing the beliefs, to produce E, a new effect or consequence. RET aims to minimize clients' self-defeating philosophies which cause anxiety and hostility and to help them to acquire a more realistic and tolerant philosophy of life.

Albert Ellis (born 1931) is the originator of rational-emotive therapy. Good introductions to his work are contained in the *Handbook of Rational-emotive Therapy*[30] and *A New Guide to Rational Living*.[31] The basic Ellis reference, now somewhat outdated, is *Reason and Emotion in Psychotherapy*.[32]

Reality

Reality therapy emphasizes the importance of acknowledging reality as a basis for responsible behaviour. Acting responsibly enables people to fulfil needs for love and worth and thus attain a success identity. Failure identities are caused by denying or ignoring reality, irresponsible behaviour and the loneliness and pain caused by lack of involvement in worthwhile relationships and activity. The Western world is now an identity society, with an emphasis on personal fulfilment, rather than a survival society, with the emphasis on the attainment of economic goals. However, the identity society contains numerous casualties with failure identities. The practice of reality therapy entails an involved relationship on the part of the counsellor. Clients are helped to understand that their current behaviour is their own choice and to evaluate whether or not it is their best choice for fulfilling their needs. If not, they are helped to develop and implement plans for more responsible behaviour.

William Glasser (born 1925) is the originator of reality therapy. His most important book is *Reality Therapy*,[33] which is an introduction to its theory and practice. His other books include: *The Identity Society*,[34] which illustrates the relevance of reality therapy to a changing Western society; *Schools Without Failure*,[35] about avoiding failure and developing success identities in the schools; and *Stations of the Mind*,[36] about the biological structure of the mind.

Psychoanalysis

Psychoanalytic theory is an elaborate system for describing mental life. People's mental apparatus consists of three agencies: the id (or it), which is constantly striving for instinctual satisfaction; the ego (or I), which aims to meet the instinctual demands of the id on the basis of reality; and the super-ego, which represents parental and moral influence. Humans are sexual from infancy, and sexual development takes place in two phases: a pregenital phase up to the end of the fifth year, a latency period, and then a genital phase starting at menarche and puberty. While the child's ego is relatively weak, it develops defensive mechanisms, in particular repression (not allowing material into consciousness), to ward off the strong sexual impulses emanating from the id. Excessive repression leads to the development of neurosis. Psychoanalysis aims to strengthen the client's ego by lifting childhood repressions. Interpreting a client's dreams is one of its major techniques.

Sigmund Freud (1856–1939) was the founder of psychoanalysis. Perhaps the best introduction to his work is his *An Outline of Psychoanalysis*,[37] written just before his death and published posthumously. A more detailed presentation of some of his later thinking is contained in his book *New Introductory Lectures on Psychoanalysis*.[38] For those who wish to read the early Freud, his two seminal books were *The Interpretation of Dreams*[39] and *Three Contributions to the Theory of*

Sex.[40] Hall's *A Primer of Freudian Psychology*[41] is a good secondary source.

Behavioural

Behavioural counselling methods are based mainly on principles of learning, though also on counselling and clinical experience. Behavioural theory incorporates such concepts as classical conditioning, operant conditioning and modelling. In classical conditioning a person may learn a phobia (e.g. fear of a dog) by the pairing of a conditioned stimulus (a dog) with an unconditioned stimulus (a loud frightening noise) so that the fear response still occurs in the presence of the dog independent of any loud, frightening noise. The idea behind operant conditioning is that people have to operate on the environment to generate consequences and that their behaviour is largely shaped and monitored by its consequences. For example, an adult who experienced negative consequences when attempting to form relationships in childhood may still be inhibited from seeking intimacy by the consequences of these early experiences. Modelling means learning from observing the behaviour of other people. Recently there has been much research on the importance of modelling to the acquisition of behaviour. One aspect of modelling is that a person may learn vicariously the consequences of a given behaviour without having to perform it directly. A relatively recent development in behavioural theory is an emphasis on self-reward, self-standards and self-instruction. This development, which owes much to rational-emotive therapy, is called 'cognitive behaviourism', since it has an emphasis on thinking.

The theory of behavioural counselling is closely tied to research and, consequently, many of the theorists have been researchers rather than practitioners. Two good books on different aspects of behavioural theory are Skinner's *Contingencies of Reinforcement*,[42] about operant conditioning, and Bandura's *Social Learning Theory*,[43] which emphasizes modelling. Wolpe, the originator of systematic desensitization, is an example of someone who has combined research with practice. His major research book is *Psychotherapy by Reciprocal Inhibition*,[44] while his *The Practice of Behaviour Therapy*[45] is a personal viewpoint on practice. Other books on the practice of behavioural counselling include: Krumboltz and Thoresen's edited book on *Counseling Methods*;[46] Goldfried and Davison's *Clinical Behaviour Therapy*;[47] and Kanter and Goldstein's edited book *Helping People Change: A Textbook of Methods*.[48] Three references in the area of cognitive behaviourism are Meichenbaum's *Cognitive Behavior Modification*,[49] the book edited by Karoly and Kanfer entitled *Self Management and Behavior Change: From Theory to Practice*,[50] and Beck's *Cognitive Therapy and the Emotional Disorders*,[51] though the latter book might be considered more representative of cognitive than of cognitive-behavioural counselling.

A final word is that many counsellors adopt a position of eclecticism in which they work from more than one theoretical position. By implication, this means that they find individual theories insufficiently comprehensive when confronted with the demands of practice. Eclecticism should not be an excuse for a shallow understanding of any of the positions on which such counsellors base their practice.

REFERENCES

1. Corsini, R.J. & contributors (1979) *Current Psychotherapies* (2nd ed.). Itasca, Illinois: Peacock.
2. Hall, G.S. & Lindzey, G. (1978) *Theories of Personality* (3rd ed.). New York: Wiley.
3. Hansen, J.C., Stevic, R.R. & Warner, R.W. (1977) *Counseling: Theory and Process* (2nd ed.). Boston: Allyn and Bacon.
4. Nelson-Jones, R. (1982) *The Theory and Practice of Counselling Psychology*. Eastbourne: Holt, Rinehart and Winston.
5. Rogers, C.R. (1961) *On Becoming a Person*. London: Constable.
6. Rogers, C.R. (1980) *A Way of Being*. London: Constable.
7. Rogers, C.R. (1942) *Counselling and Psychotherapy*. London: Constable.
8. Rogers, C.R. (1951) *Client-centred Therapy*. London: Constable.
9. Rogers, C.R. (1970) *Encounter Groups*. Harmondsworth: Penguin.
10. Rogers, C.R. (1969) *Freedom to Learn*. Columbus, Ohio: Charles E. Merrill.
11. Rogers, C.R. (1973) *Becoming Partners: Marriage and Its Alternatives*. London: Constable.
12. Rogers, C.R. (1977) *Carl Rogers on Personal Power*. London: Constable.
13. Rogers, C.R. (1959) A theory of therapy, personality, and interpersonal relationships, as developed in the client-centred framework. In Koch, S. (ed.), *Psychology: A Study of Science* (Study 1, Volume 3), pp. 184–256. New York: McGraw-Hill.
14. Perls, F.S. (1973) *The Gestalt Approach and Eyewitness to Therapy*. New York: Bantam.
15. Perls, F.S. (1969) *Gestalt Therapy Verbatim*. New York: Bantam.
16. Perls, F.S. Hefferline, R.F. & Goodman, P. (1951) *Gestalt Theory*. London: Souvenir Press.
17. Yalom, I.D. (1980) *Existential Psychotherapy*. New York: Basic Books.
18. Frankl, V.E. (1963) *Man's Search for Meaning*. Sevenoaks: Hodder & Stoughton.
19. Frankl, V.E. (1957) *The Doctor and the Soul*. Harmondsworth: Penguin.

20. Frankl, V.E. (1967) *Psychotherapy and Existentialism*. Harmondsworth: Penguin.
21. May, R. (1953) *Man's Search for Himself*. London: Souvenir Press.
22. May, R. (1977) *The Meaning of Anxiety* (Rev. ed.). New York: Norton.
23. Bugental, J.F.T. (1978) *Psychotherapy and Process: The Fundamentals of an Existential Humanistic Approach*. Reading, Massachusetts: Addison-Wesley.
24. Bugental, J.F.T. (1981) *The Search for Authenticity* (Enlarged ed.). New York: Irvington.
25. Berne, E. (1961) *Transactional Analysis in Psychotherapy*. London: Souvenir Press.
26. Berne, E. (1964) *Games People Play*. Harmondsworth: Penguin.
27. Berne, E. (1972) *What Do You Say After You Say Hello?* London: Corgi.
28. Steiner, C.M. (1974) *Scripts People Live*. New York: Bantam.
29. Woollams, S. & Brown, M. (1979) *The Total Handbook of Transactional Analysis*. Englewood Cliffs, NJ: Prentice-Hall.
30. Ellis, A. (1977) The basic clinical theory of rational-emotive therapy. In Ellis, A. & Grieger, R. (ed.) *Handbook of Rational-emotive Therapy*, pp. 3–34. New York: Springer.
31. Ellis, A. & Harper, R.A. (1977) *A New Guide to Rational Living*. Hollywood: Wilshire Book Co.
32. Ellis, A. (1962) *Reason and Emotion in Psychotherapy*. New York: Lyle Stuart.
33. Glasser, W. (1965) *Reality Therapy*. New York: Harper and Row.
34. Glasser, W. (1975) *The Identity Society* (Rev. ed.). New York: Harper and Row.
35. Glasser, W. (1969) *Schools Without Failure*. New York: Harper and Row.
36. Glasser, W. (1981) *Stations of the Mind*. New York: Harper and Row.
37. Freud, S. (1949) *An Outline of Psychoanalysis*. London: Hogarth.
38. Freud, S. (1973) *New Introductory Lectures on Psychoanalysis*. Harmondsworth: Penguin. Most of Freud's major psychological writings are available in the Pelican Freud Library.
39. Freud, S. (1976) *The Interpretation of Dreams*. Harmondsworth: Penguin.
40. Freud, S. (1962) *Three Contributions to the Theory of Sex*. New York: E.P. Dutton.
41. Hall, C.S. (1979) *A Primer of Freudian Psychology*. New York: New American Library.
42. Skinner, B.F. (1969) *Contingencies of Reinforcement*. New York: Appleton-Century-Crofts.
43. Bandura, A. (1977) *Social Learning Theory*. Englewood Cliffs, NJ: Prentice-Hall.
44. Wolpe, J. (1958) *Psychotherapy by Reciprocal Inhibition*. Stanford: Stanford University Press.
45. Wolpe, J. (1973) *The Practice of Behaviour Therapy*. Oxford: Pergamon.
46. Krumboltz, J.D. & Thoresen, C.E. (ed.) (1976) *Counseling Methods*. New York: Holt, Rinehart and Winston.
47. Goldfried, M.R. & Davison, G.C. (1976) *Clinical Behaviour Therapy*. New York: Holt, Rinehart and Winston.
48. Kanfer, F.H. & Goldstein, A.P. (1980) *Helping People Change: A Textbook of Methods* (2nd ed.). New York: Pergamon.

49. Meichenbaum, D. (1977) *Cognitive Behavior Modification*. New York: Plenum.
50. Karoly, P. and Kanfer, F.H. (1982) *Self Management and Behaviour Change: From Theory to Practice*. Oxford: Pergamon.
51. Beck, A.T. (1976) *Cognitive Therapy and the Emotional Disorders*. New York: New American Library.

RESPONSE TO EXERCISE A.1

The following answers are representative of four different theoretical positions.

Question	Behaviourist	Rational-emotive	Person-centred	Psychoanalytic
1	(d)	(b)	(c)	(a)
2	(d)	(b)	(c)	(a)
3	(b)	(c)	(a)	(d)
4	(c)	(d)	(a)	(b)
5	(a)	(d)	(b)	(c)
6	(d)	(b)	(a)	(c)

You can total your marks for each theoretical position to arrive at a theoretical preferences profile for yourself. This is a questionnaire to help you to explore yourself rather than to label yourself, so please beware of overinterpreting your profile.

A Glossary of Counselling Terms

Acceptance   Unconditional approval by the counsellor.

Actualizing tendency   A term used by Rogers to describe a drive by which people maintain and enhance themselves.

Acute   Sharp, critical, intense. Often contrasted with chronic (see below).

Adaptive behaviour   Behaviour which helps individuals to cope with their lives and to meet their physiological and psychological needs.

Advanced empathic responding   Responses to clients' statements that expand or advance their awareness yet still remain primarily within their frame of reference.

Aggressive behaviour   Hostile or attacking behaviour which is an over-reaction to a given situation and which, in personal relationships, is likely to be perceived as offensive.

Alternative frames of reference   Different ways of viewing people and situations.

Anticipating risk and gain   Assessing the positive and negative consequences of future behaviour and events. Some of this assessment may be below a person's level of awareness.

Antidepressant drugs   Drugs which are used primarily to elevate mood and to relieve depression.

Anxiety   Feelings of fear and apprehension which may be general or associated with specific people and situations.

Assertion   The ability to state positive and oppositional thoughts and feelings in an appropriate way that is neither aggressive nor inhibited.

Assertive training   Training in the outward expression of thoughts and feelings in appropriate ways. Involves rehearsing behaviours by role-playing prior to enacting them.

Assessment Collecting and analysing data about clients in order to make treatment decisions. Monitoring progress and evaluating changes. Frequently a collaborative exercise with clients.

Attribution of responsibility Ascribing or making causal inferences about the responsibility for one's own or other people's feelings, thoughts and actions and for external events.

Audio aids A range of aids, especially the cassette recorder, which can be used either in or in conjunction with counselling.

Avoidance Thinking and acting in ways that avoid dealing directly with the realities of life, for example by withdrawal.

Awareness Consciousness of and sensitivity to oneself, others and the environment.

Behavioural counselling An approach which views counselling in learning terms and focuses on anxiety reduction and on altering specific behaviours.

Behaviour rehearsal An approach which involves the counsellor coaching clients and rehearsing them in appropriate behaviours by role-playing. Clients may also be asked to rehearse appropriate behaviours in their imaginations.

Bisexuality Being sexually interested in one's own as well as in the opposite sex.

Bodily communication Conveying messages about thoughts and feelings in ways that either do not use words or frame the use of words.

Careers counselling Counselling people about initial choice of career and at decision points during their careers. Also, may refer to unemployment and redundancy counselling and to pre-retirement and retirement counselling.

Catharsis Discharge of emotional tension by talking it out.

Challenging Challenging aims to expand clients' awareness by means of reflecting and/or focusing on discrepancies in clients' thoughts, feelings and actions.

Chronic Lingering, lasting. Sometimes also with the connotation of not being as severe as when the term 'acute' is used.

Classical conditioning A form of learning in which a previously neutral stimulus assumes the capacity to elicit the response of another stimulus with which it has been paired.

Client-centred counselling An approach to counselling, developed mainly by Carl Rogers, which emphasizes the importance of clients' subjective perceptions. See *Person-centred counselling*.

Cognitive counselling Approaches to counselling which attempt to alter clients' feelings and actions by altering the ways in which they think.

Concreteness Responding to clients' utterances in a clear and specific manner. Clear and specific communication by clients.

Conditioning See *Classical conditioning* and *Operant conditioning*.

Confidentiality Keeping trust with clients by not divulging personal information about them unless granted permission.

Confrontation 'Confrontation' is another term for 'challenging' (see above).

Congruence Genuineness and lack of facade. Having one's actions match one's thoughts, feelings and words.

Continuation responses Brief counsellor responses designed to give the client the message 'I am with you. Please continue'.

Continuous reward A schedule of reward or reinforcement in which a reward is automatically given after each correct response.

Contracting Making agreements with clients which may be implicit, verbal, written and unsigned, or written and signed by both counsellor and client.

Counselling Counselling aims to help clients, who are mainly seen outside medical settings, to help themselves. The counsellor's repertoire of psychological skills includes both those of forming an understanding relationship with clients and those focused on helping them to change specific aspects of their feeling, thinking and behaviour.

Countertransference Negative and positive feelings, based on unresolved areas in their own lives, which arise in counsellors towards their clients.

Couples counselling Counselling two partners in a relationship either jointly or with a mixture of counselling them separately and jointly.

Crises Situations of excessive stress in which people feel that their coping resources are severely stretched or inadequate to meet the adjustive demands being made upon them.

Crisis interviewing Interviewing focused on providing counselling assistance at periods of crisis in clients' lives.

Decision-making interviewing Interviewing focused on providing counselling assistance at periods of decision in clients' lives.

Defences The processes by which people deny and distort information at variance with their conceptions of self when this information threatens their feelings of adequacy and worth.

Delusions Strongly held false ideas.

Denial Denial is a defensive process by which individuals protect themselves from unpleasant aspects of themselves and of external reality by refusing to recognize them.

Dependency Clients who are dependent maintain themselves by relying on support from others, for example their counsellors, or from drugs rather than by relying on self-support.

Developmental interviewing Focuses on providing clients with a nurturing emotional relationship to remedy real or imagined deficiencies in the quality of previous relationships, especially those provided by parents.

Directive counselling Counselling in which the counsellor gives direction to much or all of an interview.

Distortion Distortion is a defensive process involving altering unpleasant or discrepant aspects of reality in order to make them less threatening and more consistent with existing conceptions of self.

Dream interpretation Dream interpretation is used in counselling approaches such as psychoanalysis and gestalt counselling. It involves providing explanations of the manifest and latent content of clients' dreams.

Eclecticism Basing one's counselling practice on more than one theoretical position.

Educational counselling Counselling in educational settings which often focuses on educational concerns, for example study and examination difficulties.

Ego In psychoanalysis, the rational part of the mental apparatus which mediates between the demands of the id, the super-ego and reality. Other meanings include self-concept and self-worth.

Ego states A term used in transactional analysis to describe patterns of feeling, thinking and behaviour. Each person has three ego states: Parent, Adult and Child.

Elaboration responses Counsellor responses which encourage clients to elaborate and clarify their previous statements.

Empathic responding Accurately understanding, from their frames of reference, what your clients are telling you and then sensitively communicating back your understanding in a language attuned to your clients' needs. More colloquially, being a good listener and then responding with understanding.

Encounter groups An intensive method of group counselling with an emphasis on focusing on feelings and on group interaction.

Endogenous depression Depression predominantly originating within the physiology of the organism.

Existence Existence literally means 'to stand out'.

Existential counselling An approach to counselling emphasizing helping clients to take responsibility for affirming and defining their existence within the parameters of death and other limiting and contingent factors in life.

Extinction   The weakening or disappearance of a response when it is no longer rewarded or reinforced.

Family counselling   Form of counselling focusing on the relationships within the family.

Feelings   Emotions, affective states of varying degrees of positiveness and negativeness.

Focused exploration   Counsellor and client together explore a specific area or areas of a client's feeling, thinking and/or acting.

Free association   A psychoanalytic procedure in which clients are encouraged to share without censorship their every thought and feeling.

Gay counselling   Counselling homosexually and bisexually oriented clients.

Genuineness   Absence of facade and insincerity. Having one's actions match one's thoughts, feelings and words.

Gestalt   Gestalt means form, shape, pattern or configuration.

Gestalt counselling   Gestalt counselling and therapy consists of the application of a number of techniques focused on making clients aware of how they are blocking making good contact or strong gestalts with their own senses and with the environment.

Goals   Goals are the implicit or explicit objectives of counselling relationships and of specific counselling methods or client plans.

Group counselling   The relationships, activities and skills involved in counselling two or more people at the same time.

Guilt   Feelings of subjective distress, involving self-devaluation and anxiety, resulting from having transgressed a code of behaviour to which one subscribes.

Habit   A settled tendency based on learning to respond in a consistent way to a person or situation.

Hallucination   Illusions regarding external objects which are not actually present. Most commonly these are auditory, for example hearing voices.

Helping contacts   The use of practical counselling skills in situations outside formal counselling.

Helping relationships   Relationships which may or may not take place in interview settings and where the use of counselling skills is likely to be only part of the helper's relationship with the client.

Hierarchies   Refers in behavioural counselling to lists of progressively more anxiety-evoking scenes, for example in systematic desensitization, and to lists of progressively more difficult tasks.

Homework   Tasks assigned inside to be completed outside and usually between counselling interviews.

Homosexuality Sexual interest in people of the same sex.

Hostility Thoughts, feelings and behaviours aimed at attacking, destroying or damaging a perceived source of frustration or threat.

Hypnotic drugs Drugs that induce sleep.

Illusion False perception or belief.

Imaginal rehearsal Role-playing desired behaviours in imagination prior to enacting them.

'I' messages Acknowledging and directly stating what you think and feel by starting with the words 'I think . . .' or 'I feel . . .' etc.

Immediacy Counsellor and, possibly, client comments that focus on the 'here and now' of the counselling relationship, perhaps by focusing on what has previously been left unsaid. Sometimes expressed as 'you–me' talk.

Information Material relevant to clients' concerns and decisions which they may seek out for themselves or which may be provided by their counsellors, for example careers information provided in occupational counselling.

Inhibition Restraining, weakening, inadequately acknowledging and shrinking from an impulse, desire or action.

Intermittent reward A schedule of reward or reinforcement in which rewards are given intermittently rather than after every correct response.

Internal dialogue Inner verbalizations and conversations. Sometimes used as a synonym for thinking.

Internal frame of reference The subjective perceptions of an individual rather than an external viewpoint.

Interpretation Explanations from the counsellor's frame of reference of clients' behaviours, thought processes or dreams.

Introjection Taking something from another person or other people and treating it as part of oneself. See *Projection.*

In vivo Taking place in a real-life setting as contrasted with taking place in a counsellor's office or in a person's imagination.

Leisure counselling Counselling peoople about their use of free or discretionary time.

Life skills The skills necessary for effective living, for example commuciation skills.

Maladaptive behaviour Behaviour that hinders, prevents and defeats people's ability to cope with their lives and to meet their physiological and psychological needs.

Manic depressive psychoses Psychotic disorders characterized by elation and overactivity (mania), pessimism and underactivity (depression), or by an alternation of the two.

Manipulation of feedback A defensive process by which individuals put overt and covert pressure on others to provide feedback that is consistent with their conceptions of themselves.

Marathon group Intensive group experience in a restricted environment lasting 24 hours or more.

Marital counselling Counselling marital partners or people thinking of marrying, and possibly providing a conciliation service for divorced people in the interests of their children.

Medication Medically prescribed drugs used independently or in conjunction with counselling.

Men's counselling Counselling focused on developing the human potential of men by freeing them from gender-stereotyped feeling, thinking and behaviour.

Misattribution of responsibility Inaccurately ascribing the causes of one's own or of other people's feelings, thoughts and actions and of external events.

Modelling Learning by observing another perform a desired behaviour. Demonstrating a desired behaviour.

Monitoring Observing and checking on behaviour either inside or outside counselling interviews.

Nervous breakdown Collapse or drastic lessening of ability to cope with one's life. Involves physiological and psychological debilitation.

Non-verbal communication See *Bodily communication.*

Occupational counselling Counselling people about their occupational concerns, especially decisions and problems related to the world of work, though increasingly referring to a wider spectrum of activity.

Opening remarks Counsellor statements made at the start of initial and subsequent interviews.

Operant conditioning Making reward or reinforcement contingent on behaviour that operates on the environment to produce the desired consequences.

Paranoia A psychosis characterized by a delusional system, most often of a persecutory nature.

Paranoid state Transient psychotic disorder characterized by a delusional system, most often of a persecutory nature.

Para-verbal communication Vocal communications that frame verbal utterances.

Personal and social education Educating pupils, students and others in life skills.

Person-centred counselling A more recent term for client-centred counselling, possibly reflecting a shift in emphasis to group work with 'normal' people.

Plan A step-by-step outline, verbal or written, of the specific actions necessary to attain the client's goals.

Presenting concerns The concerns and problems that clients say have brought them to counselling.

Problem-focused counselling Counselling focused on helping clients to cope with or manage specific problems in their lives.

Projection Taking something from oneself and treating it as part of another person or other people. See *Introjection.*

Psychiatry The branch of medicine dealing with understanding, treating and preventing mental disorders.

Psychoanalysis A theoretical model and counselling and therapeutic approach originated by Freud. Also, the term applies to approaches which are later variations of Freud's model.

Psychodrama A counselling and therapeutic approach originated by Moreno involving the use of dramatic enactments of scenes.

Psychological education Primarily means educating people in psychological or life skills. Other meanings may include humanistic education and paraprofessional training.

Psychology The science and study of human behaviour.

Psychosis Severe mental disorder involving loss of contact with reality and usually characterized by delusions and/or hallucinations.

Psychosomatic disorders Psychophysiological disorders caused and maintained primarily by psychological and emotional rather than by physical or organic factors.

Psychotherapy Often used as another term for counselling. May have connotations of moderately to severely disturbed clients seen in medical settings, but not necessarily so. More accurate to speak of the psychotherapies, since there are many theoretical and practical approaches to psychotherapy.

Questions Questions may be used by counsellors to get clients to specify, to elaborate, to focus on feelings, to explore alternatives and to make decisions.

Rational-emotive counselling A form of counselling and therapy originated by Albert Ellis which views clients as being the victims of their own irrational belief systems.

Reactive depression Depression which is a disproportionate and continuing reaction to a precipitating event, such as a bereavement or setback. Reactive depressions are often contrasted with endogenous depressions, though depressions may contain both elements.

Realistic standards Standards for behaviour and self-evaluation which are functional in helping individuals to cope with their lives and meet their physiological and psychological needs.

Reality therapy Form of counselling and therapy, originated by William Glasser, which emphasizes the importance of acknowledging reality as a basis for responsible behaviour that enables people to fulfil needs for love and worth and thus attain a success identity.

Records Counsellors may keep records focusing on initial assessment, progress during counselling, and termination details. Records may also take the form of statistical summaries.

Reflection Mirroring the verbal and/or emotional content of the client's communications through empathic responding.

Regard Counsellor liking or prizing of the client. Unconditional acceptance of the client as a person.

Reinforcement. See *Reward.*

Relaxation A technique whereby clients are taught to relax by tensing and relaxing various muscle groups. Sometimes also combined with mental relaxation involving imagining restful scenes.

Reluctant clients Clients who have been referred or assigned to counselling against their will.

Repression A defensive process by means of which anxiety-evoking material and memories are kept out of awareness or consciousness.

Resistance All processes in clients that oppose their progress towards self-awareness and psychological well-being.

Responding decisions Decisions on the part of counsellors about how best to respond to single or to a series of client statements.

Responsibility Responsibility for creating one's existence and meeting one's physiological and psychological needs within the constraints of reality. Involves attributing responsibility accurately.

Reward A reward or reinforcement is an event which, when following a response, strengthens the probability of that response re-occurring.

Role decisions Counsellor decisions about how best to allocate their time between various possibilities for their role.

Role-playing Learning by enacting behaviours, usually in simulated settings.

Schedules of reward See *Continuous reward* and *Intermittent reward.*

Schizophrenia A psychosis characterized by the disintegration of personality, emotional withdrawal, and disorders of perception, thought and behaviour.

Self-acceptance Accepting oneself as a person while remaining aware of one's strengths and limitations.

Self-awareness Being aware of one's significant thoughts, feelings and experiences and of the impact that one makes on others.

Self-conceptions The ways in which people see themselves and to which they attach terms like 'I' or 'me'.

Self-disclosure Revealing personal information, especially by intentional verbal communication.

Self-evaluation The process of placing positive and negative values on one's personal characteristics.

Self-exploration Exploring one's own feelings, thoughts and actions and learning to experience one's emotions.

Self-instruction The process of talking to oneself with coping statements that reduce anxiety and facilitate the performance of tasks.

Self-protective thinking Defensive ways of thinking whose object is to preserve one's sense of adequacy and self-concept from discrepant or otherwise threatening information.

Self-standards The standards by which one leads one's life and which form the basis of positive and negative evaluations of self.

Self-worth Sense of adequacy, positive or negative evaluation of oneself as a person.

Shaping of behaviour The fashioning of new patterns of behaviour by rewarding successively close approximations until the desired behaviour is attained.

Social rules The implicit and explicit rules of conduct which vary according to the social contexts in which communication takes place.

Social skills Skills for communicating in personal and work relationships and in social groupings.

Specificity Responding to clients' utterances in a clear and specific manner. Avoidance of vague generalities. Clear and specific communication by clients.

Stages of counselling Timing counselling interventions according to the state or readiness of clients in the counselling process. If necessary, nurturing clients prior to focusing on thinking and acting.

Stress Perceived demands on one's energy and coping abilities.

Stressor An individual item that causes stress.

Stress tolerance The level of stress or cumulative amount of stressors that an individual can tolerate before experiencing distinct physiological and psychological distress.

Structuring The behaviours by which counsellors let their clients know their respective roles at various stages of the counselling process.

Successive approximation See *Shaping of behaviour*. Successive approximation is also used in anxiety-reduction techniques whereby clients, in vivo or in imagination, are placed or imagine themselves in increasingly anxiety-evoking situations.

Summarizing Counsellor summaries clarify and reflect back what the client has been saying over a period of time. Summaries may also include some feedback from the counsellor.

Supportive interviewing Counselling clients who, while not in a state of crisis, feel that some extra support would be helpful to help them through an awkward phase in their lives.

Systematic desensitization A behavioural counselling method aimed at reducing anxiety by presenting items from a hierarchy of progressively more anxiety-evoking scenes to clients when they are relaxed.

Tension Feeling mentally and physically stretched and under strain.

Termination The ending of counselling interviews and relationships.

Tests Psychological tests are ways of gathering information about people by taking objective and standardized measures of samples of their behaviour.

Thinking difficulties Ways of thinking that cause clients to have negative emotions and to behave less effectively than they might.

Threat Perception of real or imagined danger.

Timing The 'when' of making counsellor responses and of making and implementing treatment decisions.

Toxic Poisonous. Most commonly used regarding the unwanted side-effects of drugs, but sometimes used to describe people.

Tranquillizing drugs Drugs for the reduction of anxiety and tension.

Transactional analysis A form of counselling originated by Eric Berne based on the analysis of 'Parent', 'Adult' and 'Child' ego states.

Transference Process by which a client transfers feelings and emotions applicable to a previous relationship onto the counsellor; emphasized in psychoanalysis.

Transition counselling Counselling people about to go through or undergoing major changes in their lives.

Transition statements Counsellor statements which move or suggest moving the content of an interview from one topic area to another or from one stage of the interview to another.

Treatment decisions Treatment decisions refer to what method or methods to adopt with which client or clients and when.

Tunnel vision A narrowing of perception under threat so that the individual focuses only on certain factors in a situation and excludes others which may be important.

Unconscious Beneath the level of conscious awareness.

Unrealistic standards Standards for behaviour and self-evaluation which are dysfunctional in helping individuals to cope with their lives and meet their physiological and psychological needs.

Verbal communication What people actually say with words as contrasted with what they say by their vocal and bodily communication.

Vicarious reward A vicarious reward is an observed event which, when following a response by another, strengthens the possibility of that response recurring.

Visual aids   A range of aids, for example video recorders or flip-charts, which can be used either in or in conjunction with counselling.

Vocal communication   Para-verbal communications, for example pitch and loudness, that frame spoken words.

Withdrawal   Retreating or pulling back with one's feelings, thoughts and/or actions.

Women's counselling   Counselling focused on developing the human potential of women by freeing them from gender-stereotyped feeling, thinking and behaviour.

Working through   Facing up to a problem or decision and working on it until a satisfactory resolution or adjustment is reached.

Written aids   Written aids are used in or in conjunction with counselling to collect information about clients, to get them to do homework and to provide information for clients.

Name Index

Ackroyd, A. 209, 210
Alberti, R.E. 126
Allen, W. 91
Authier, J. 199, 212

Bandura, A. 225
Barach, R. 211
Barrett-Lennard, G.T. 60–61
Beck, A.T. 226
Bergin, A.E. 212
Berne, E. 222–223, 239
Bernstein, D.A. 125
Borkovec, T.D. 125
Bower, G.H. 127
Bower, S.A. 127
Brammer, L.M. 212
Brown, M. 223
Bugental, J.F.T. 222

Carkhuff, R.R. 199, 211, 212
Coleman, J.C. 173
Corimer, L.S. 212
Corsini, R. 220

Daley, M.F. 133
Davison, G.C. 125, 225
Dreiblatt, I.S. 211

Egan, G. 94, 199, 212
Ellis, A. 27, 92, 97, 223, 236
Emmons, M.L. 126

Feiffer, J. 18
Frankl, V.E. 222
Freud, S. 105, 113, 116, 224–225, 236

Garfield, S.L. 212
Gilmore, S.K. 212
Glasser, W. 223–224, 237
Goldfried, M.R. 125, 225
Goldstein, A.P. 225
Goodman, P. 221
Gordon, T. 212
Gregg, G. 27

Hackney, H. 212
Hall, C.S. 220, 225
Hansen, J.C. 212, 220
Harper, R.A. 223
Hefferline, R.F. 221
Hopson, B. 199

Ingham, H. 24–25
Ivey, A.E. 199, 212

Jones, J. 199

Kanfer, F.H. 225, 226
Karoly, F. 226
Kennedy, E. 166, 211
Krumboltz, J. 225

Lâo-Tsze 26
Lewinsohn, P.M. 133
Lindzey, G. 220
Loughary, J.W. 165
Luft, J. 24–25

MacPhillamy, D.J. 133
May, R. 222
Meichenbaum, D. 226
Mitchell, K.M. 60
Moreno, J.L. 236
Murgatroyd, S. 162

Nedelman, D.J. 211
Nelson-Jones, R. 29, 125, 212, 220

Patterson, C.H. 29, 211
Perls, F.S. 27, 221
Pfeiffer, J. 199

Ripley, T.M. 165
Rogers, C.R. 3, 4, 5, 27, 40–41, 135, 189, 200, 201, 208, 212, 220–221, 229, 230

Scally, M. 199
Selye, H. 155
Shostrom, E.L. 212
Skinner, B.F. 225
Steiner, C.M. 223
Stevic, R.R. 212, 220

Thoresen, C.E. 225
Trethowan, W.H. 170
Truax, C.B. 60, 135

Warner, R.W. 212, 220
Willis, J. 170
Wolfe, R. 162
Wolpe, J. 125, 225
Woollams, S. 223

Yalom, I.D. 212, 222

Zaro, J.S. 211

Subject Index

Advanced empathic responding 59–60

Aggression
in group counselling 194–195

Alternative frames of reference 107–109

American Personnel and Guidance Association 210, 213

American Psychological Association 210, 213

Anticipation —
in counselling 12
of risk and gain 103–107

Antidepressant drugs 174–175

Anxiety —
about group counselling 180
counsellor anxiety 30–34
instructing oneself with coping statements 120–124, 126–130, 130–132
levels of intensity 52
self-protective thinking 104–107

Assertive training 126–130

Assessment —
in assertive training 126–130
in initial interviews 66–73, 83–84
intake interviewing for groups 187–188
other methods of assessment 83–84

Attending behaviour 34–36

Attitudes of counsellor 28–30

Attribution —
attribution of responsibility 100–103
misattribution 106

Audio aids 152-155

Australian Psychological Society 209

Avoidance 106

Behavioural counselling and therapy 116–142, 225–226

Behaviour rehearsal 126–130

Bodily communication 21–25, 34–36

British Association for Counselling 209, 210, 213

British Journal of Guidance and Counselling 213

British Psychological Society 209, 210

Bulletin of the British Psychological Society 209

Canadian Counsellor 213

Canadian Guidance and Counselling Association 210, 213

Canadian Psychological Association 210

Careers counselling 6, 114

Careers Research and Advisory Centre 213

Challenging 111–113

Classical conditioning 225

Client-centred *see* Person-centred

Cognitive-behavioural counselling 225–226

Concreteness *see* Specificity

Conditioning —
classical 225
operant 225
see also Reward

Confidentiality 149

Confrontation *see* Challenging

Congruence *see* Genuineness

Consultancy —
life skills training 200
role decisions 203–205

Continuation responses 35–38

Contracting —
in group counselling 185–186
in initial interviews 72

Coping statements 120–124

Counseling Psychologist 213

Counselling —
definitions of 1–3
kinds of interview 4–7
professional associations 209–210
theoretical positions 218–227

Counselling 213

Counsellor
as decision-maker 14–15, 73, 178–182, 203–205
anxiety 30–34, 183
attitudes of 28–30
co-counsellors, use of 183
reactions 31–32
secrets 32–33
self-disclosure 32–33, 163–169

Counsellor training —
courses and workshops 209–210

Countertransference 166

Couples counselling 179

Crisis —
handling crises 155–163
helping contacts 9–10
interviews 6–7

Daley's 'reinforcement menu' 132
Decision-making–
   and problem solving 138–141
   counsellors as decision-makers 14,
   73, 178–182, 203–205
   recommending group counselling
   178–182
Defences *see* Self-protective thinking
Denial 106
Depression —
   antidepressant drugs 174–175
   manic depression 170–173
   reward approaches 133
   suicide indicators 160
Developmental —
   helping contacts 8
   interviews 4–5
Development of counselling skills
   206–217
Distortion 105–106
Drugs —
   Australian MIMS 174
   British MIMS 174
   in psychiatric use 174–175
Duration, frequency and number of
   sessions 146–147, 184–187

Eclecticism 116
Egan, Gerard —
   model of helping 94, 212
Empathic understanding —
   defining 41–42
   evaluating 45–48, 60–62
   in groups 190–191
   observing and listening 17–39
   responding with 40–64
Encounter groups 177–196
Existential counselling and therapy
   222

Family counselling 179
'Feelings talk' 51–52
Focused exploration —
   of alternative frames of reference
   107–109
   of anticipating risk and gain 103–
   107
   of attribution of responsibility
   100–103
   of self-protective thinking 104–107
   of standards 95–100
Formulating realistic standards 95–
   100

Genuineness 25, 164
Gestalt counselling and therapy 221

Goals —
   in group counselling 182–183
   in initial interviews 72
   in life skills training 196–203
   in planning 138–141
   setting 116–120
Group counselling —
   defining 178
   leading 188–196
   preparing 182–188
   recommending 178–182
   terminating 196

Hypnotic drugs 174–175

Identifying rewards 133–134
Imagination —
   imaginal rehearsal 126–130
   in systematic desensitization 125
I messages —
   counsellor self-disclosure 163–169
   in group counselling 192
Information-providing 114–115
Instructing oneself with coping statements 120–124, 126–130
Intake interviewing —
   for group counselling 187–188
Internal frame of reference 19–21
Interpretation —
   characteristics of 113–114
Introjection 105
Interviews
   kinds of 3–7
   stages of 68–73

Johari window 24–25
Journal of Counseling Psychology
   213

Life skills training —
   definition 196–197
   designing a programme 200–203
   preparatory skills 197–199
   trainer skills 199–200
Listening *see* Empathic
   understanding

MacPhillamy and Lewinsohn's
   Pleasant Events Schedule 133
Manic-depressive psychoses 170–173
Marathon groups 185
Marital counselling 114, 178
Marriage Guidance 213
Medication, use of 174–175
Misattribution of responsibility 106

Modelling —
  behaviour rehearsal and assertive training 126–130
  facilitating acting 130–132, 225
National Marriage Guidance Council 213
Necessary and sufficient conditions for client change 40
Newsheet 209
Non-verbal communication *see* Bodily communication
Note-taking *see* Record-keeping

Opening remarks 35–38
Operant conditioning 225

Paranoia 170–173
Paranoid state 170–173
Para–verbal communication *see* Vocal communication
Perceptions —
  of self and others 11–14
  of social rules 13
Personal and social education *see* Life skills training
Personal development 213–216
Person-centred counselling and therapy 1, 220–221
  see also Empathic understanding
Planning 138–141
Presenting concerns 70–72
Problem-focused —
  counselling 5–6, 116–142
  helping 8–9
Problem-solving 138–141
Professional associations —
  in counselling 209–210
  in psychology 209–210
Projection 105
Psychoanalysis 224–225
Psychological education *see* Life skills training
Psychoses 170–173
Psychotherapist *see* Counsellor
Psychotherapy *see* Counselling

Questioning —
  errors 74–76
  skills 76–80

Rational-emotive counselling and therapy 92, 97, 223
Realistic standards 95–100
Reality counselling and therapy 223–224
Reconnaissance in initial interviews 72

Record-keeping 150–152
Referrals 143–146
Reflection —
  of content 48–50
  of feeling 51–54
  of feeling and content 54–55
Reinforcement *see* Reward
Relationships —
  counselling and helping 3–14
  in groups 178–179, 191–194
Relaxation 125
Reluctant clients 87–88
Resistance —
  and self-protective thinking 104–107
  in group counselling 190
Responding decisions 14
Responsibility —
  attributing 100–103
  in reality therapy 223–224
  misattributing 106
  use of language 101–102, 106
Reward —
  classical and operant 225
  identifying rewards 133–134
  schedules of 135–136
  self-instruction 120–124
  self-reward 137–138
  using rewards in counselling 130–138
Role decisions 14, 203–205
Role-playing —
  assertive training 126–130
  modelling 130–132
Rules —
  of social contexts 13

Schizophrenia 170–173
Self-awareness 12
Self-defeating verbalizations 95–100, 120–124
Self-disclosure —
  client 14, 26
  counsellor 32–33, 163–169
  in groups 192–195
Self-evaluation 95–100
Self-exploration 26, 95–109
Self-instruction 95–100, 120–124, 126–130, 130–132
Self-protective thinking 104–107
Social skills —
  in group counselling 191–194
  life skills training 196–203
Specificity 109–111
Stages in counselling —
  and goals 93–94

in initial interviews 69–73
Stress —
   defining 155–158
   effects of 156–157
   stressors 157–158
   see also Crisis
Structuring —
   in groups 188–190
   in individual counselling 84–87
Summarizing 82–83
Support —
   in counselling interviews 7
   in helping contacts 10
Systematic desensitization 125

Telephone counselling 153
Termination —
   of groups 196
   of initial interviews 72–73, 88–89
   of subsequent interviews and relationships 147–148
Tests 114
Theoretical positions —
   behavioural 116–142, 225–226
   existential 222
   gestalt 221

person-centred 1, 220–221
psychoanalysis 224–225
rational–emotive 92, 97, 223
reality 223–224
transactional analysis 222–223
Timing —
   providing information 114–115
   see also Stages in counselling
Tranquillizing drugs 174–175
Transactional analysis 222–223
Transference 13, 166
Transition statements 80–82
Treatment decisions —
   individual counselling 65–73
   regarding groups 178–182
   see also Termination

Visual aids 152–155
Vulnerability —
   client 93–94
   counsellor 30–34
   group counselling 194–195
Vocal communication 21–25

Written aids 152–155